LADY BALTIMORE

The Witch Queens

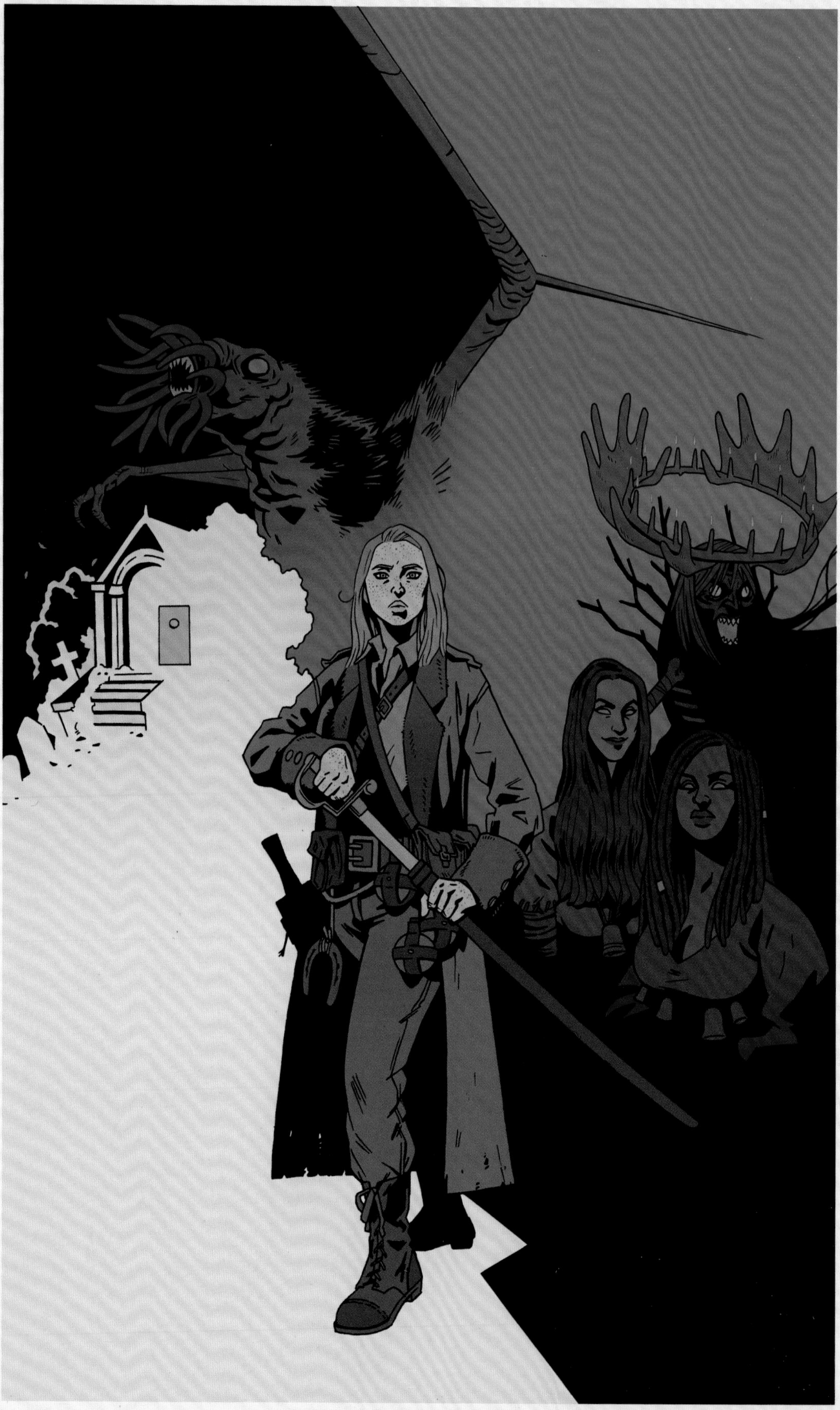

LADY BALTIMORE: THE WITCH QUEENS

VOLUME ONE

Story by
MIKE MIGNOLA
CHRISTOPHER GOLDEN

Art by
BRIDGIT CONNELL

Colors by
MICHELLE MADSEN

Letters by
CLEM ROBINS

Cover Art and Chapter Break Art by
ABIGAIL LARSON

Publisher **MIKE RICHARDSON**

Editor **KATII O'BRIEN**

Associate Editor **JENNY BLENK**

Assistant Editor **ANASTACIA FERRY**

Collection Designer **PATRICK SATTERFIELD**

Digital Art Technician **ANN GRAY**

DARK HORSE BOOKS

Neil Hankerson *Executive Vice President* • Tom Weddle *Chief Financial Officer* • Dale LaFountain *Chief Information Officer* • Tim Wiesch *Vice President of Licensing* • Matt Parkinson *Vice President of Marketing* Vanessa Todd-Holmes *Vice President of Production and Scheduling* • Mark Bernardi *Vice President of Book Trade and Digital Sales* • Randy Lahrman *Vice President of Product Development* • Ken Lizzi *General Counsel* Dave Marshall *Editor in Chief* • Davey Estrada *Editorial Director* • Chris Warner *Senior Books Editor* • Cary Grazzini *Director of Specialty Projects* • Lia Ribacchi *Art Director* • Matt Dryer *Director of Digital Art and Prepress* • Michael Gombos *Senior Director of Licensed Publications* • Kari Yadro *Director of Custom Programs* Kari Torson *Director of International Licensing*

DarkHorse.com

Published by Dark Horse Books
A division of Dark Horse Comics LLC
10956 SE Main Street
Milwaukie, OR 97222

Comic Shop Locator Service: comicshoplocator.com

First edition:February 2022
Ebook ISBN 978-1-50671-943-6
Hardcover ISBN 978-1-50671-942-9

1 3 5 7 9 10 8 6 4 2

Printed in China

This volume collects *Lady Baltimore: The Witch Queens* #1–#5, published by Dark Horse Comics.

Library of Congress Cataloging-in-Publication Data

Names: Mignola, Mike, author. | Golden, Christopher, author. | Connell,
  Bridgit, artist. | Madsen, Michelle (Illustrator), colourist. | Robins,
  Clem, 1955- letterer. | Larson, Abigail (Illustrator), cover artist.
Title: Lady Baltimore : the witch queens / story by Mike Mignola,
  Christopher Golden ; art by Bridgit Connell ; colors by Michelle Madsen
  ; letters by Clem Robins ; cover art and chapter break art by Abigail
  Larson.
Description: First edition. | Milwaukie, OR : Dark Horse Books, 2022. |
  "This volume collects Lady Baltimore: The Witch Queens #1-#5, published
  by Dark Horse Comics." | Summary: "Once she was Sofia Valk, living in a
  village overrun by evil. In time she became Lord Baltimore's most
  trusted ally. Now, more than a decade after his death, Europe has
  erupted with the early battles of World War II and dark forces are
  rising again. With witches, vampires, and Nazis on the march, Sofia must
  embrace the title of Lady Baltimore! But can she fight monsters without
  becoming a monster herself?"-- Provided by publisher.
Identifiers: LCCN 2021026608 (print) | LCCN 2021026609 (ebook) | ISBN
  9781506719429 (hardcover) | ISBN 9781506719436 (ebook)
Subjects: LCGFT: Paranormal comics. | Horror comics.
Classification: LCC PN6728.L2286 M54 2022 (print) | LCC PN6728.L2286
  (ebook) | DDC 741.5/973--dc23
LC record available at https://lccn.loc.gov/2021026608
LC ebook record available at https://lccn.loc.gov/2021026609

CHAPTER ONE

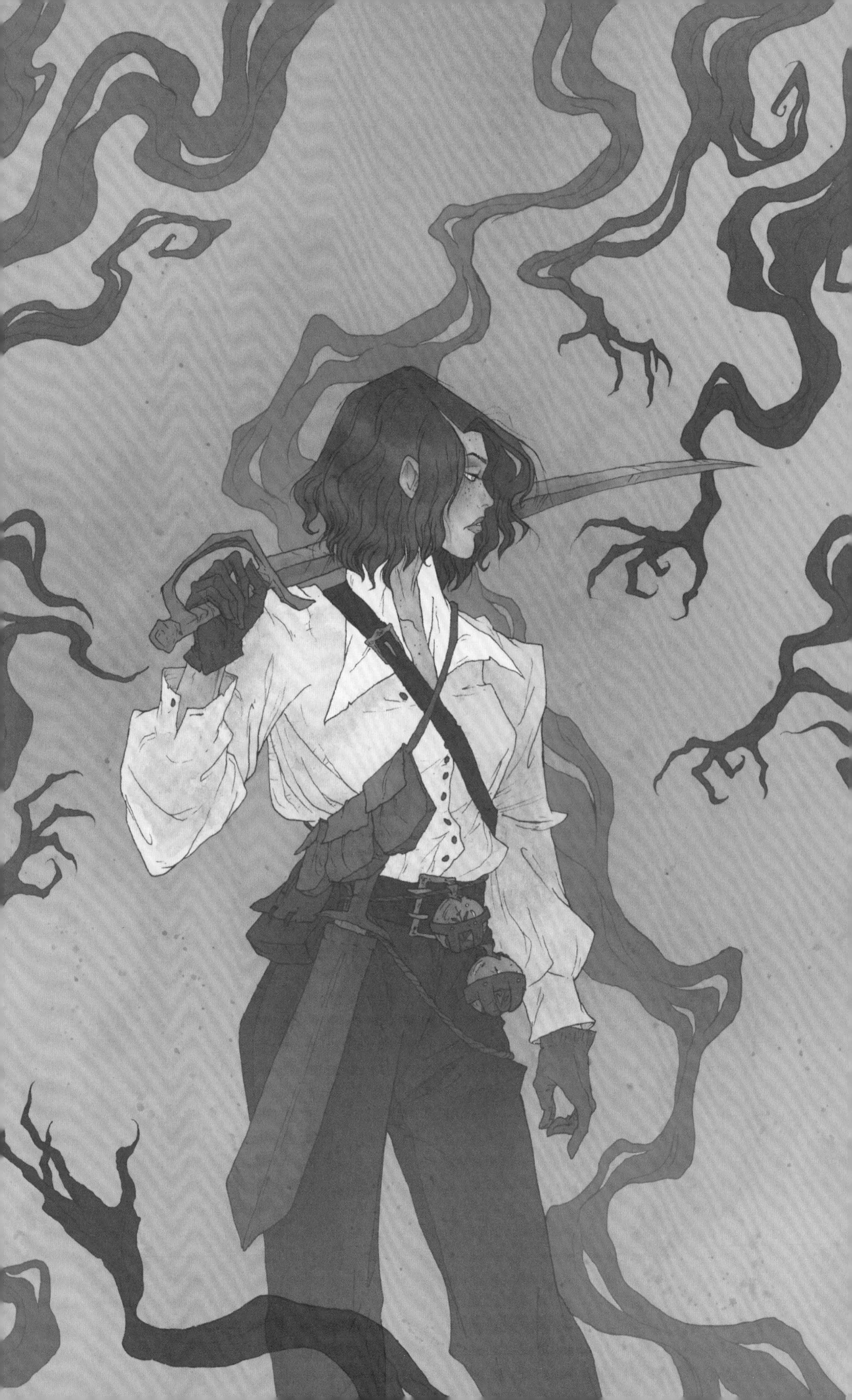

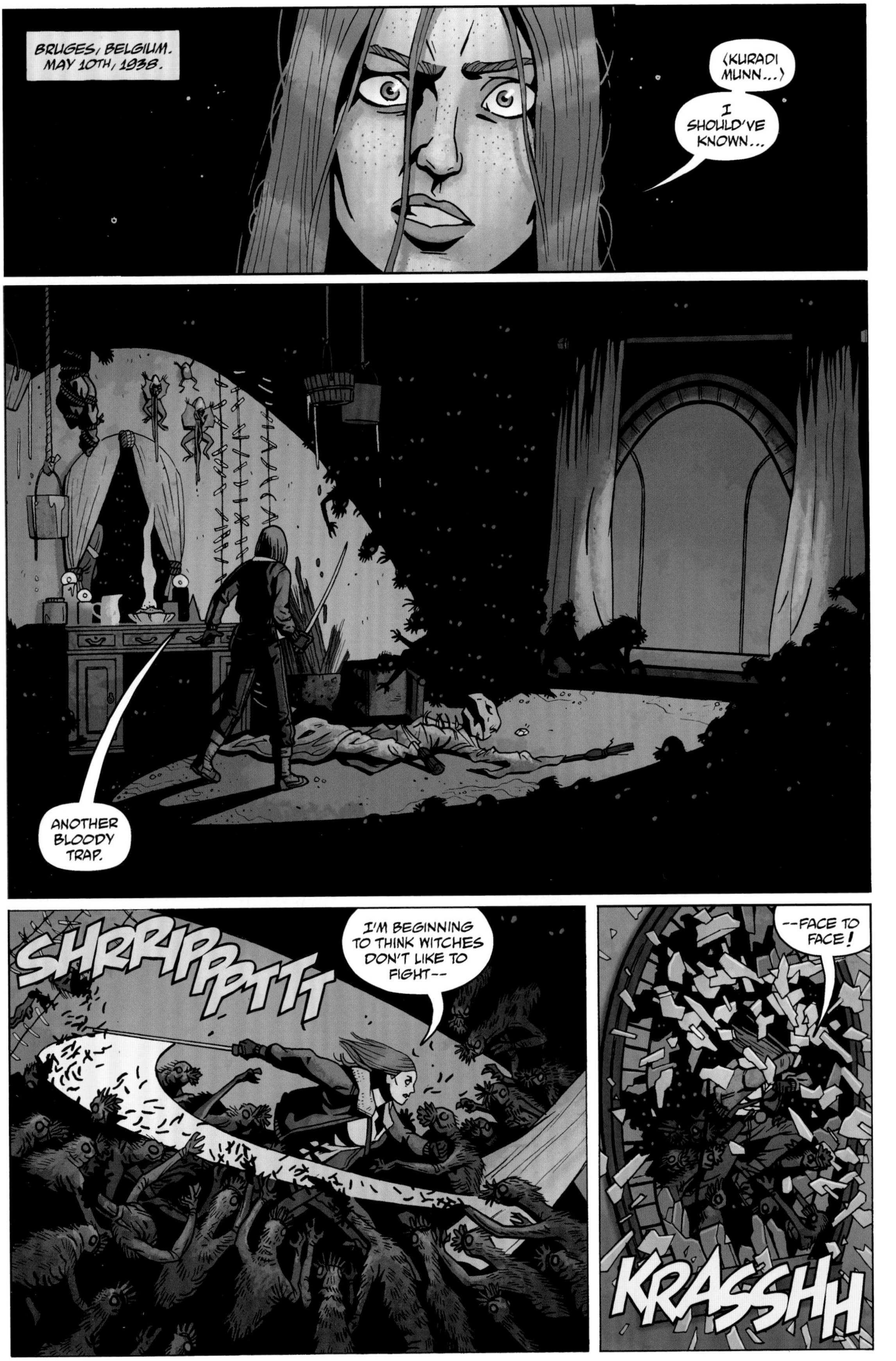
BRUGES, BELGIUM. MAY 10TH, 1938.
‹KURADI MUNN...›
I SHOULD'VE KNOWN...
ANOTHER BLOODY TRAP.
SHRRIPPPTTTT
I'M BEGINNING TO THINK WITCHES DON'T LIKE TO FIGHT--
--FACE TO FACE!
KRASSHH

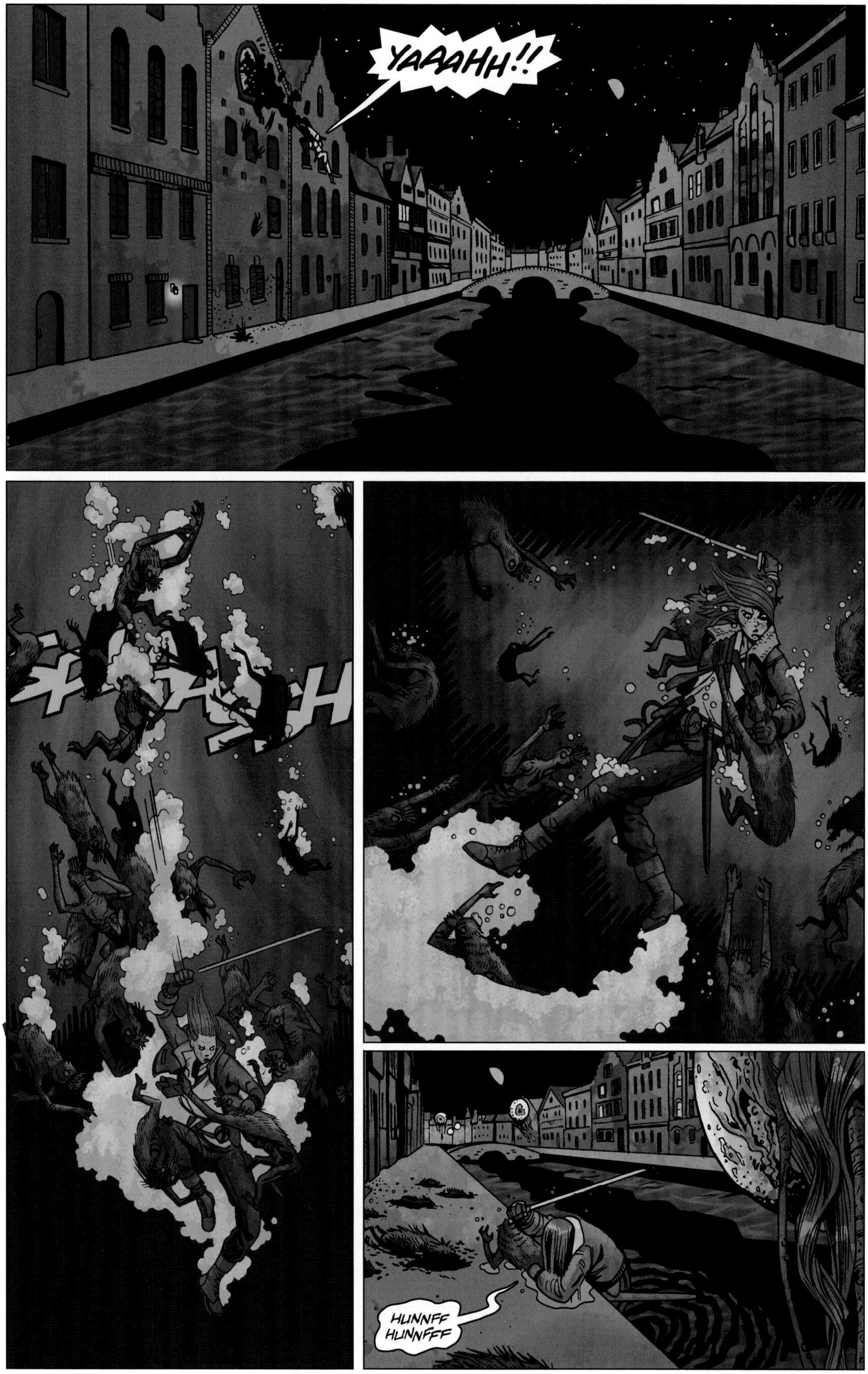
YAAAHH!!
HUNNFF
HUNNFFF

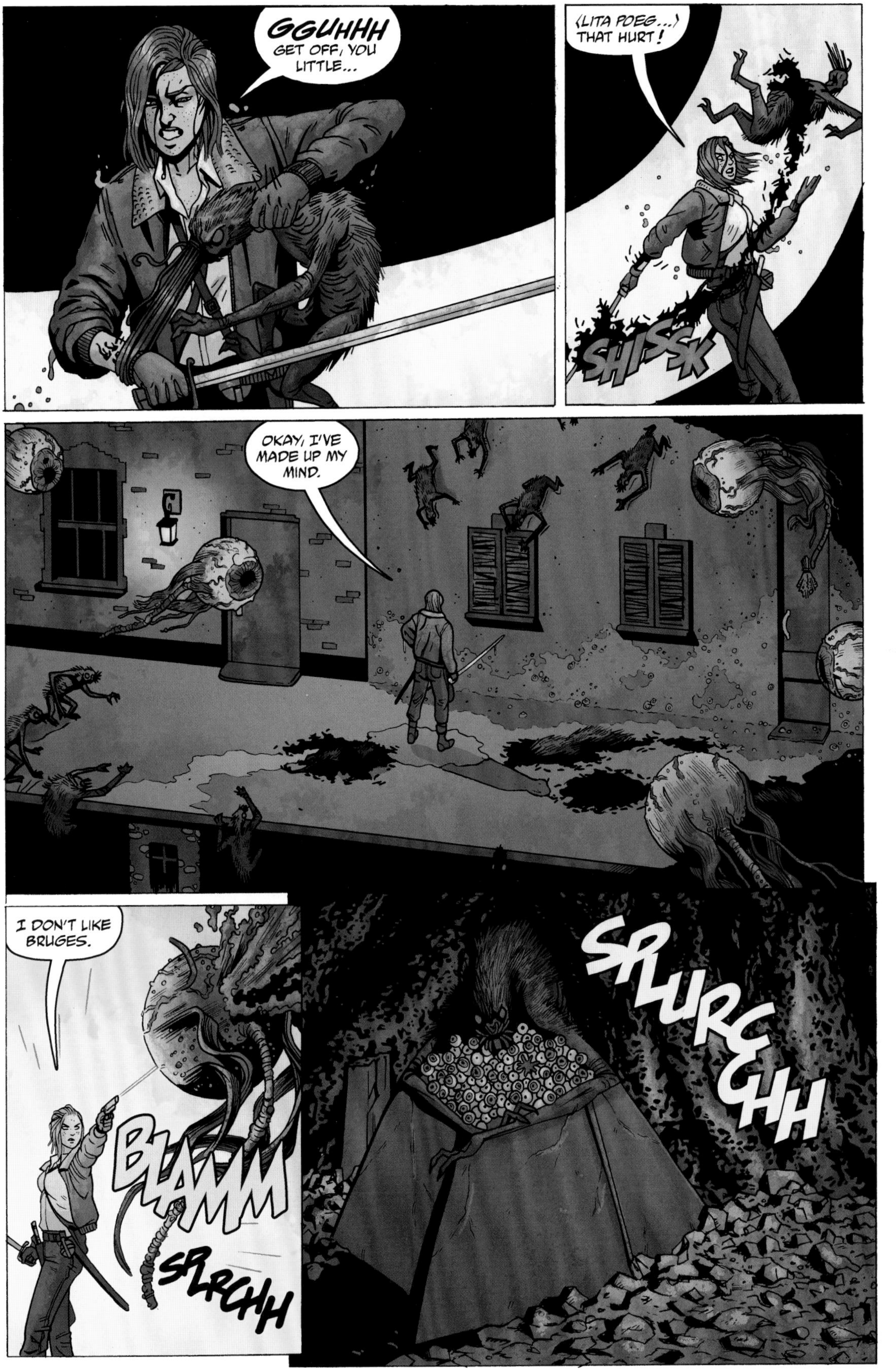
GGUHHH
GET OFF, YOU LITTLE...
(LITA POEG...) THAT HURT!
SHISSK
OKAY, I'VE MADE UP MY MIND.
I DON'T LIKE BRUGES.
BLAMM
SPLRCHH
SPLURCHH

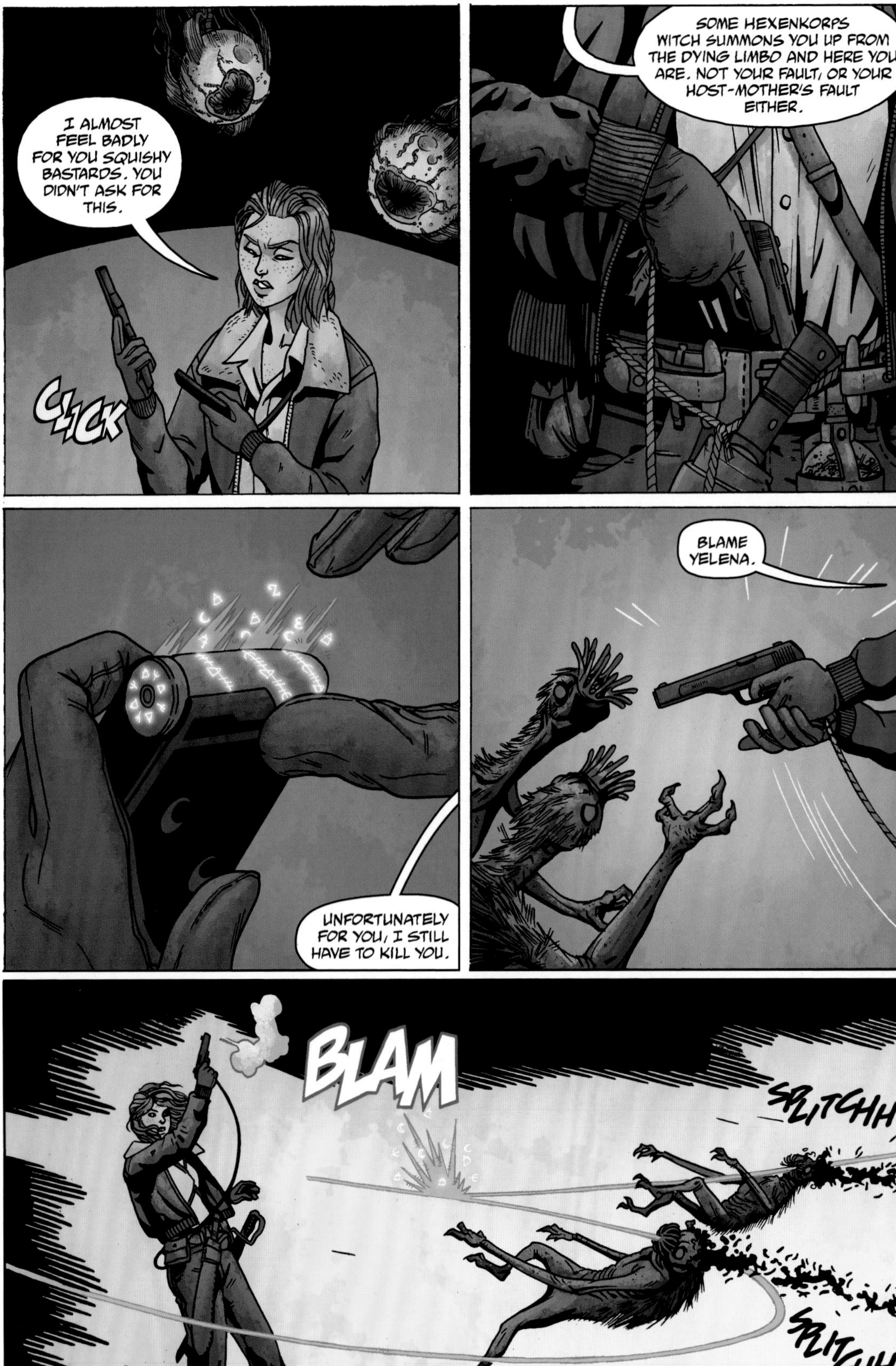
I ALMOST FEEL BADLY FOR YOU SQUISHY BASTARDS. YOU DIDN'T ASK FOR THIS.
CLICK
SOME HEXENKORPS WITCH SUMMONS YOU UP FROM THE DYING LIMBO AND HERE YOU ARE. NOT YOUR FAULT, OR YOUR HOST-MOTHER'S FAULT EITHER.
UNFORTUNATELY FOR YOU, I STILL HAVE TO KILL YOU.
BLAME YELENA.
BLAM
SPLITCHH
SPLITCHH

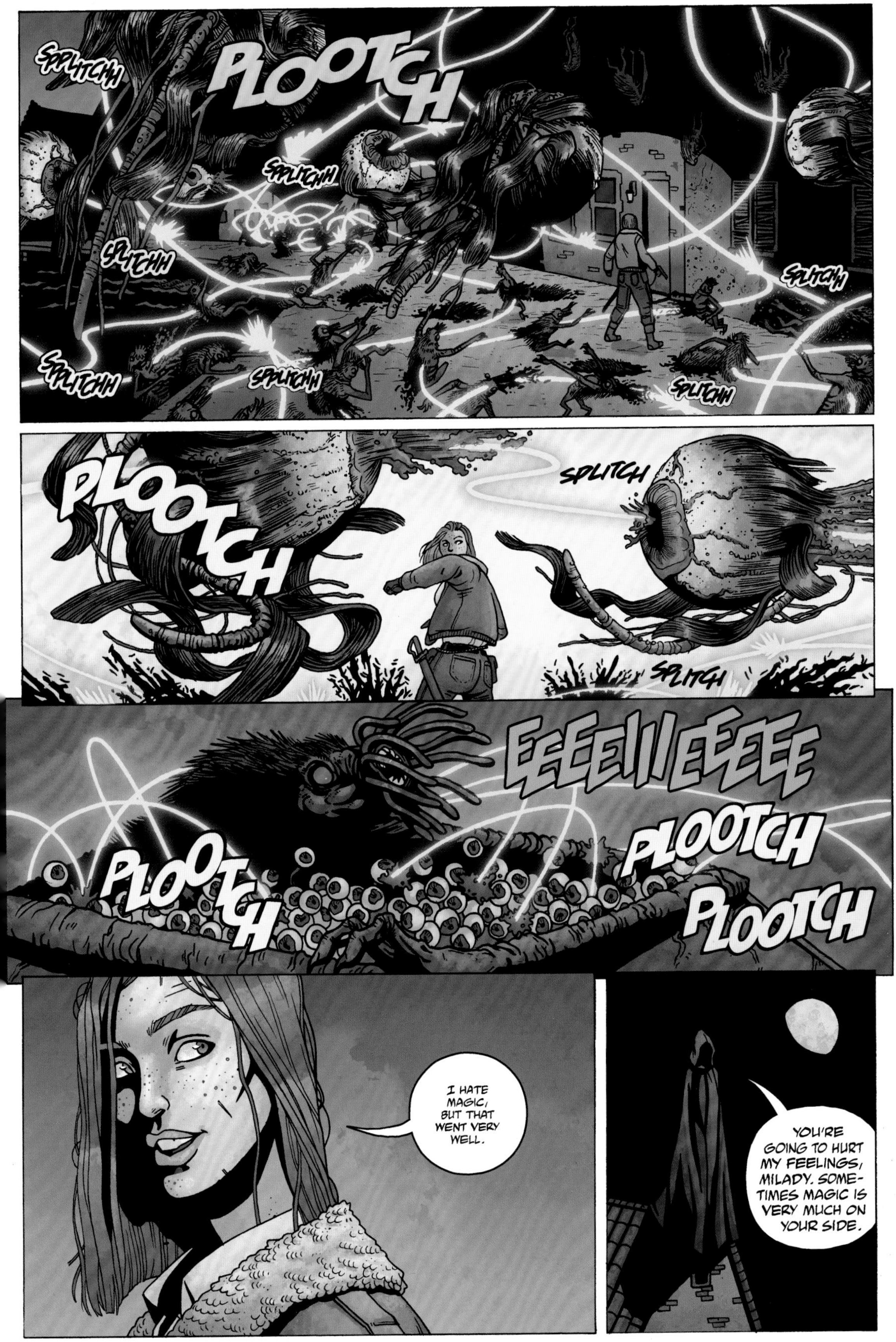
SPPLITCHH
PLOOTCH
SPPLITCHH
SPLITCHH
SPLITCHH
SPPLITCHH
SPPLITCHH
SPLITCHH
PLOOTCH
SPLITCH
SPLITCH
EEEEIIIEEEEE
PLOOTCH
PLOOTCH
PLOOTCH
I HATE MAGIC, BUT THAT WENT VERY WELL.
YOU'RE GOING TO HURT MY FEELINGS, MILADY. SOMETIMES MAGIC IS VERY MUCH ON YOUR SIDE.

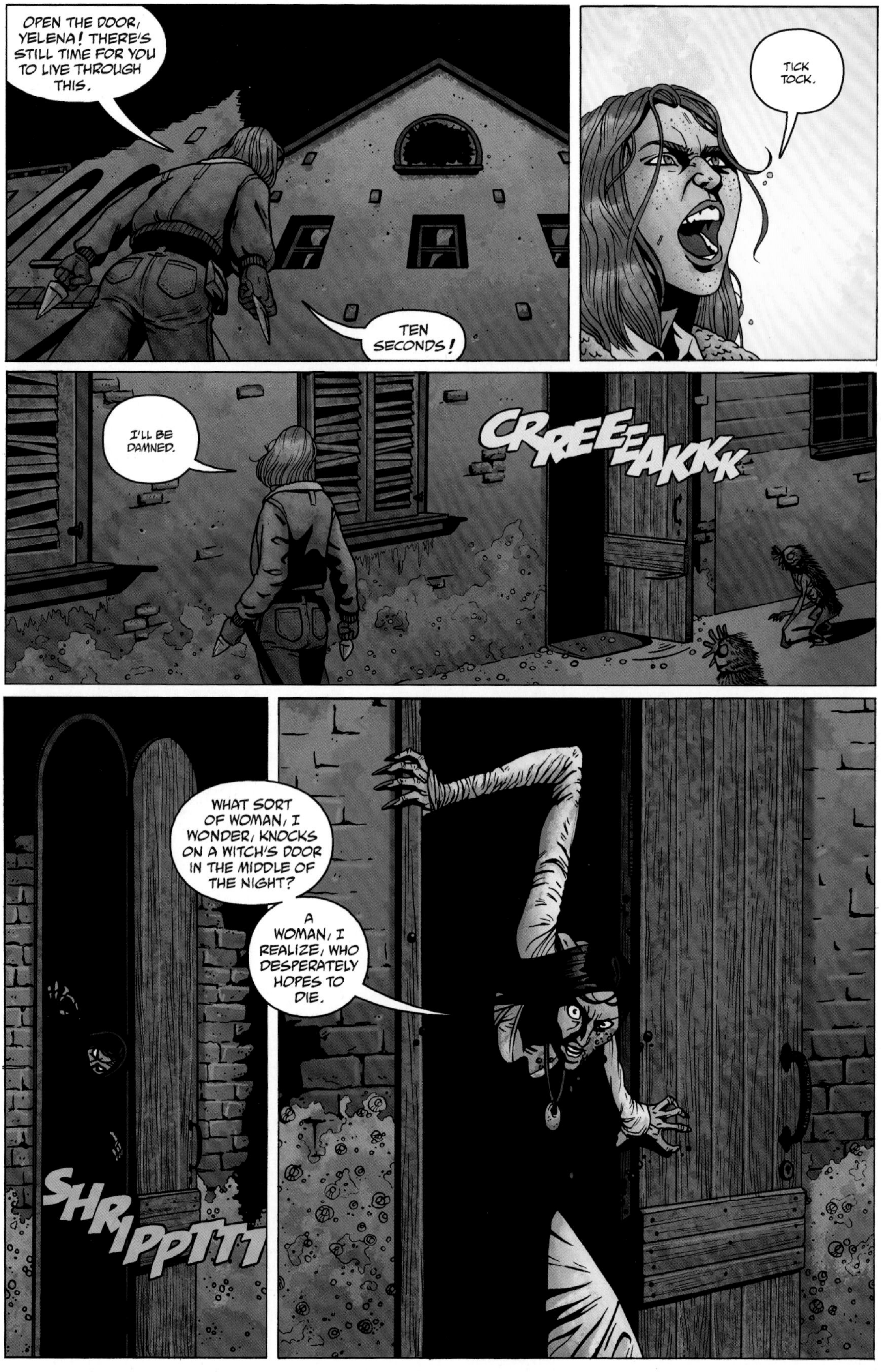
OPEN THE DOOR, YELENA! THERE'S STILL TIME FOR YOU TO LIVE THROUGH THIS.
TEN SECONDS!
TICK TOCK.
I'LL BE DAMNED.
CRREEEEAKKKK
WHAT SORT OF WOMAN, I WONDER, KNOCKS ON A WITCH'S DOOR IN THE MIDDLE OF THE NIGHT?
A WOMAN, I REALIZE, WHO DESPERATELY HOPES TO DIE.
SHRIPPTTT

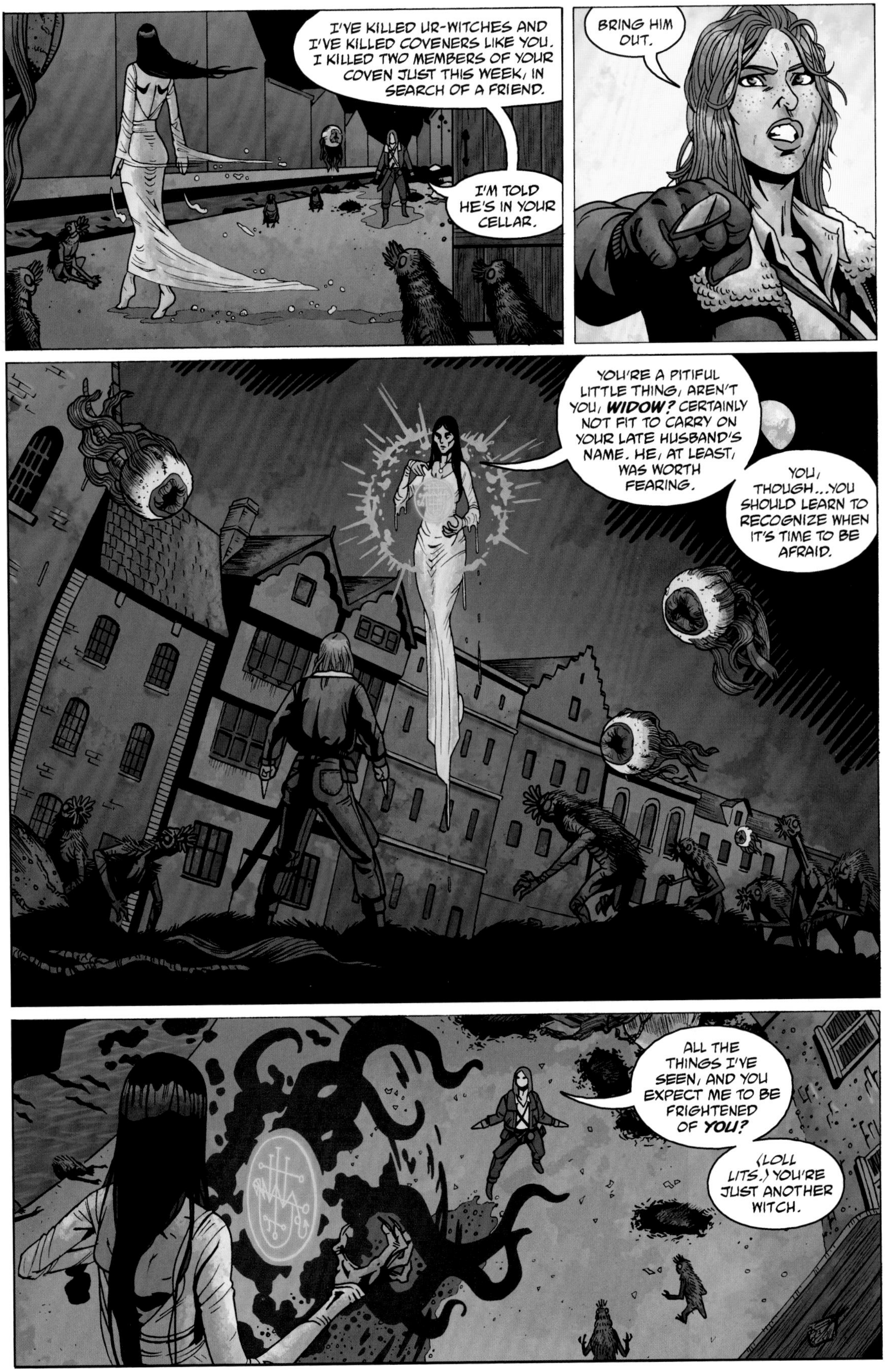
I'VE KILLED UR-WITCHES AND I'VE KILLED COVENERS LIKE YOU. I KILLED TWO MEMBERS OF YOUR COVEN JUST THIS WEEK, IN SEARCH OF A FRIEND.
I'M TOLD HE'S IN YOUR CELLAR.
BRING HIM OUT.
YOU'RE A PITIFUL LITTLE THING, AREN'T YOU, **WIDOW?** CERTAINLY NOT FIT TO CARRY ON YOUR LATE HUSBAND'S NAME. HE, AT LEAST, WAS WORTH FEARING.
YOU, THOUGH...YOU SHOULD LEARN TO RECOGNIZE WHEN IT'S TIME TO BE AFRAID.
ALL THE THINGS I'VE SEEN, AND YOU EXPECT ME TO BE FRIGHTENED OF **YOU?**
<LOLL LITS.> YOU'RE JUST ANOTHER WITCH.

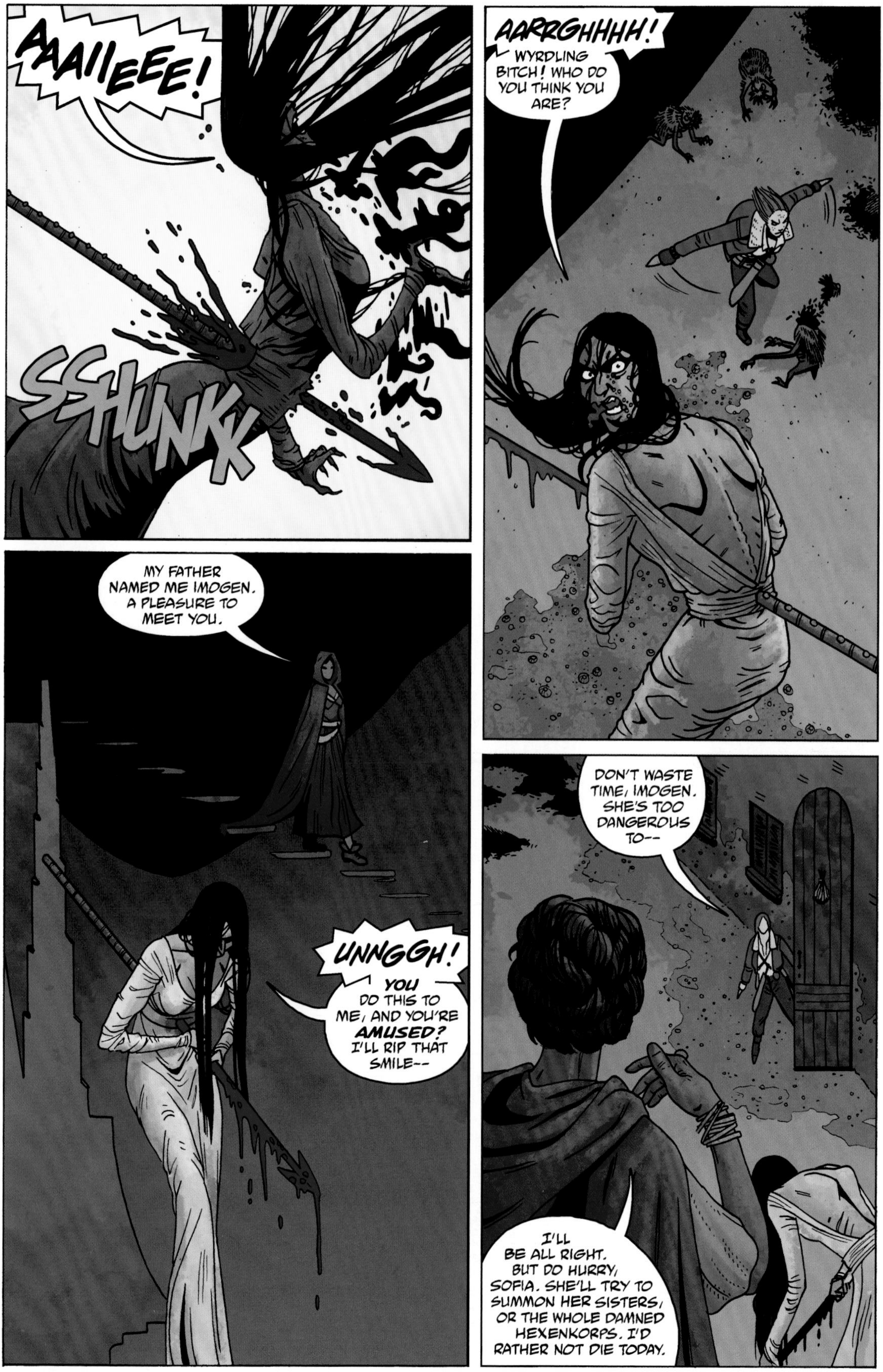
AAAIIEEE!
SSHUNKK
AARRGHHHH!
WYRDLING BITCH! WHO DO YOU THINK YOU ARE?
MY FATHER NAMED ME IMOGEN. A PLEASURE TO MEET YOU.
UNNGGH!
YOU DO THIS TO ME, AND YOU'RE AMUSED? I'LL RIP THAT SMILE--
DON'T WASTE TIME, IMOGEN. SHE'S TOO DANGEROUS TO--
I'LL BE ALL RIGHT. BUT DO HURRY, SOFIA. SHE'LL TRY TO SUMMON HER SISTERS, OR THE WHOLE DAMNED HEXENKORPS. I'D RATHER NOT DIE TODAY.

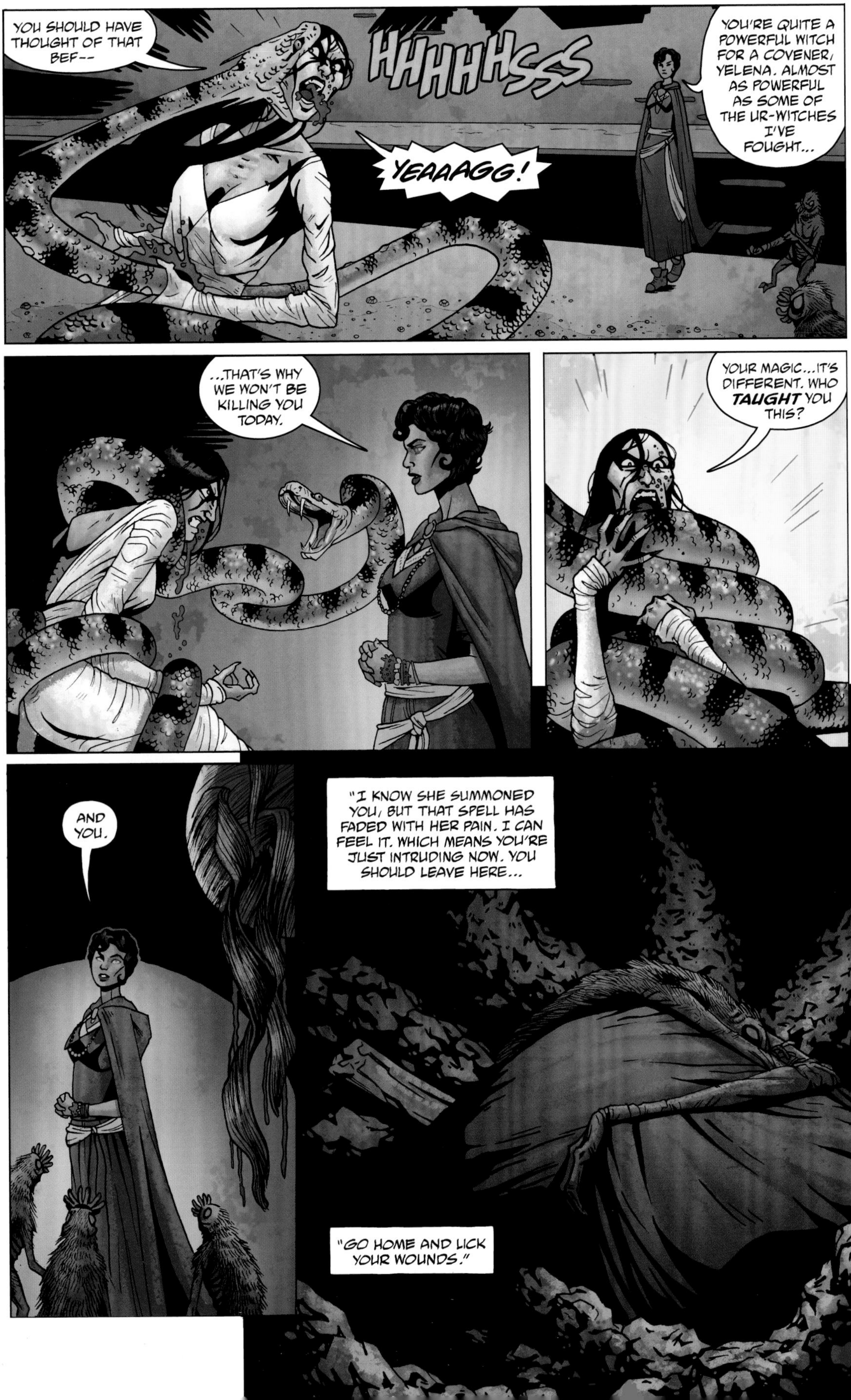
YOU SHOULD HAVE THOUGHT OF THAT BEF--
HHHHHSSS
YEAAAGG!
YOU'RE QUITE A POWERFUL WITCH FOR A COVENER, YELENA. ALMOST AS POWERFUL AS SOME OF THE UR-WITCHES I'VE FOUGHT...
...THAT'S WHY WE WON'T BE KILLING YOU TODAY.
YOUR MAGIC...IT'S DIFFERENT. WHO TAUGHT YOU THIS?
AND YOU.
"I KNOW SHE SUMMONED YOU, BUT THAT SPELL HAS FADED WITH HER PAIN. I CAN FEEL IT. WHICH MEANS YOU'RE JUST INTRUDING NOW. YOU SHOULD LEAVE HERE...
"GO HOME AND LICK YOUR WOUNDS."

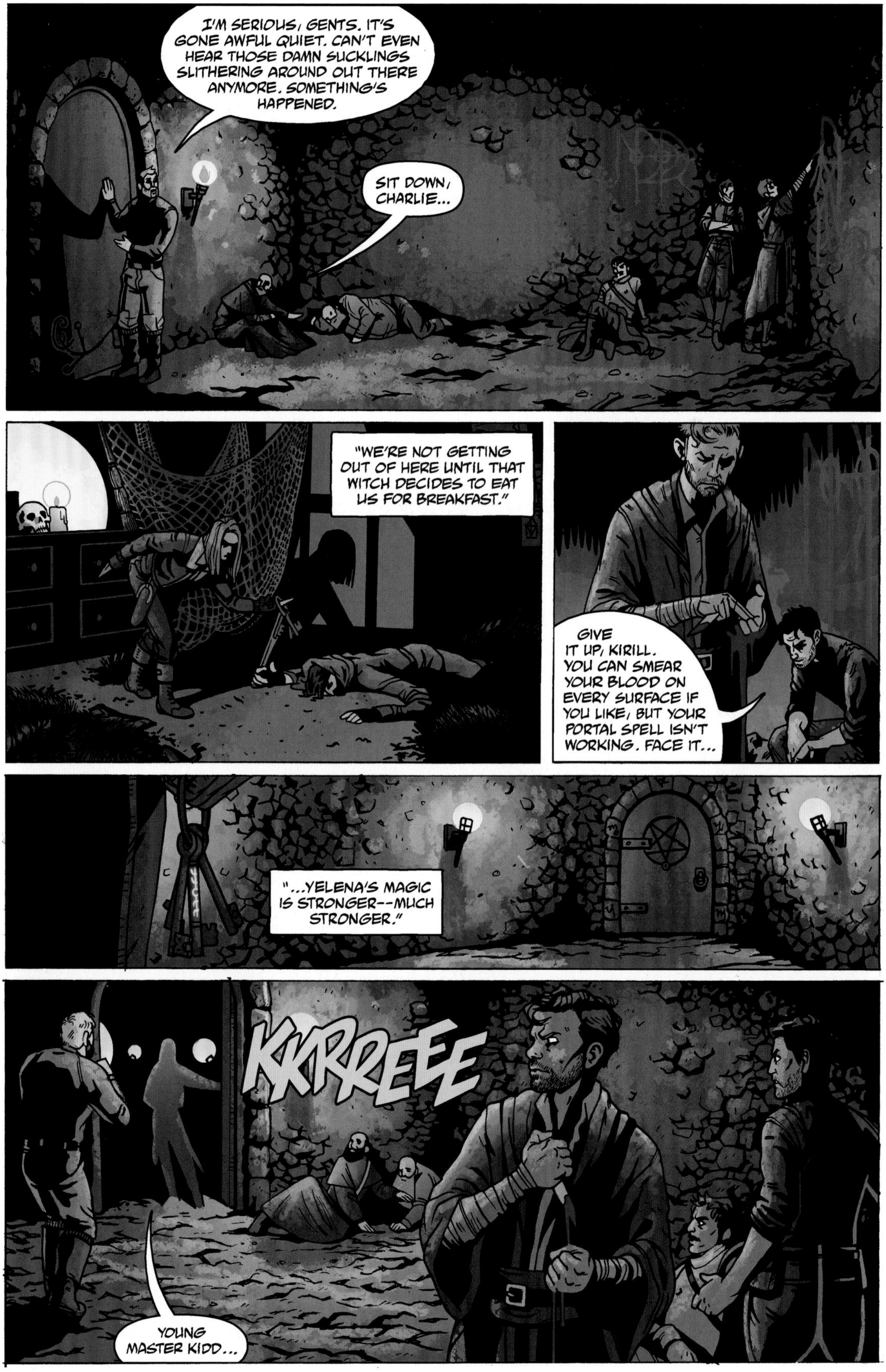
I'M SERIOUS, GENTS. IT'S GONE AWFUL QUIET. CAN'T EVEN HEAR THOSE DAMN SUCKLINGS SLITHERING AROUND OUT THERE ANYMORE. SOMETHING'S HAPPENED.
SIT DOWN, CHARLIE...
"WE'RE NOT GETTING OUT OF HERE UNTIL THAT WITCH DECIDES TO EAT US FOR BREAKFAST."
GIVE IT UP, KIRILL. YOU CAN SMEAR YOUR BLOOD ON EVERY SURFACE IF YOU LIKE, BUT YOUR PORTAL SPELL ISN'T WORKING. FACE IT...
"...YELENA'S MAGIC IS STRONGER--MUCH STRONGER."
KKRREEE
YOUNG MASTER KIDD...

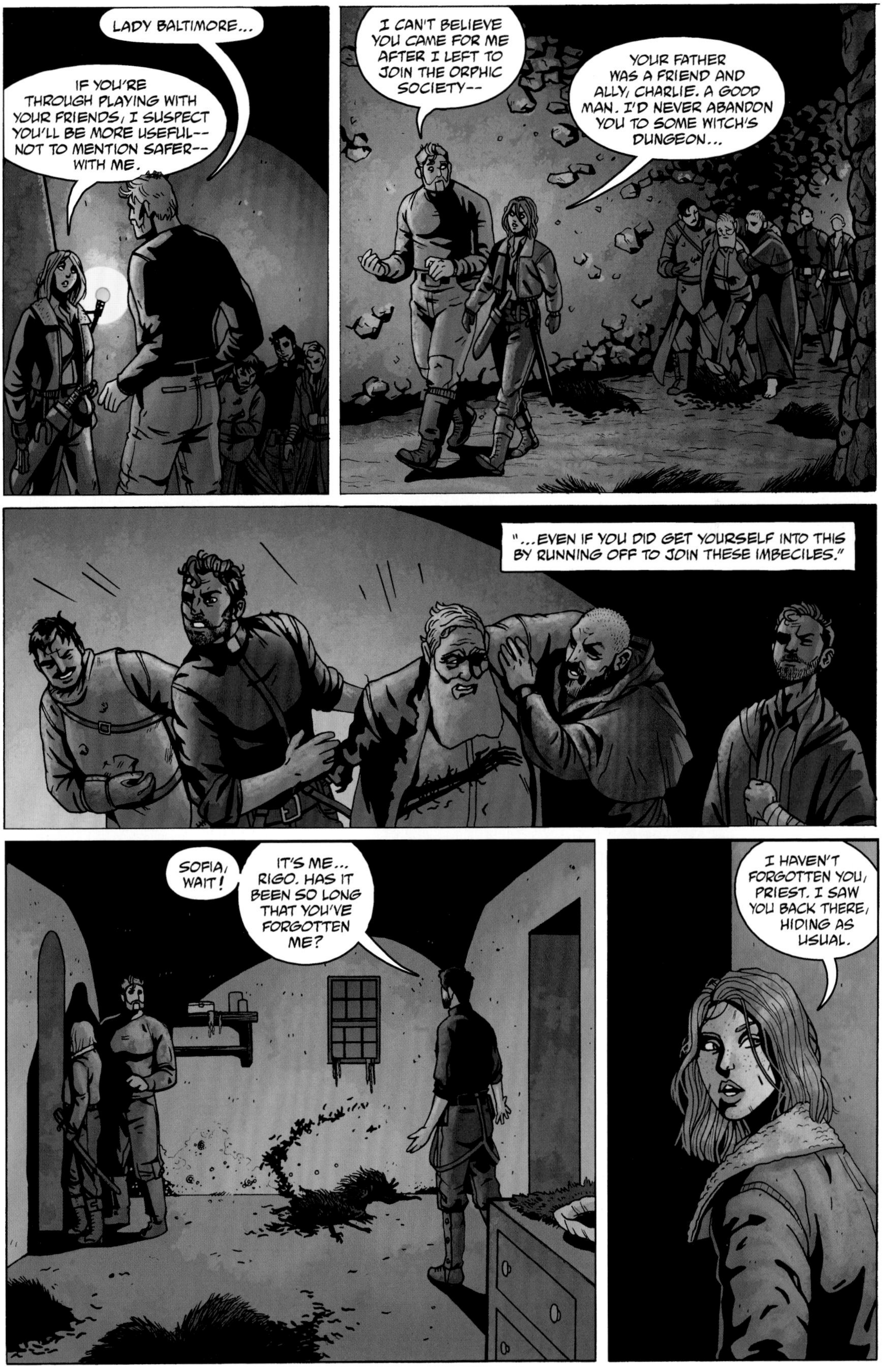
LADY BALTIMORE...
IF YOU'RE THROUGH PLAYING WITH YOUR FRIENDS, I SUSPECT YOU'LL BE MORE USEFUL-- NOT TO MENTION SAFER-- WITH ME.
I CAN'T BELIEVE YOU CAME FOR ME AFTER I LEFT TO JOIN THE ORPHIC SOCIETY--
YOUR FATHER WAS A FRIEND AND ALLY, CHARLIE. A GOOD MAN. I'D NEVER ABANDON YOU TO SOME WITCH'S DUNGEON...
"...EVEN IF YOU DID GET YOURSELF INTO THIS BY RUNNING OFF TO JOIN THESE IMBECILES."
SOFIA, WAIT!
IT'S ME... RIGO. HAS IT BEEN SO LONG THAT YOU'VE FORGOTTEN ME?
I HAVEN'T FORGOTTEN YOU, PRIEST. I SAW YOU BACK THERE, HIDING AS USUAL.

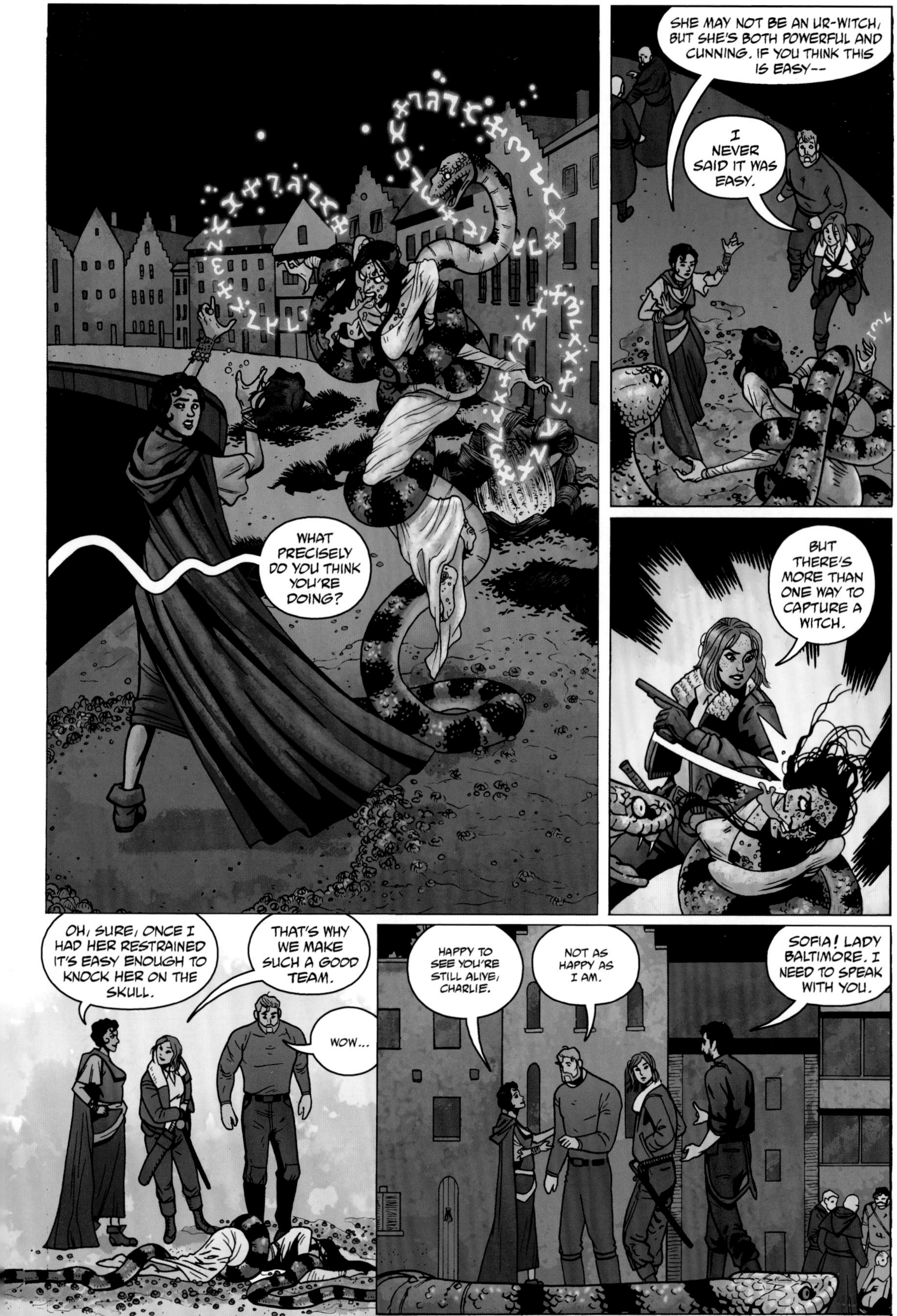
WHAT PRECISELY DO YOU THINK YOU'RE DOING?
SHE MAY NOT BE AN UR-WITCH, BUT SHE'S BOTH POWERFUL AND CUNNING. IF YOU THINK THIS IS EASY--
I NEVER SAID IT WAS EASY.
BUT THERE'S MORE THAN ONE WAY TO CAPTURE A WITCH.
OH, SURE, ONCE I HAD HER RESTRAINED IT'S EASY ENOUGH TO KNOCK HER ON THE SKULL.
THAT'S WHY WE MAKE SUCH A GOOD TEAM.
WOW...
HAPPY TO SEE YOU'RE STILL ALIVE, CHARLIE.
NOT AS HAPPY AS I AM.
SOFIA! LADY BALTIMORE. I NEED TO SPEAK WITH YOU.

IN THE PAST, YOU'VE BEEN RELUCTANT TO JOIN FORCES WITH THE ORPHIC SOCIETY--

I'M TOLD YOUR BAND OF MAGICIANS, OCCULTISTS, AND BROKEN PRIESTS HAS BEEN QUITE HELPFUL IN RESISTING THE GROWING NAZI THREAT.

DON'T MISUNDERSTAND, RIGO.

WITH SO MANY WITCH COVENS BANDING TOGETHER TO FORM THE HEXENKORPS, SUPPORTING MEISSNER'S TROOPS IN THE SUDETENLAND, WHAT YOU'RE DOING IS NECESSARY AND ADMIRABLE.

BUT?

BUT...

...I'VE SEEN THE PAIN AND SUFFERING THIS WORLD HAS TO OFFER. HAD PLENTY OF MY OWN. I DON'T NEED A BUNCH OF EX-HOLY MEN AND DABBLERS IN MAGIC TELLING *ME* HOW TO FIGHT BACK.

BEEP BEEP

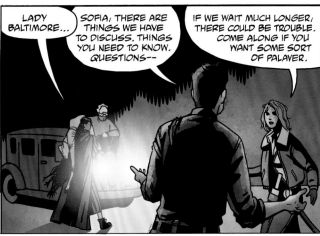

LADY BALTIMORE...

SOFIA, THERE ARE THINGS WE HAVE TO DISCUSS. THINGS YOU NEED TO KNOW. QUESTIONS--

IF WE WAIT MUCH LONGER, THERE COULD BE TROUBLE. COME ALONG IF YOU WANT SOME SORT OF PALAVER.

REPORT BACK TO THE BISHOP. I'LL BE IN TOUCH AS SOON AS I CAN...

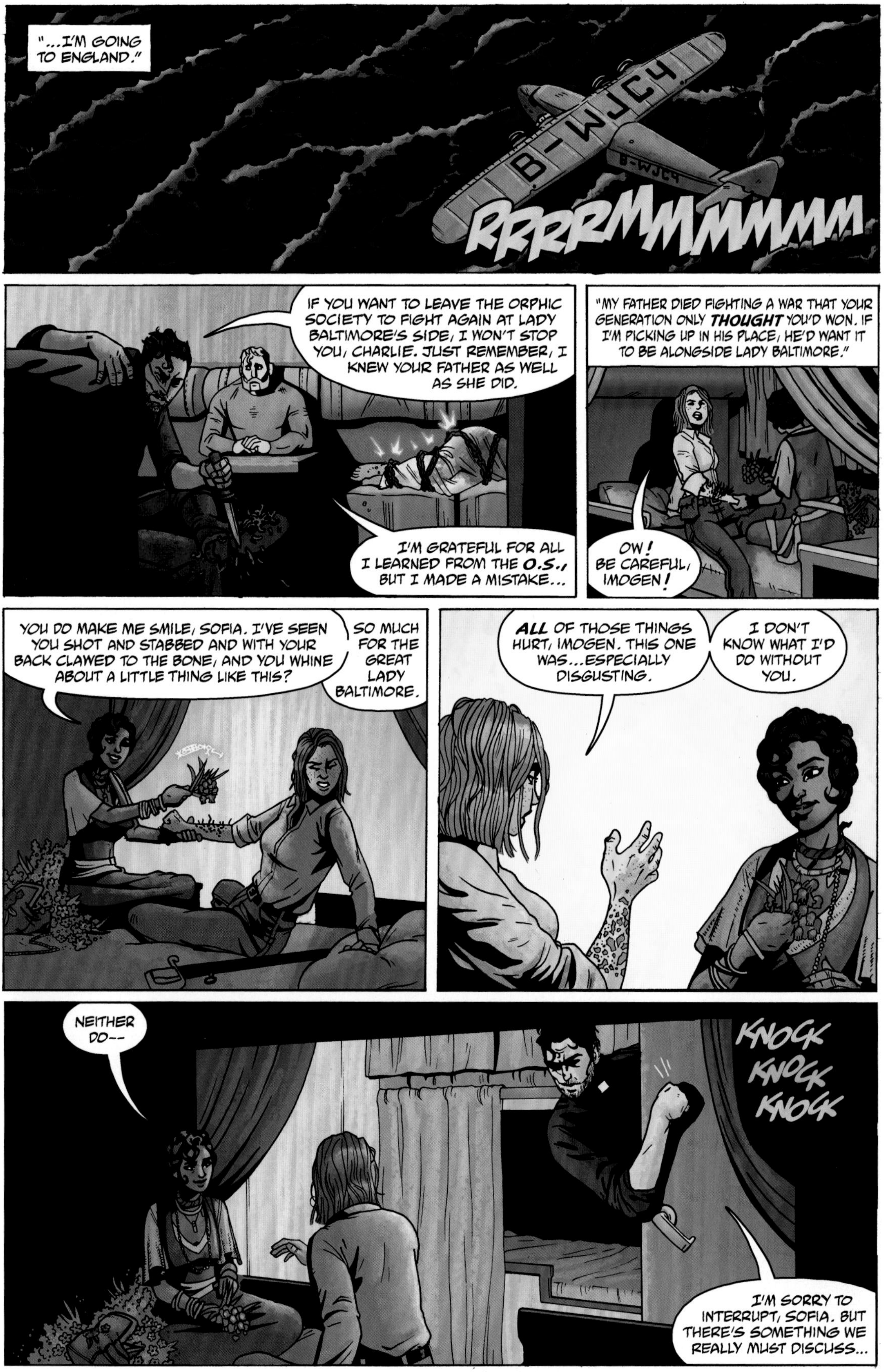
"...I'M GOING TO ENGLAND."
B-WJCY
RRRRMMMMMM
IF YOU WANT TO LEAVE THE ORPHIC SOCIETY TO FIGHT AGAIN AT LADY BALTIMORE'S SIDE, I WON'T STOP YOU, CHARLIE. JUST REMEMBER, I KNEW YOUR FATHER AS WELL AS SHE DID.
I'M GRATEFUL FOR ALL I LEARNED FROM THE O.S., BUT I MADE A MISTAKE...
"MY FATHER DIED FIGHTING A WAR THAT YOUR GENERATION ONLY THOUGHT YOU'D WON. IF I'M PICKING UP IN HIS PLACE, HE'D WANT IT TO BE ALONGSIDE LADY BALTIMORE."
OW! BE CAREFUL, IMOGEN!
YOU DO MAKE ME SMILE, SOFIA. I'VE SEEN YOU SHOT AND STABBED AND WITH YOUR BACK CLAWED TO THE BONE, AND YOU WHINE ABOUT A LITTLE THING LIKE THIS?
SO MUCH FOR THE GREAT LADY BALTIMORE.
ALL OF THOSE THINGS HURT, IMOGEN. THIS ONE WAS...ESPECIALLY DISGUSTING.
I DON'T KNOW WHAT I'D DO WITHOUT YOU.
NEITHER DO--
KNOCK KNOCK KNOCK
I'M SORRY TO INTERRUPT, SOFIA. BUT THERE'S SOMETHING WE REALLY MUST DISCUSS...

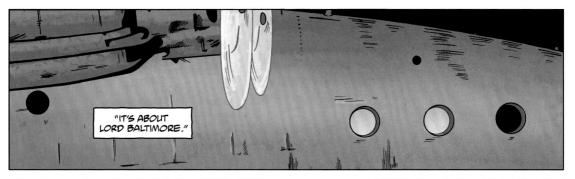

"IT'S ABOUT LORD BALTIMORE."

THE HEXENKORPS HAS BEEN SPREADING ITS INFLUENCE ACROSS EUROPE. INFILTRATING POLITICAL MACHINERY, FOMENTING HATRED AND NATIONALISM. I MUST AGAIN SUGGEST THAT WE MERGE OUR EFFORTS.

BALTIMORE MAY HAVE WARRED AGAINST THE DARKNESS WITH ONLY A HANDFUL OF ALLIES, BUT WITH ALL DUE RESPECT, YOU ARE NOT LORD--

I AM NOT LORD BALTIMORE?

SSHING

DO YOU HONESTLY THINK I'M UNAWARE? WHATEVER THE GODS MAY HAVE MADE HIM, HENRY WAS NO LONGER HUMAN AND I'M MADE OF *FAR* MORE ORDINARY STUFF...

BUT THIS WAS HIS BLADE. HE LET ME IN, RIGO. TRUSTED ME AND UNDERSTOOD ME AS I TRUSTED AND UNDER-STOOD HIM.

HE MARRIED ME BECAUSE HE INTENDED TO DIE BUT DID NOT WANT TO LEAVE HIS FAMILY'S ESTATE AND LEGACY TO CRUMBLE TO DUST. THIS WAS HIS SWORD... AND NOW IT'S MINE...

IT DOESN'T HAVE TO BE THIS WAY. YOUR LIFE COULD BE DIFFERENT.

OUR LIVES COULD BE DIFFERENT.

"I DON'T NEED YOUR PROTECTION TODAY ANY MORE THAN I DID ALL THOSE YEARS AGO."

WHY DON'T YOU JUST GET TO WHAT YOU WANT FROM ME?

ALL RIGHT, THEN, PUT BLUNTLY...

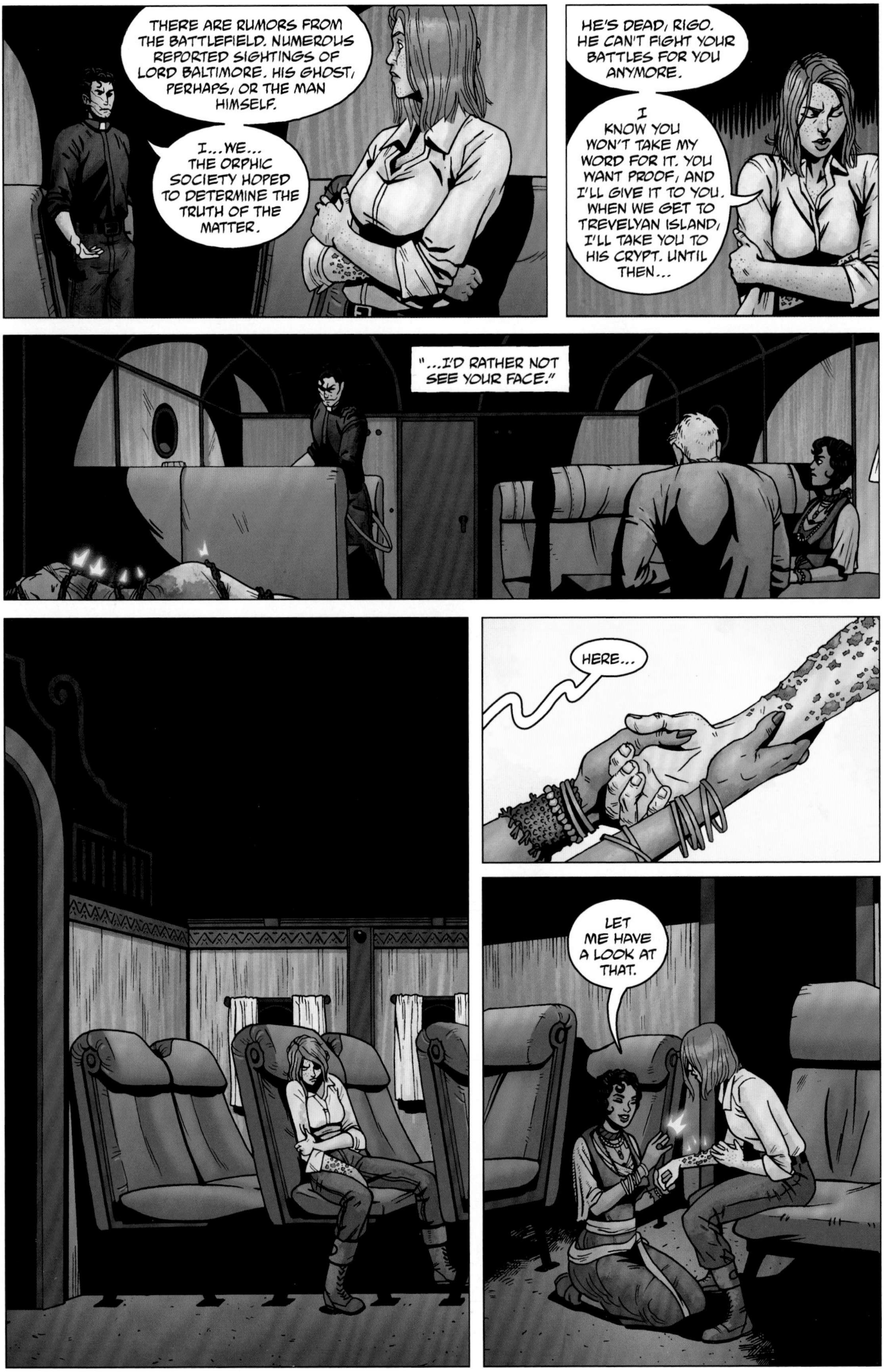
THERE ARE RUMORS FROM THE BATTLEFIELD. NUMEROUS REPORTED SIGHTINGS OF LORD BALTIMORE. HIS GHOST, PERHAPS, OR THE MAN HIMSELF.
I...WE... THE ORPHIC SOCIETY HOPED TO DETERMINE THE TRUTH OF THE MATTER.
HE'S DEAD, RIGO. HE CAN'T FIGHT YOUR BATTLES FOR YOU ANYMORE.
I KNOW YOU WON'T TAKE MY WORD FOR IT. YOU WANT PROOF, AND I'LL GIVE IT TO YOU. WHEN WE GET TO TREVELYAN ISLAND, I'LL TAKE YOU TO HIS CRYPT. UNTIL THEN...
"...I'D RATHER NOT SEE YOUR FACE."
HERE...
LET ME HAVE A LOOK AT THAT.

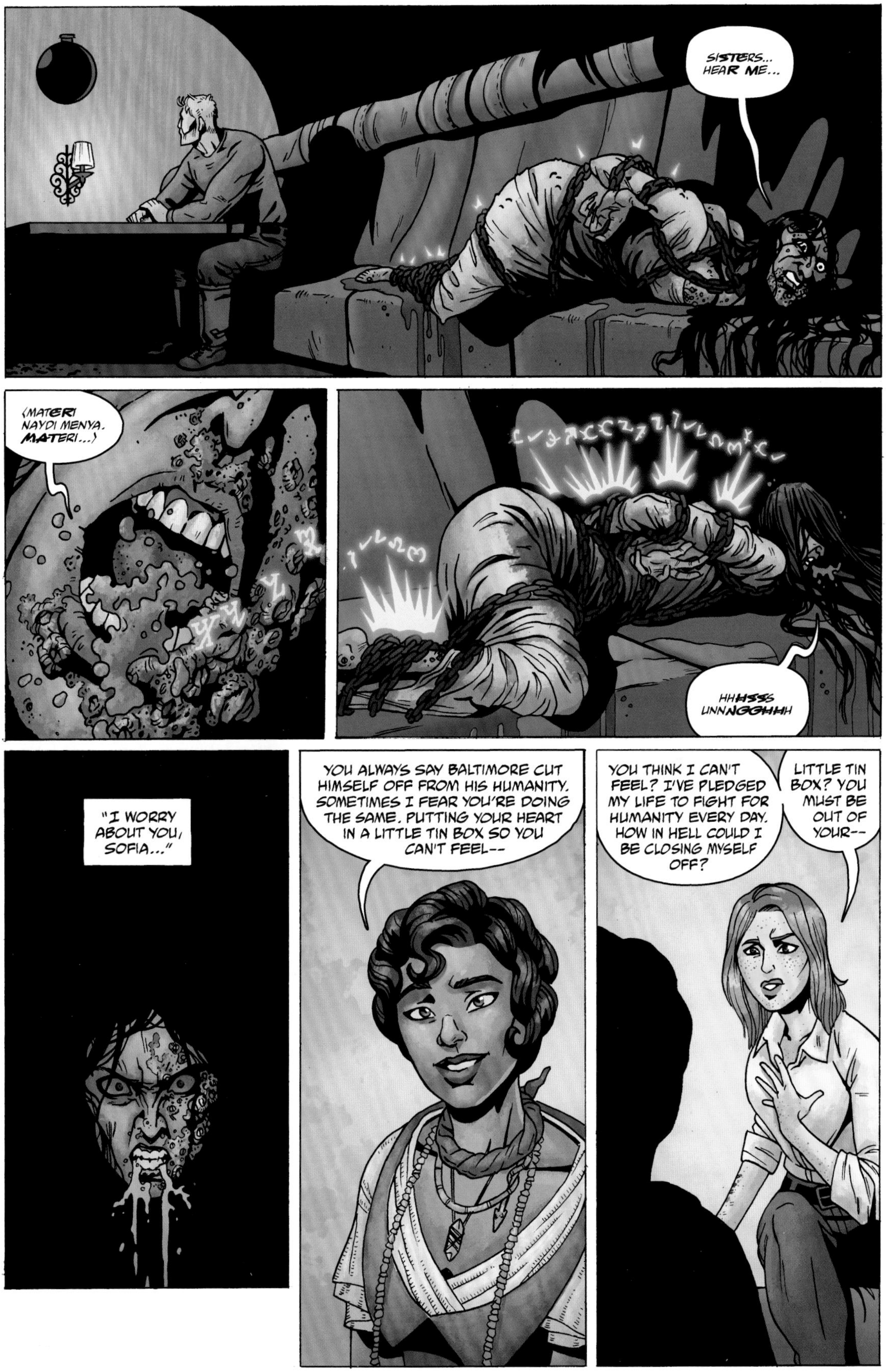
SISTERS... HEAR ME...
‹MATERI NAYDI MENYA. MATERI...›
HHHSSS UNNNGGHHH
"I WORRY ABOUT YOU, SOFIA..."
YOU ALWAYS SAY BALTIMORE CUT HIMSELF OFF FROM HIS HUMANITY. SOMETIMES I FEAR YOU'RE DOING THE SAME. PUTTING YOUR HEART IN A LITTLE TIN BOX SO YOU CAN'T FEEL--
YOU THINK I CAN'T FEEL? I'VE PLEDGED MY LIFE TO FIGHT FOR HUMANITY EVERY DAY. HOW IN HELL COULD I BE CLOSING MYSELF OFF?
LITTLE TIN BOX? YOU MUST BE OUT OF YOUR--

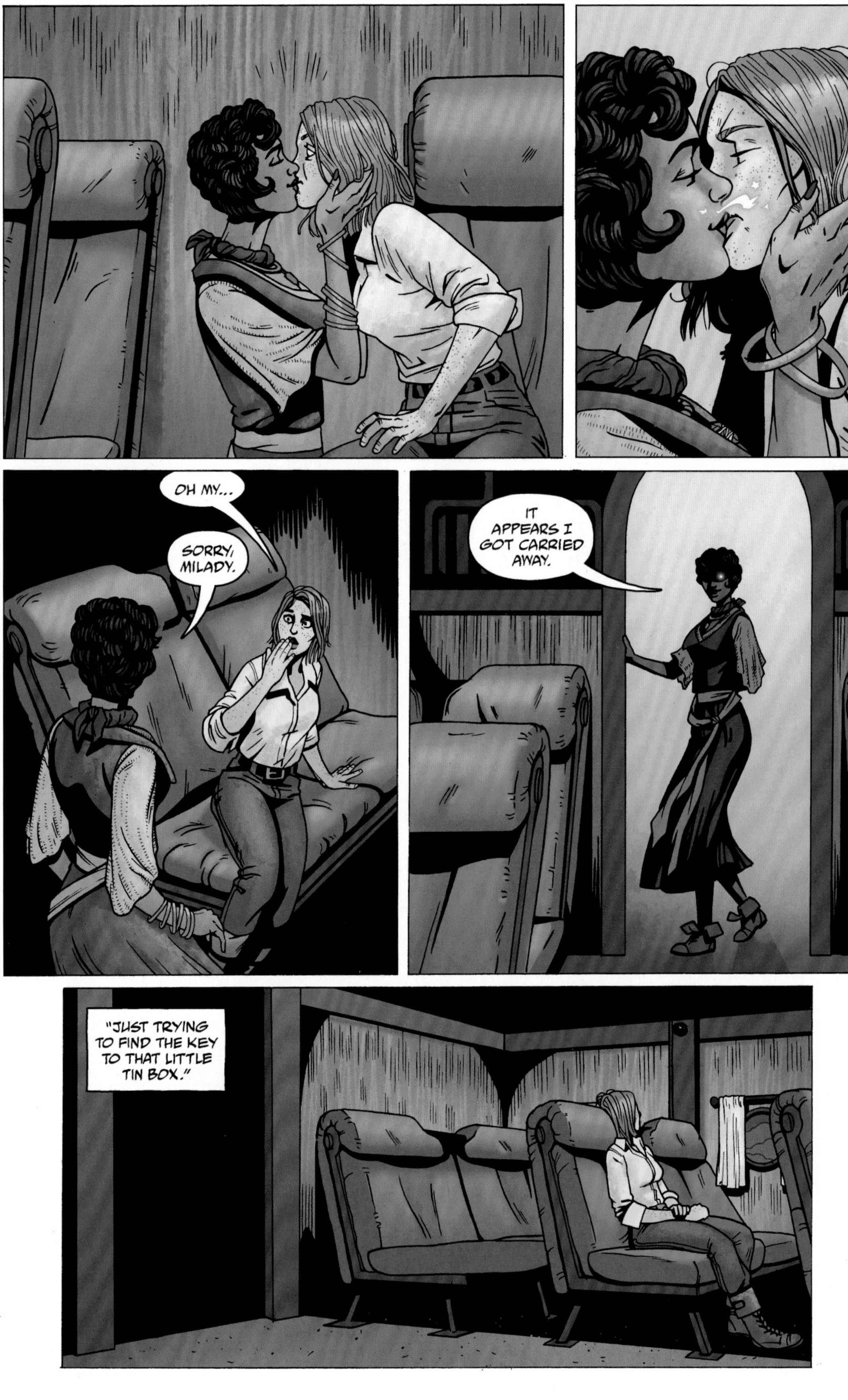
OH MY...
SORRY, MILADY.
IT APPEARS I GOT CARRIED AWAY.
"JUST TRYING TO FIND THE KEY TO THAT LITTLE TIN BOX."

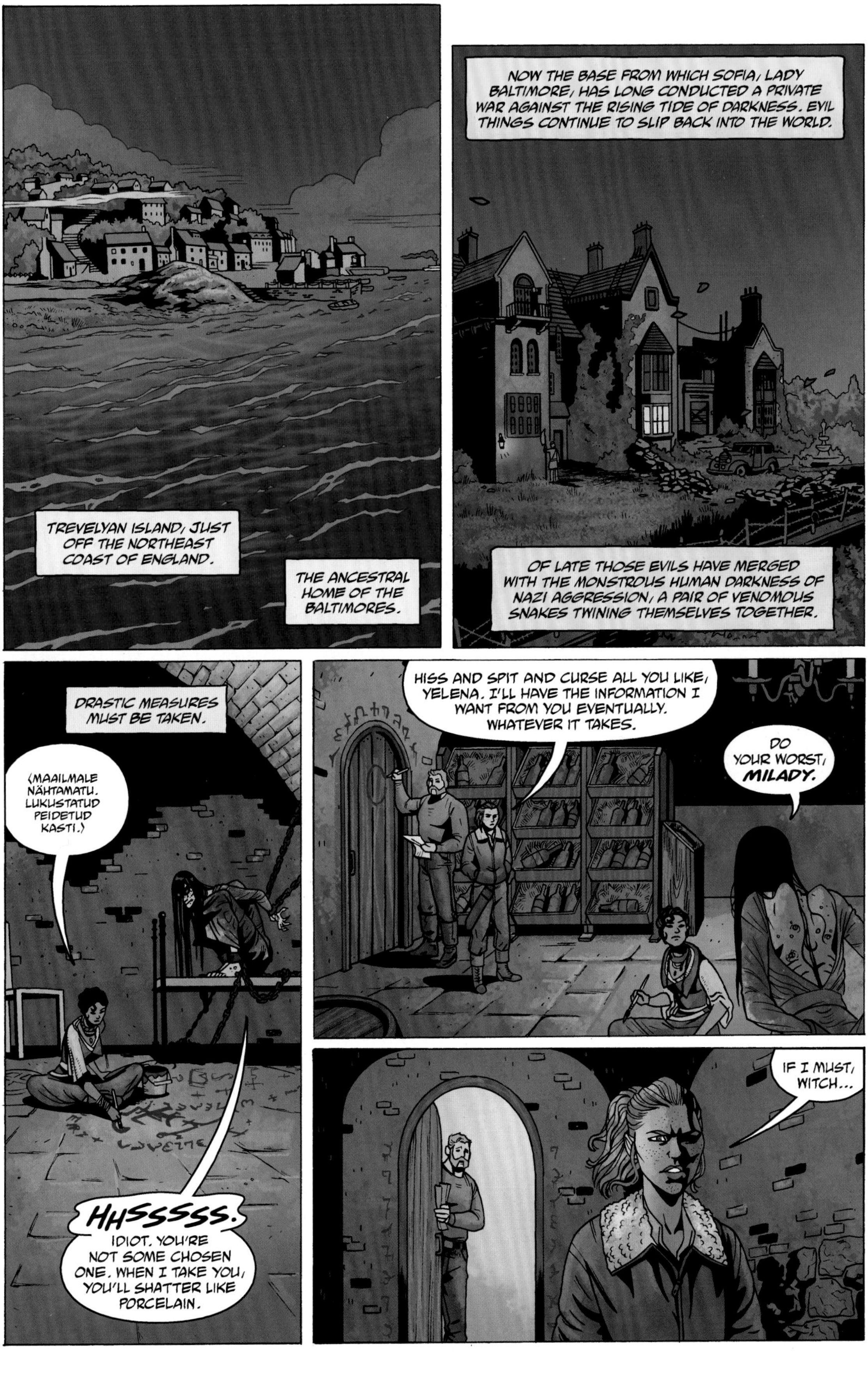

TREVELYAN ISLAND, JUST OFF THE NORTHEAST COAST OF ENGLAND.
THE ANCESTRAL HOME OF THE BALTIMORES.
NOW THE BASE FROM WHICH SOFIA, LADY BALTIMORE, HAS LONG CONDUCTED A PRIVATE WAR AGAINST THE RISING TIDE OF DARKNESS. EVIL THINGS CONTINUE TO SLIP BACK INTO THE WORLD.
OF LATE THOSE EVILS HAVE MERGED WITH THE MONSTROUS HUMAN DARKNESS OF NAZI AGGRESSION, A PAIR OF VENOMOUS SNAKES TWINING THEMSELVES TOGETHER.
DRASTIC MEASURES MUST BE TAKEN.
(MAAILMALE NÄHTAMATU. LUKUSTATUD PEIDETUD KASTI.)
HHSSSSS.
IDIOT. YOU'RE NOT SOME CHOSEN ONE. WHEN I TAKE YOU, YOU'LL SHATTER LIKE PORCELAIN.
HISS AND SPIT AND CURSE ALL YOU LIKE, YELENA. I'LL HAVE THE INFORMATION I WANT FROM YOU EVENTUALLY. WHATEVER IT TAKES.
DO YOUR WORST, MILADY.
IF I MUST, WITCH...

"...IF I MUST."

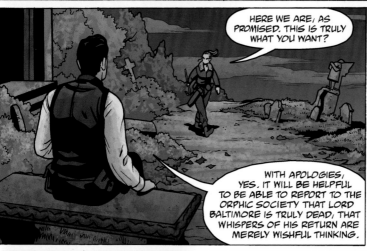

HERE WE ARE, AS PROMISED. THIS IS TRULY WHAT YOU WANT?

WITH APOLOGIES, YES. IT WILL BE HELPFUL TO BE ABLE TO REPORT TO THE ORPHIC SOCIETY THAT LORD BALTIMORE IS TRULY DEAD, THAT WHISPERS OF HIS RETURN ARE MERELY WISHFUL THINKING.

SKREEEEEE

I WISH HE WERE ALIVE. PARTLY BECAUSE I ADMIRED AND CARED FOR HIM...

...BUT MOSTLY BECAUSE IF HE WERE HERE, I COULD REST. I COULD HAND RESPONSIBILITY FOR THIS WAR BACK TO HIM.

COME ON, THEN. GIVE ME A HAND.

RRMMMBLLL

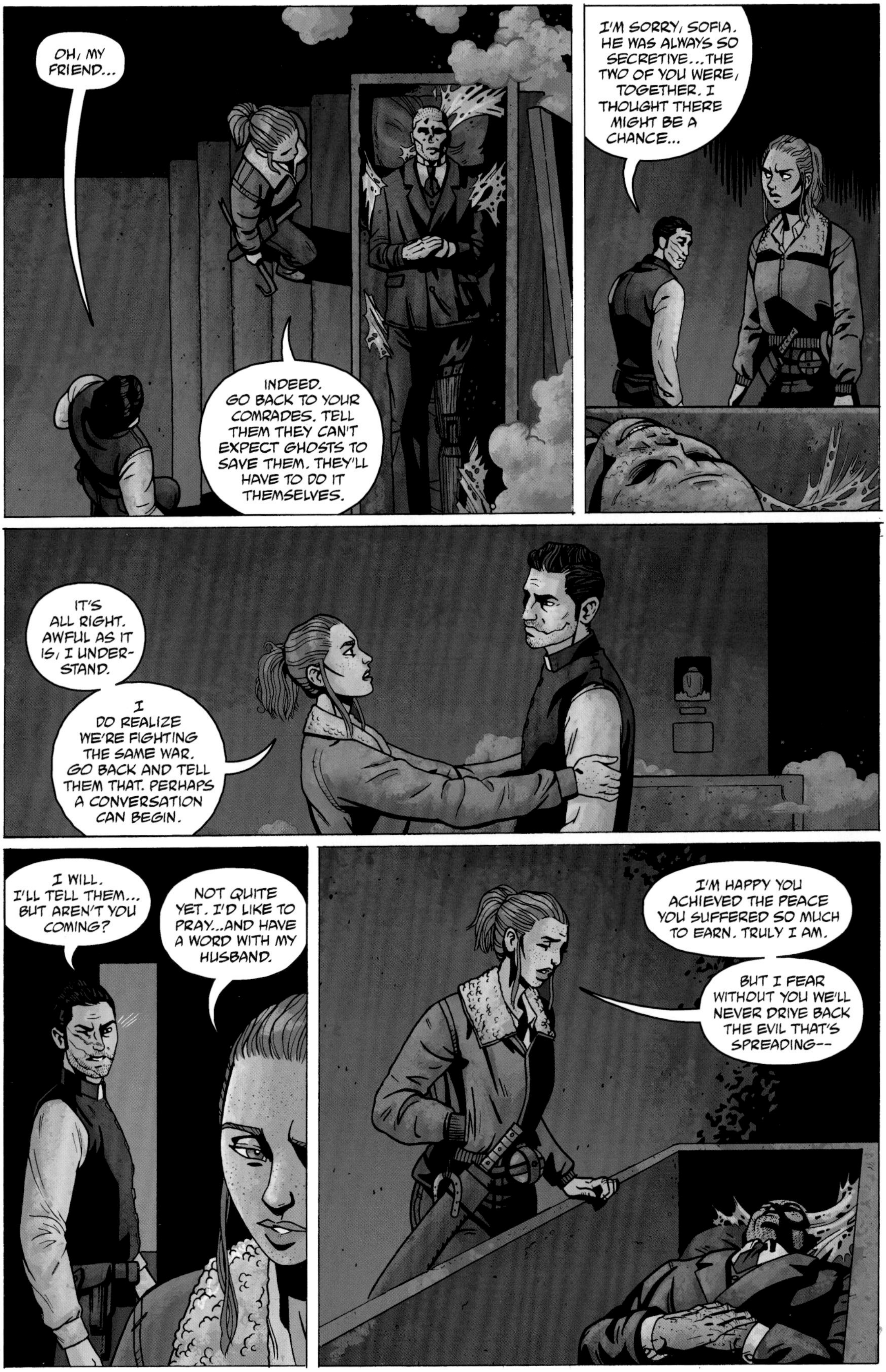
OH, MY FRIEND...
INDEED. GO BACK TO YOUR COMRADES. TELL THEM THEY CAN'T EXPECT GHOSTS TO SAVE THEM. THEY'LL HAVE TO DO IT THEMSELVES.
I'M SORRY, SOFIA. HE WAS ALWAYS SO SECRETIVE...THE TWO OF YOU WERE, TOGETHER. I THOUGHT THERE MIGHT BE A CHANCE...
IT'S ALL RIGHT. AWFUL AS IT IS, I UNDER-STAND.
I DO REALIZE WE'RE FIGHTING THE SAME WAR. GO BACK AND TELL THEM THAT. PERHAPS A CONVERSATION CAN BEGIN.
I WILL. I'LL TELL THEM... BUT AREN'T YOU COMING?
NOT QUITE YET. I'D LIKE TO PRAY...AND HAVE A WORD WITH MY HUSBAND.
I'M HAPPY YOU ACHIEVED THE PEACE YOU SUFFERED SO MUCH TO EARN. TRULY I AM.
BUT I FEAR WITHOUT YOU WE'LL NEVER DRIVE BACK THE EVIL THAT'S SPREADING--

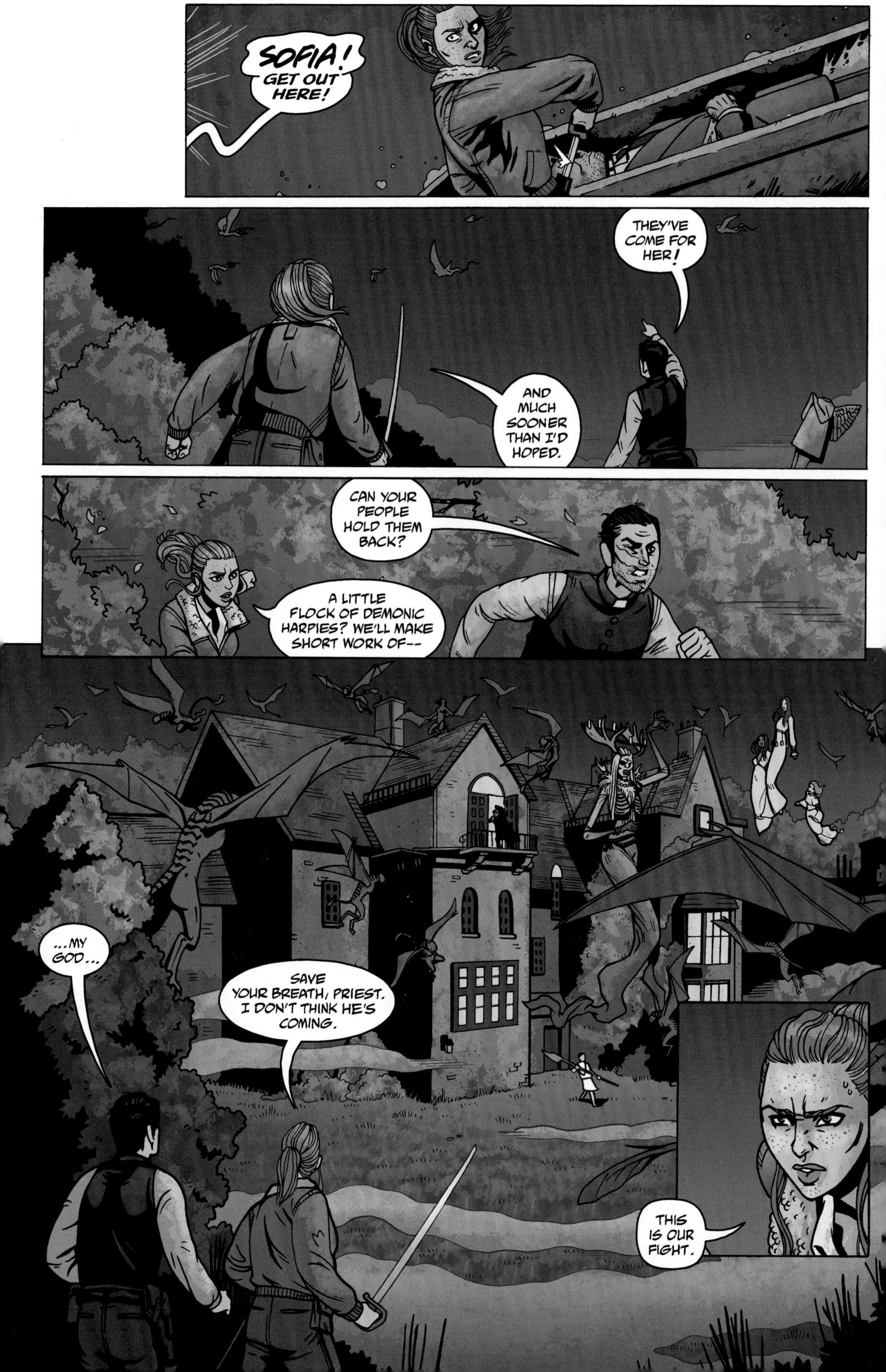
SOFIA! GET OUT HERE!
THEY'VE COME FOR HER!
AND MUCH SOONER THAN I'D HOPED.
CAN YOUR PEOPLE HOLD THEM BACK?
A LITTLE FLOCK OF DEMONIC HARPIES? WE'LL MAKE SHORT WORK OF--
...MY GOD...
SAVE YOUR BREATH, PRIEST. I DON'T THINK HE'S COMING.
THIS IS OUR FIGHT.

CHAPTER TWO

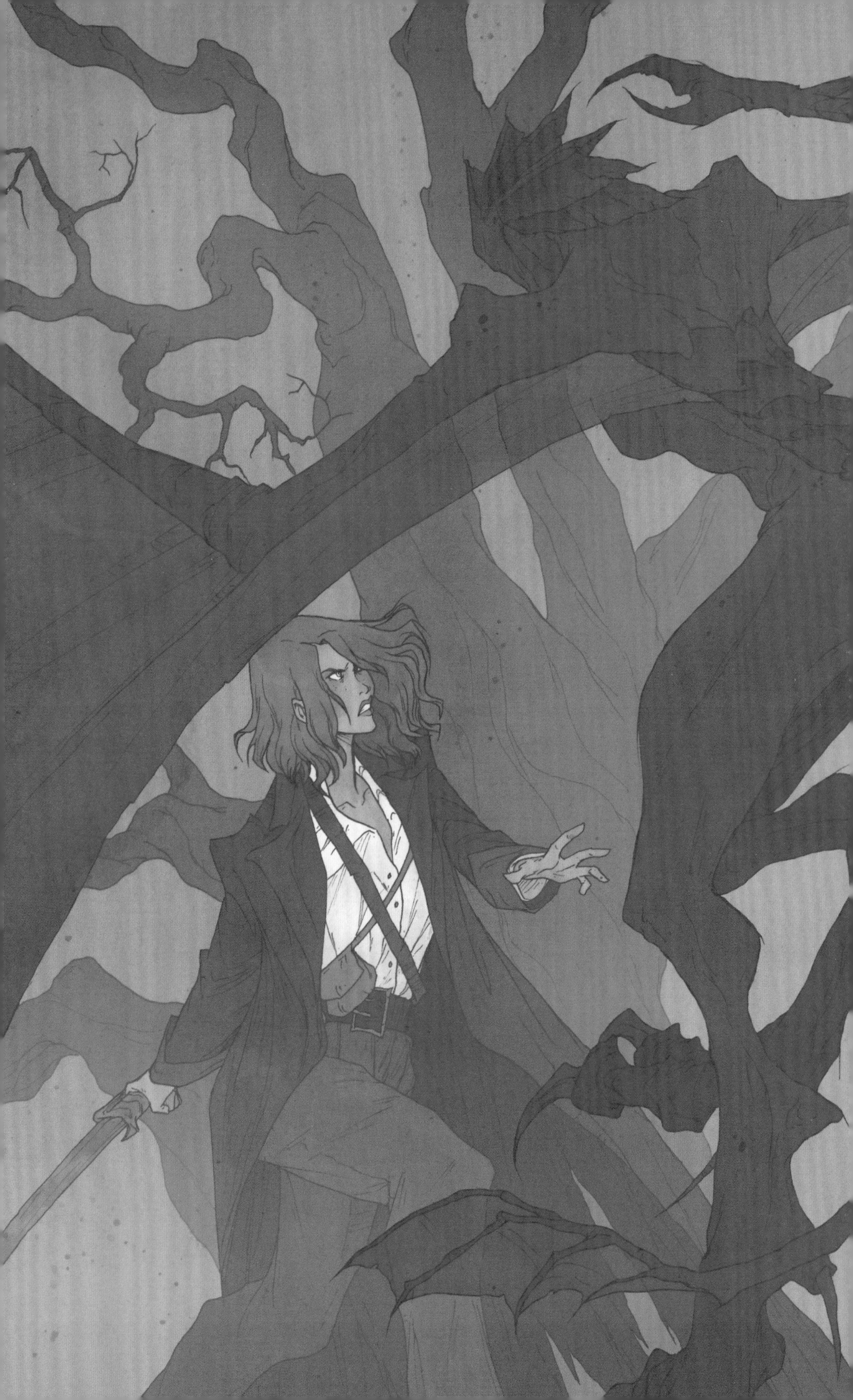

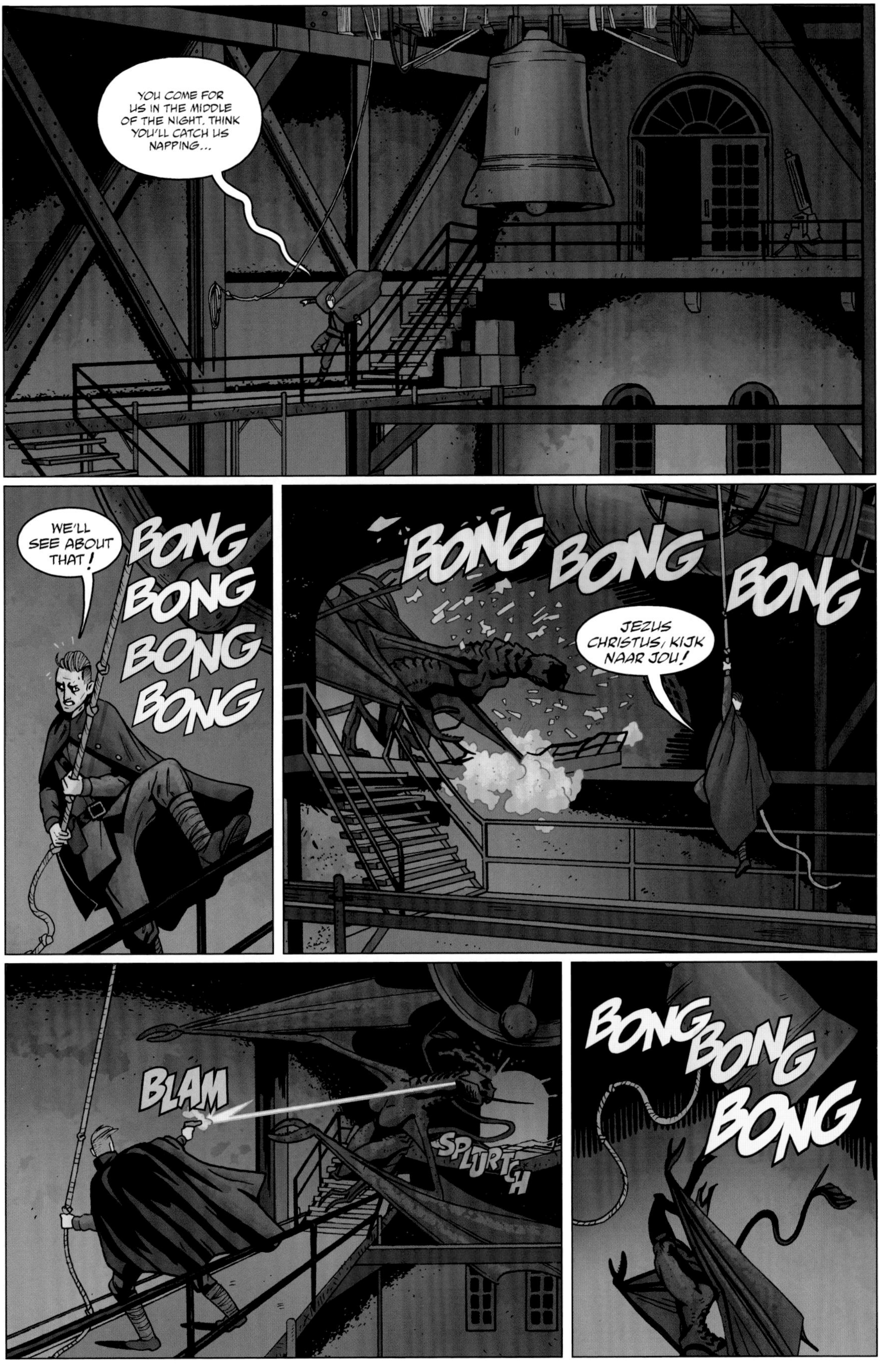
YOU COME FOR US IN THE MIDDLE OF THE NIGHT. THINK YOU'LL CATCH US NAPPING...
WE'LL SEE ABOUT THAT!
BONG
BONG
BONG
BONG
BONG BONG BONG
JEZUS CHRISTUS, KIJK NAAR JOU!
BLAM
SPLURTCH
BONG BONG BONG

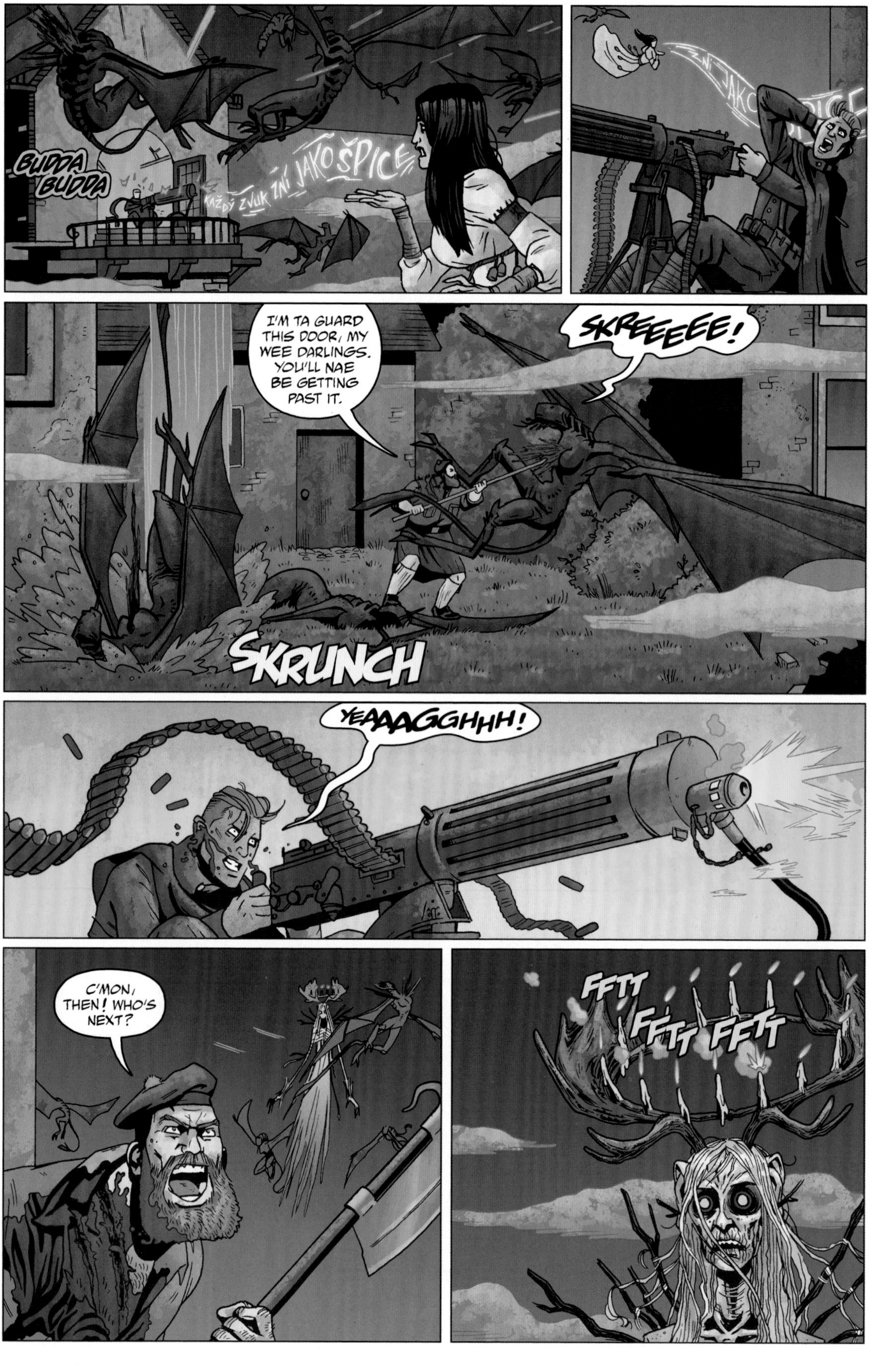
BUDDA BUDDA
KAŽDÝ ZVUK ZNÍ JAKO ŠPICE
ZNÍ JAKO
I'M TA GUARD THIS DOOR, MY WEE DARLINGS. YOU'LL NAE BE GETTING PAST IT.
SKREEEEEE!
SKRUNCH
YEAAAGGHHH!
C'MON, THEN! WHO'S NEXT?
FFTT FFTTT FFTT

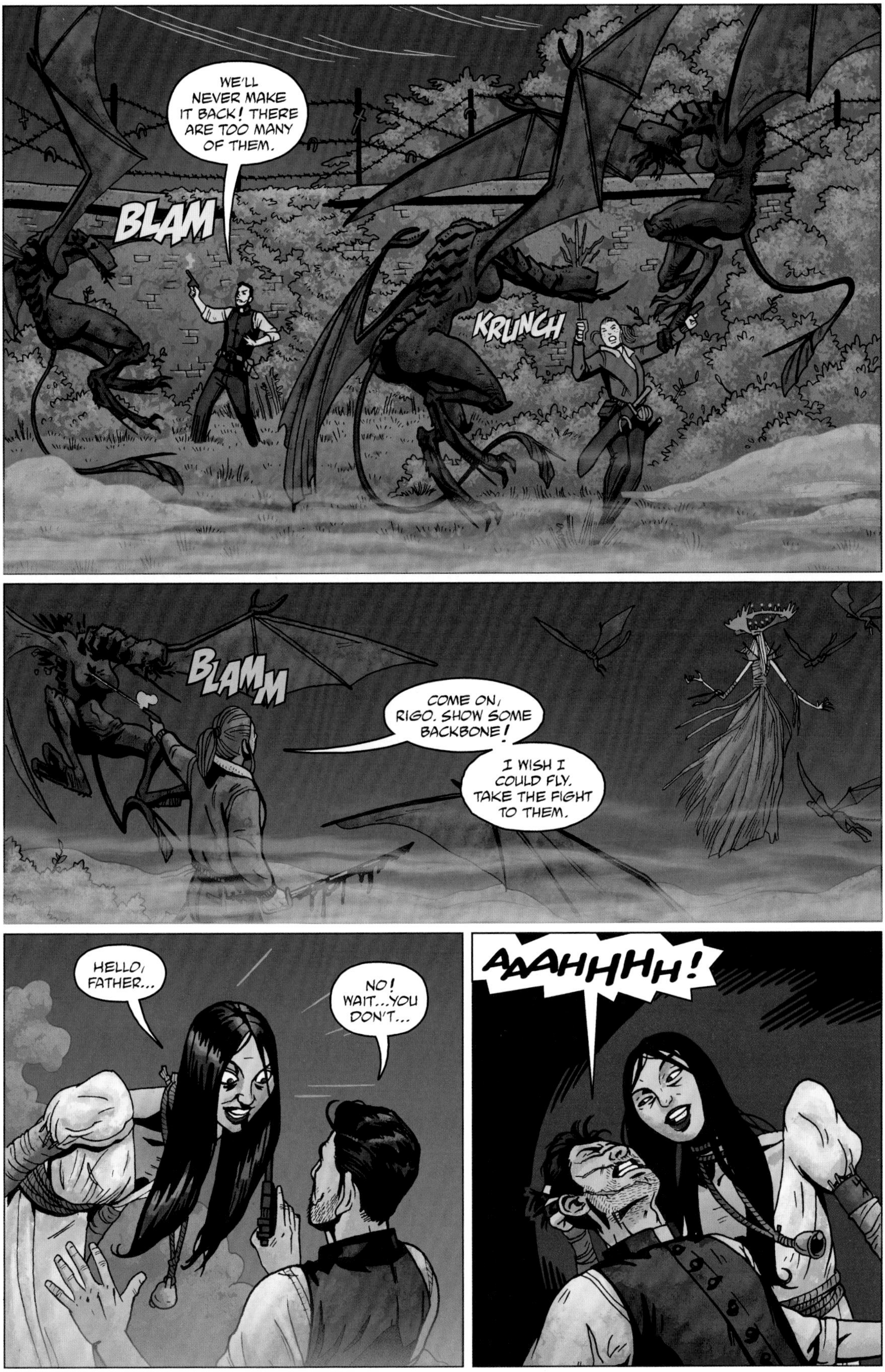
WE'LL NEVER MAKE IT BACK! THERE ARE TOO MANY OF THEM.
BLAM
KRUNCH
BLAMM
COME ON, RIGO. SHOW SOME BACKBONE!
I WISH I COULD FLY. TAKE THE FIGHT TO THEM.
HELLO, FATHER...
NO! WAIT...YOU DON'T...
AAAHHHH!

OH, MY POOR LITTLE FRIEND. THEY'VE COME FOR ME, AND I'M AFRAID THEY'LL HAVE YOUR GUTS FOR GARTERS.

YOU'RE A SENSIBLE YOUNG MAN, CHARLIE KIDD. RELEASE ME NOW, AND I'LL ASK THEM TO SHOW MERCY WITH YOU.

THAT'S RIGHT... NOW'S THE TIME.

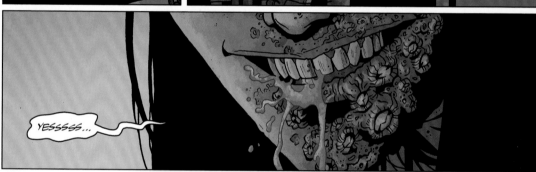

YESSSSS...

NJAL! JOSEPHINE! THE TWO OF YOU GO HELP MacGOLDRICK AT THE DOOR!

LADY BALTIMORE WENT TO THE CEMETERY. IF YOU DON'T SEE HER OUTSIDE, CLEAR A PATH AND GO RETRIEVE HER!

WE WON'T COME BACK WITHOUT HER!

YEEAAGH!

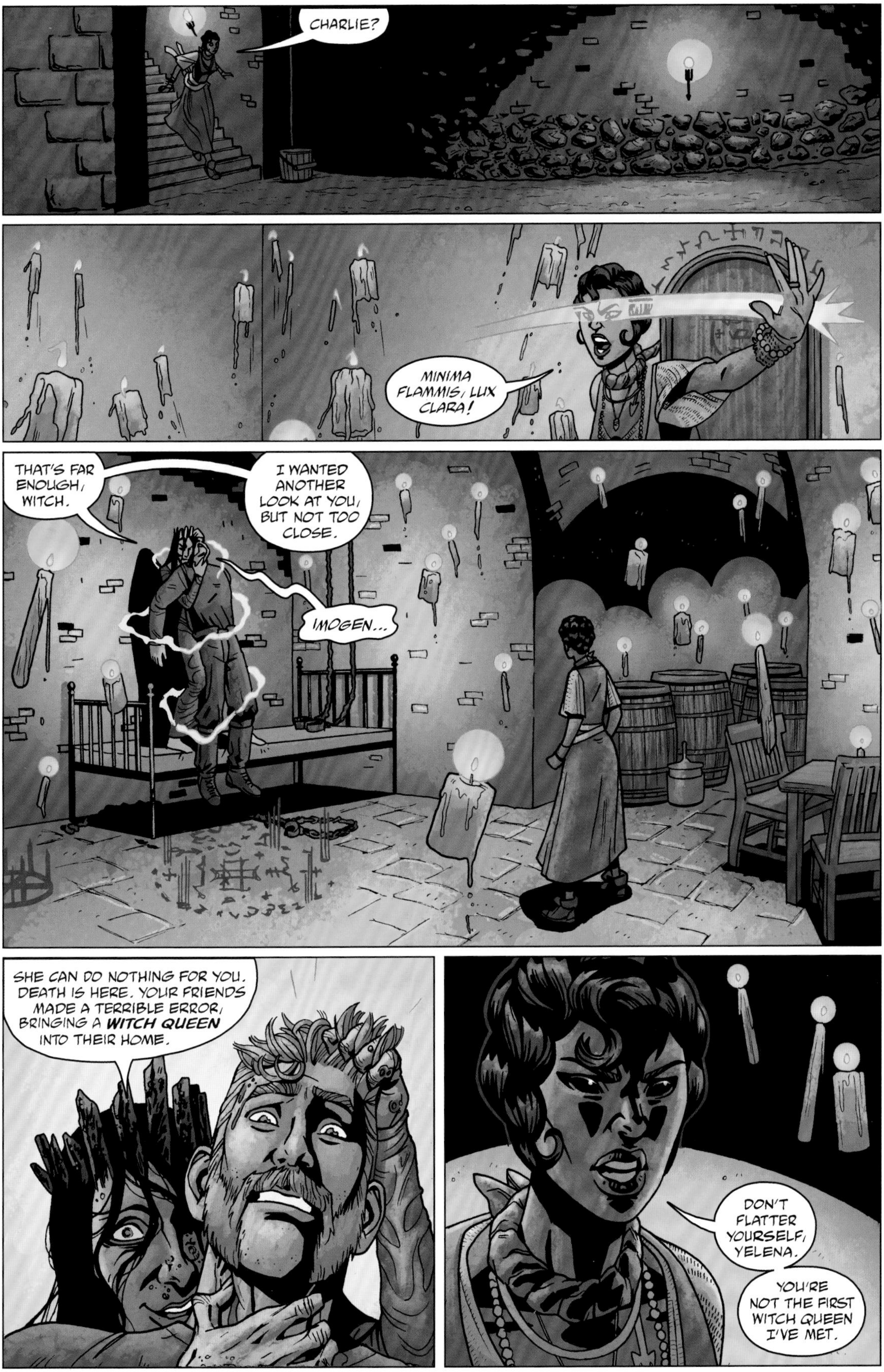
CHARLIE?
MINIMA FLAMMIS, LUX CLARA!
THAT'S FAR ENOUGH, WITCH.
I WANTED ANOTHER LOOK AT YOU, BUT NOT TOO CLOSE.
IMOGEN...
SHE CAN DO NOTHING FOR YOU. DEATH IS HERE. YOUR FRIENDS MADE A TERRIBLE ERROR, BRINGING A **WITCH QUEEN** INTO THEIR HOME.
DON'T FLATTER YOURSELF, YELENA.
YOU'RE NOT THE FIRST WITCH QUEEN I'VE MET.

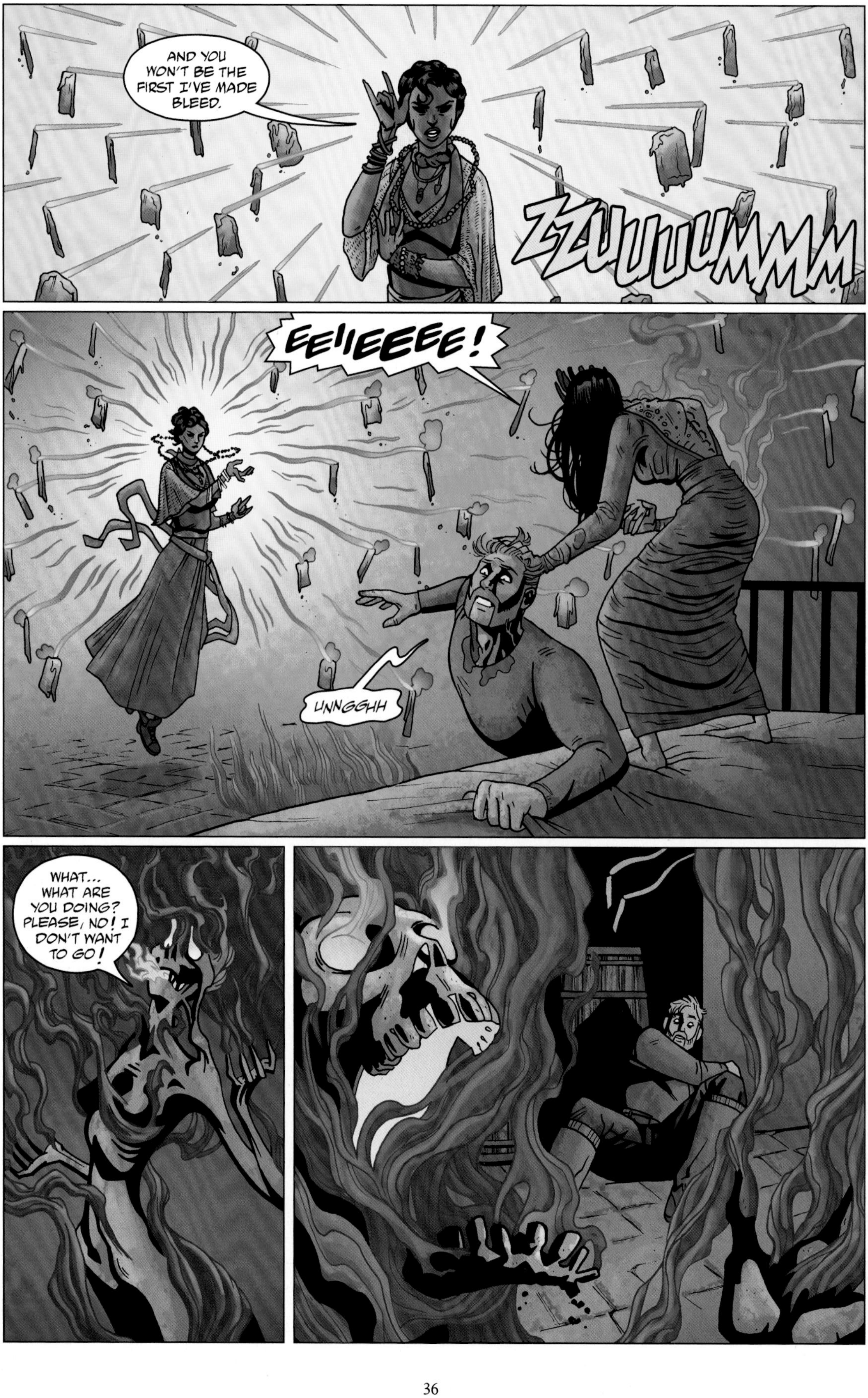
AND YOU WON'T BE THE FIRST I'VE MADE BLEED.
ZZUUUUMMMM
EEEIEEEE!
UNNGGHH
WHAT... WHAT ARE YOU DOING? PLEASE, NO! I DON'T WANT TO GO!

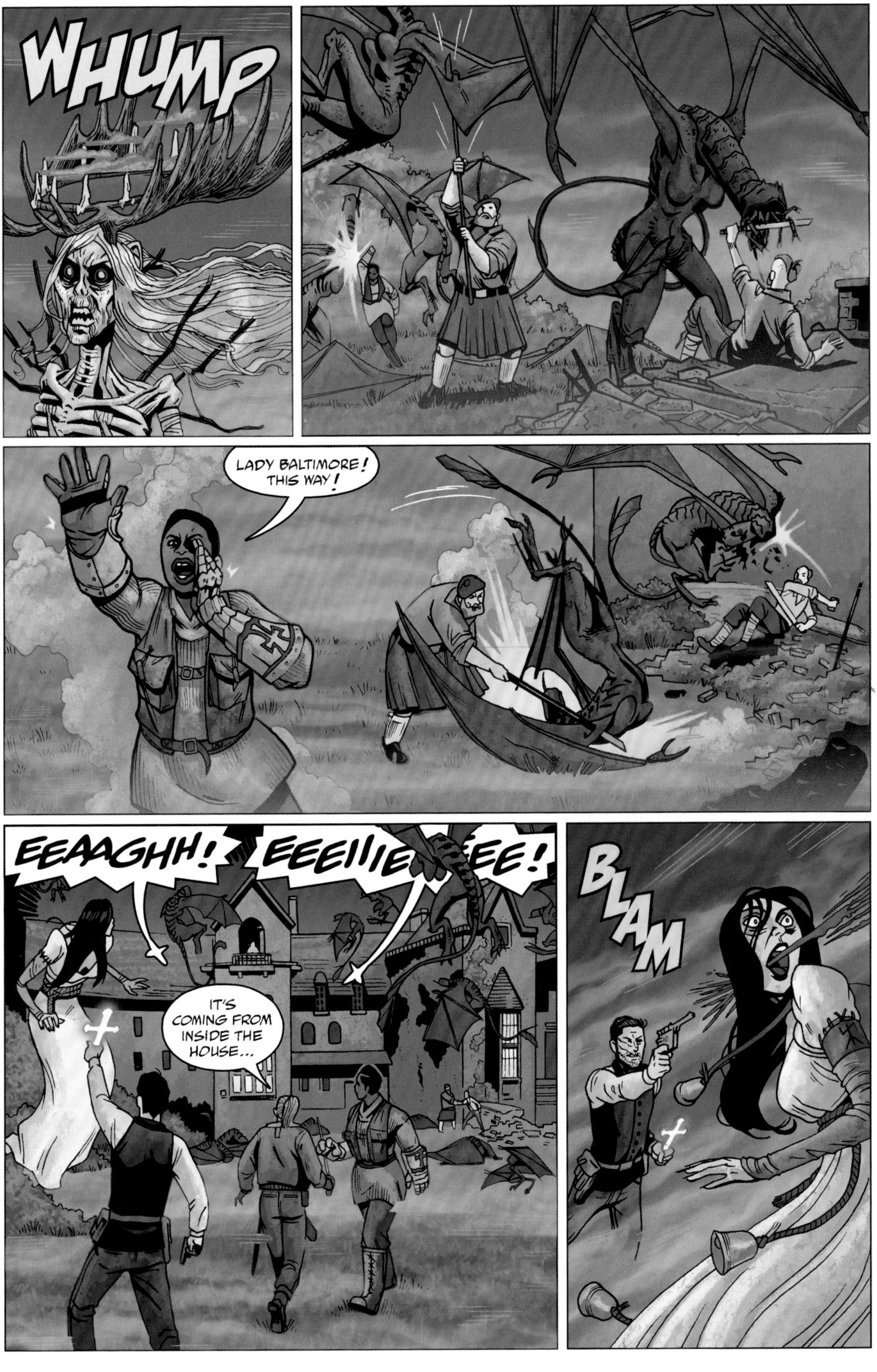
WHUMP
LADY BALTIMORE! THIS WAY!
EEAAGHH!
EEEIIIE EEE!
IT'S COMING FROM INSIDE THE HOUSE...
BLAM

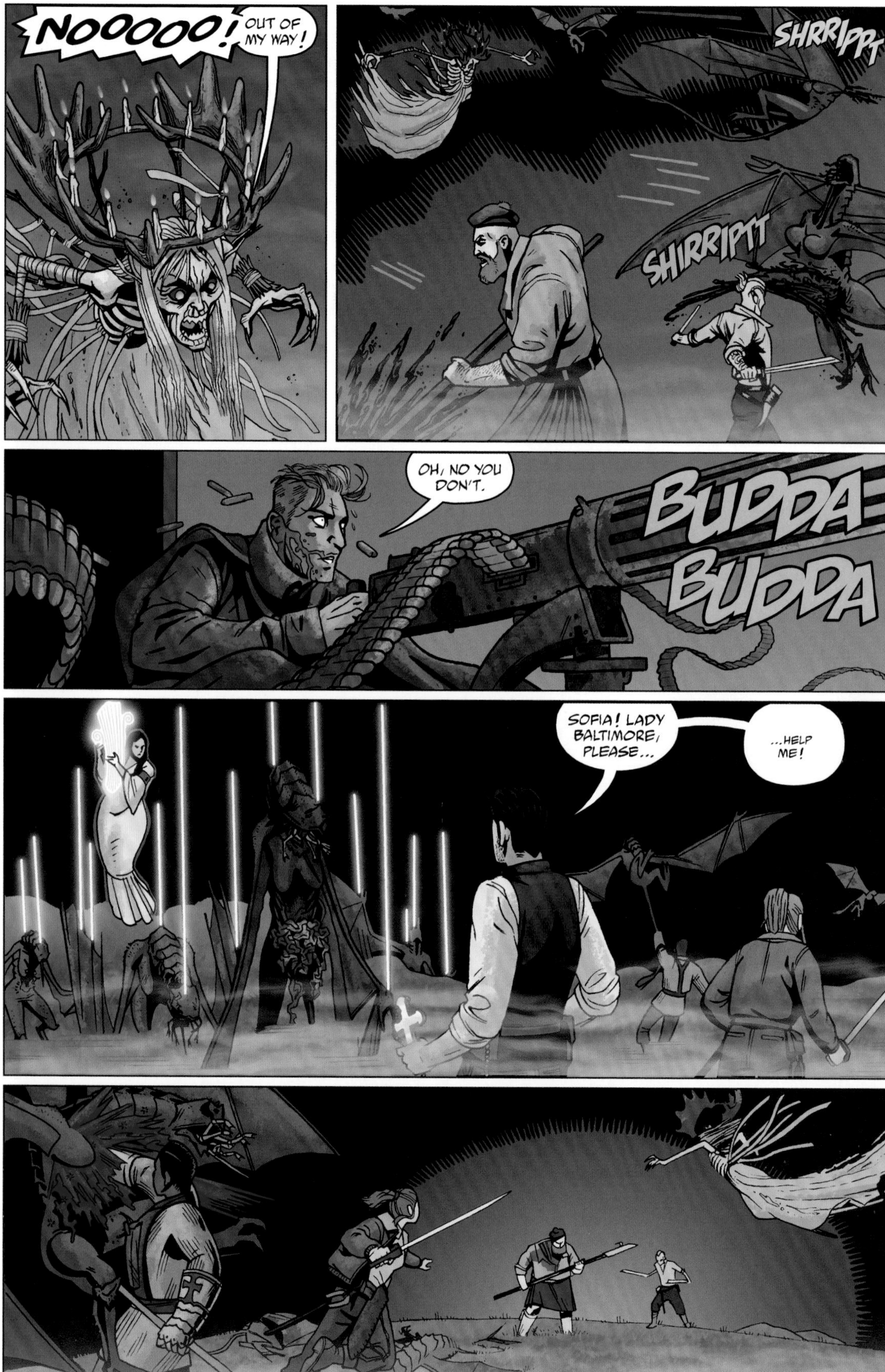
NOOOOO!
OUT OF MY WAY!
SHRRIPPT
SHRRIPTT
OH, NO YOU DON'T.
BUDDA BUDDA
SOFIA! LADY BALTIMORE, PLEASE...
...HELP ME!

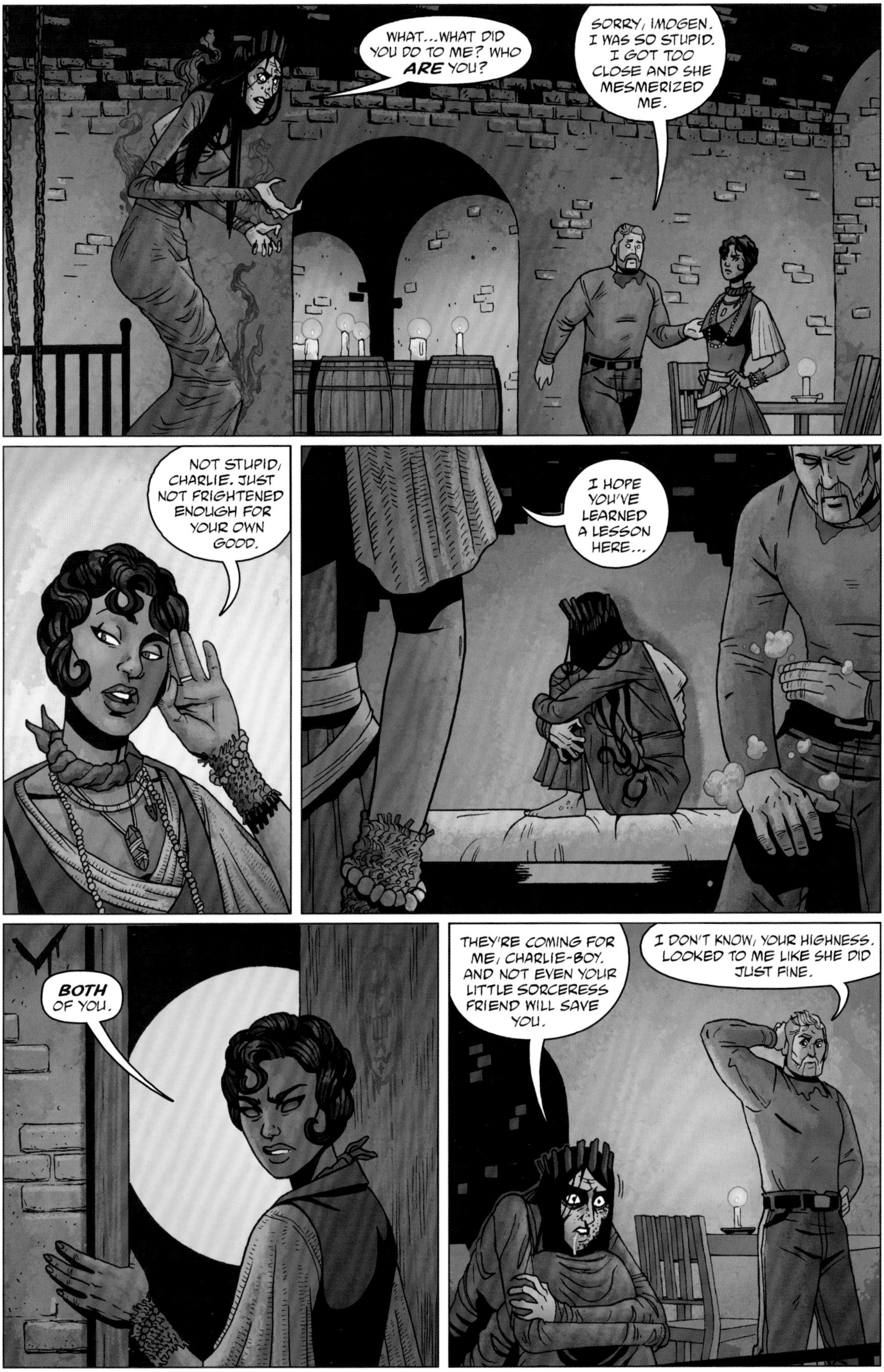
WHAT...WHAT DID YOU DO TO ME? WHO ARE YOU?
SORRY, IMOGEN. I WAS SO STUPID. I GOT TOO CLOSE AND SHE MESMERIZED ME.
NOT STUPID, CHARLIE. JUST NOT FRIGHTENED ENOUGH FOR YOUR OWN GOOD.
I HOPE YOU'VE LEARNED A LESSON HERE...
BOTH OF YOU.
THEY'RE COMING FOR ME, CHARLIE-BOY. AND NOT EVEN YOUR LITTLE SORCERESS FRIEND WILL SAVE YOU.
I DON'T KNOW, YOUR HIGHNESS. LOOKED TO ME LIKE SHE DID JUST FINE.

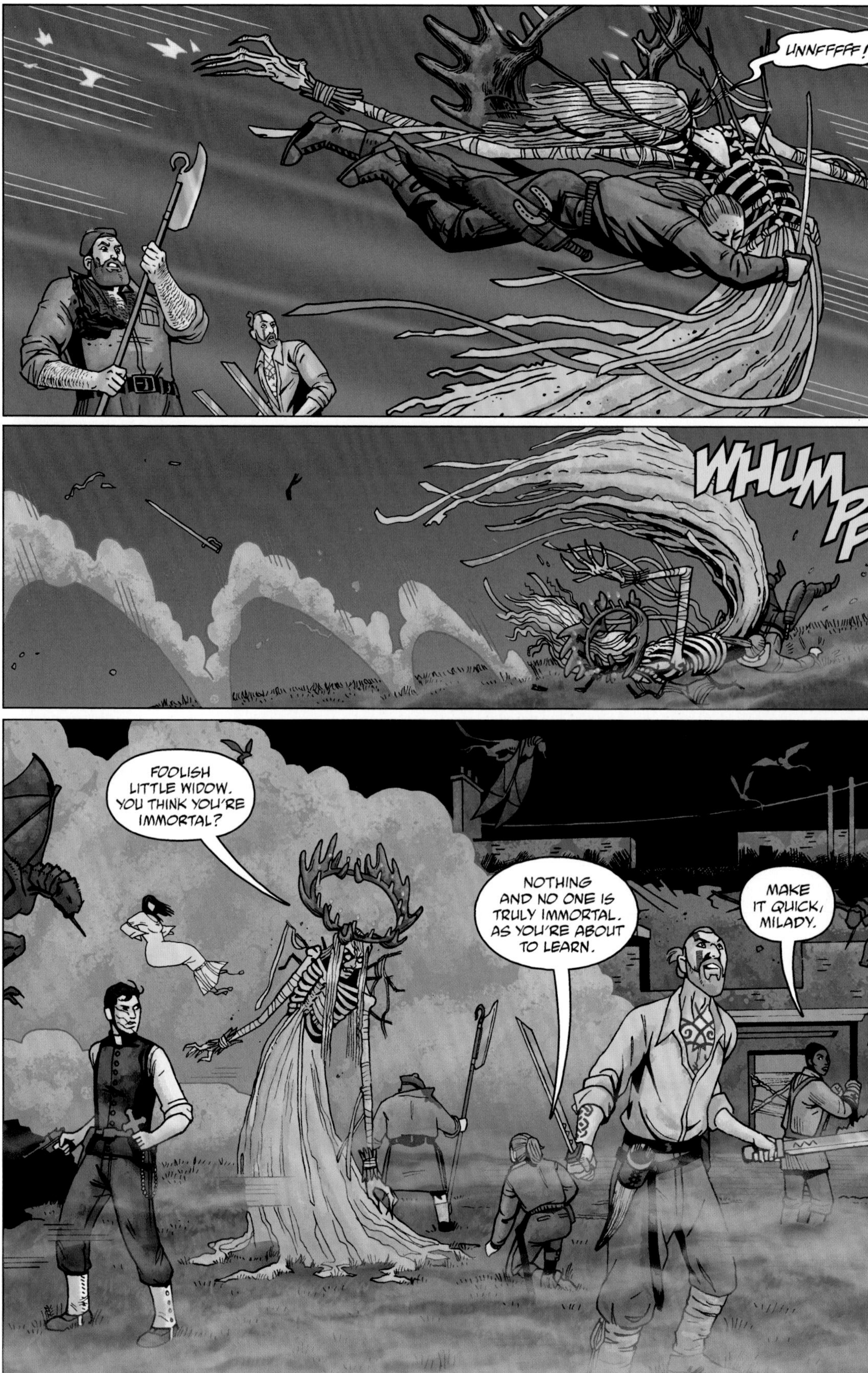
UNNFFFFF!
WHUMPP
FOOLISH LITTLE WIDOW. YOU THINK YOU'RE IMMORTAL?
NOTHING AND NO ONE IS TRULY IMMORTAL. AS YOU'RE ABOUT TO LEARN.
MAKE IT QUICK, MILADY.

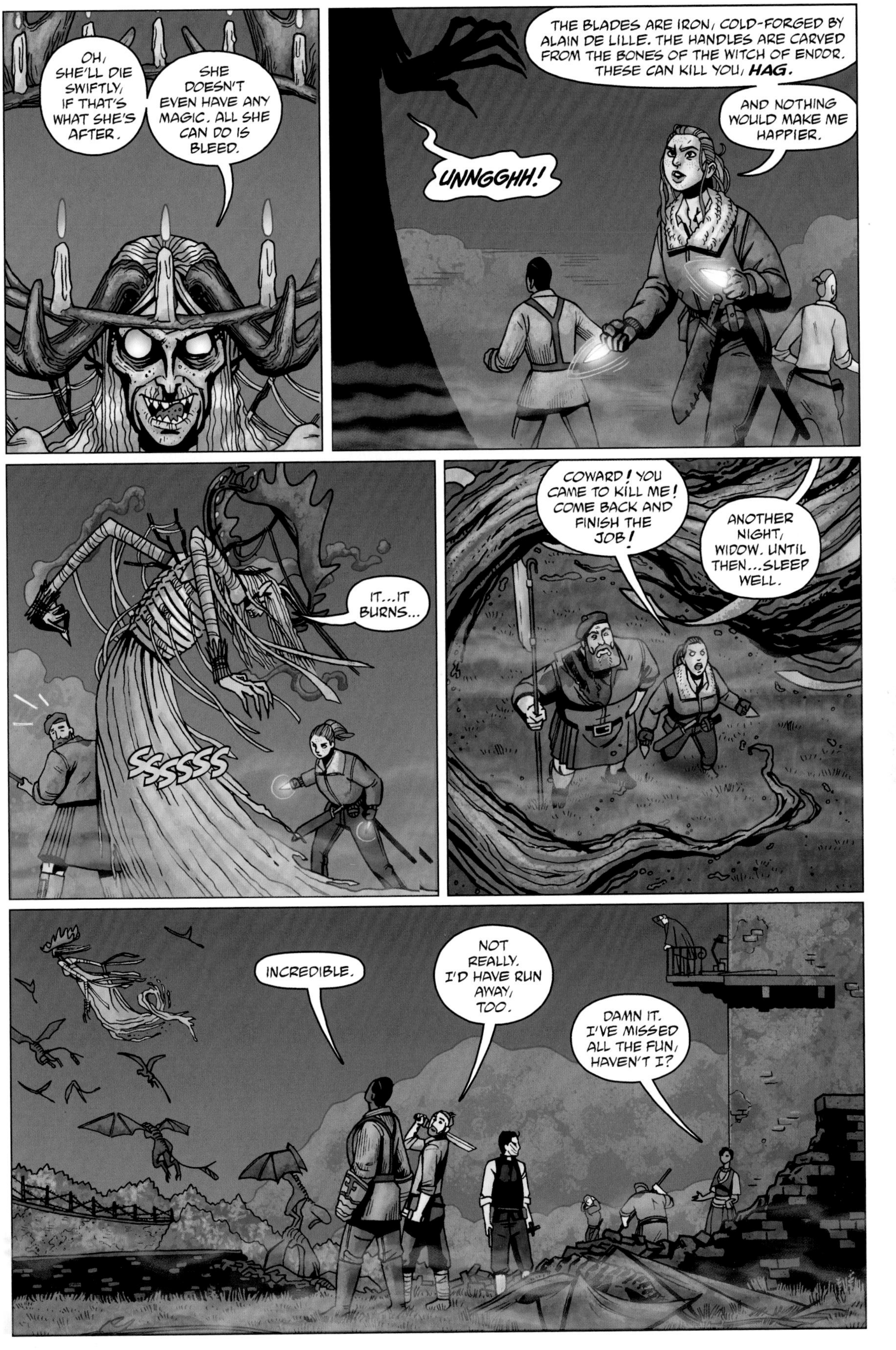
OH, SHE'LL DIE SWIFTLY, IF THAT'S WHAT SHE'S AFTER.
SHE DOESN'T EVEN HAVE ANY MAGIC. ALL SHE CAN DO IS BLEED.
THE BLADES ARE IRON, COLD-FORGED BY ALAIN DE LILLE. THE HANDLES ARE CARVED FROM THE BONES OF THE WITCH OF ENDOR. THESE CAN KILL YOU, HAG.
AND NOTHING WOULD MAKE ME HAPPIER.
UNNGGHH!
IT...IT BURNS...
SSSSSS
COWARD! YOU CAME TO KILL ME! COME BACK AND FINISH THE JOB!
ANOTHER NIGHT, WIDOW. UNTIL THEN...SLEEP WELL.
INCREDIBLE.
NOT REALLY. I'D HAVE RUN AWAY, TOO.
DAMN IT. I'VE MISSED ALL THE FUN, HAVEN'T I?

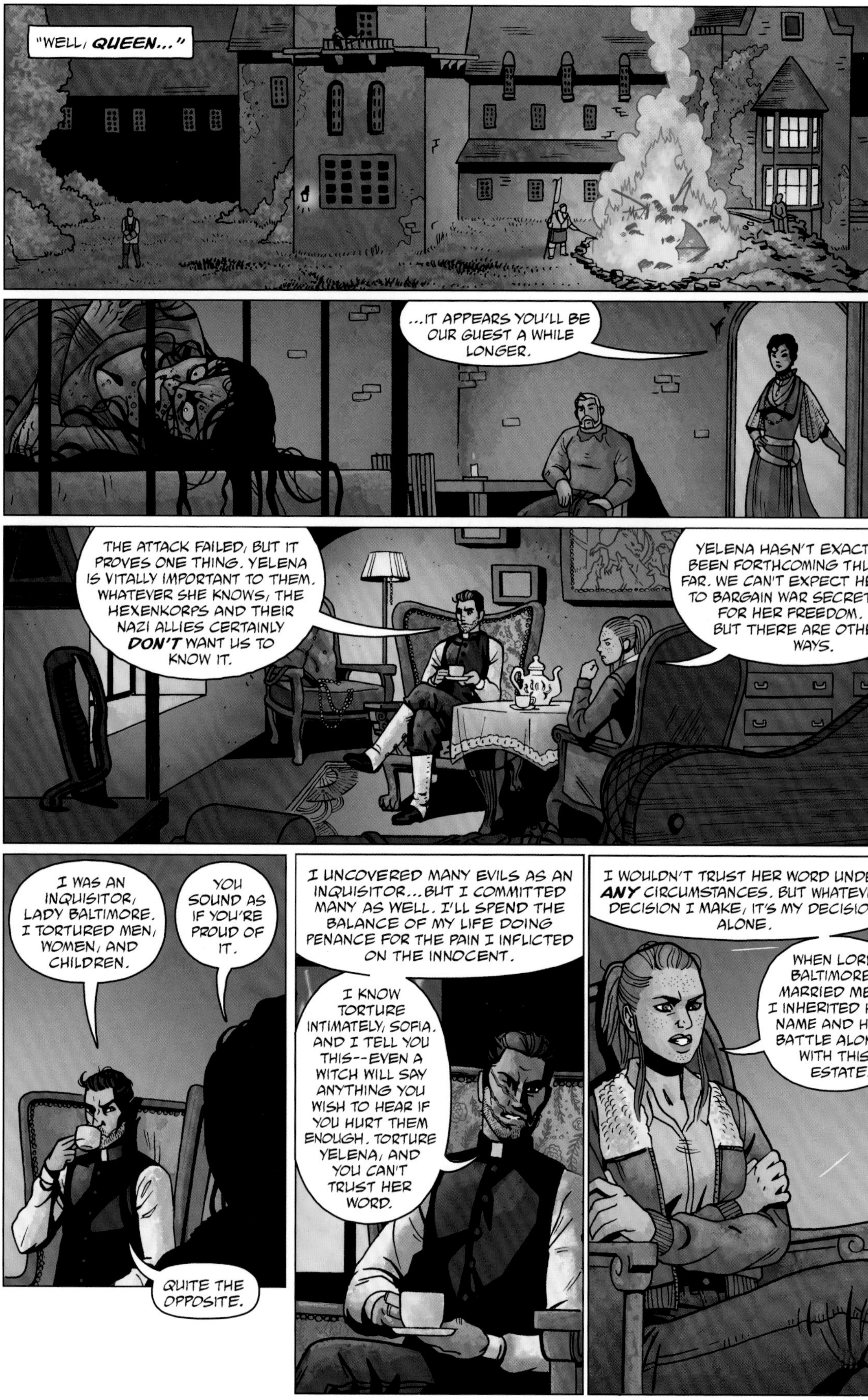
"WELL, QUEEN..."
...IT APPEARS YOU'LL BE OUR GUEST A WHILE LONGER.
THE ATTACK FAILED, BUT IT PROVES ONE THING. YELENA IS VITALLY IMPORTANT TO THEM. WHATEVER SHE KNOWS, THE HEXENKORPS AND THEIR NAZI ALLIES CERTAINLY DON'T WANT US TO KNOW IT.
YELENA HASN'T EXACTLY BEEN FORTHCOMING THUS FAR. WE CAN'T EXPECT HER TO BARGAIN WAR SECRETS FOR HER FREEDOM. BUT THERE ARE OTHER WAYS.
I WAS AN INQUISITOR, LADY BALTIMORE. I TORTURED MEN, WOMEN, AND CHILDREN.
YOU SOUND AS IF YOU'RE PROUD OF IT.
QUITE THE OPPOSITE.
I UNCOVERED MANY EVILS AS AN INQUISITOR... BUT I COMMITTED MANY AS WELL. I'LL SPEND THE BALANCE OF MY LIFE DOING PENANCE FOR THE PAIN I INFLICTED ON THE INNOCENT.
I KNOW TORTURE INTIMATELY, SOFIA. AND I TELL YOU THIS--EVEN A WITCH WILL SAY ANYTHING YOU WISH TO HEAR IF YOU HURT THEM ENOUGH. TORTURE YELENA, AND YOU CAN'T TRUST HER WORD.
I WOULDN'T TRUST HER WORD UNDER ANY CIRCUMSTANCES. BUT WHATEVER DECISION I MAKE, IT'S MY DECISION ALONE.
WHEN LORD BALTIMORE MARRIED ME, I INHERITED HIS NAME AND HIS BATTLE ALONG WITH THIS ESTATE.

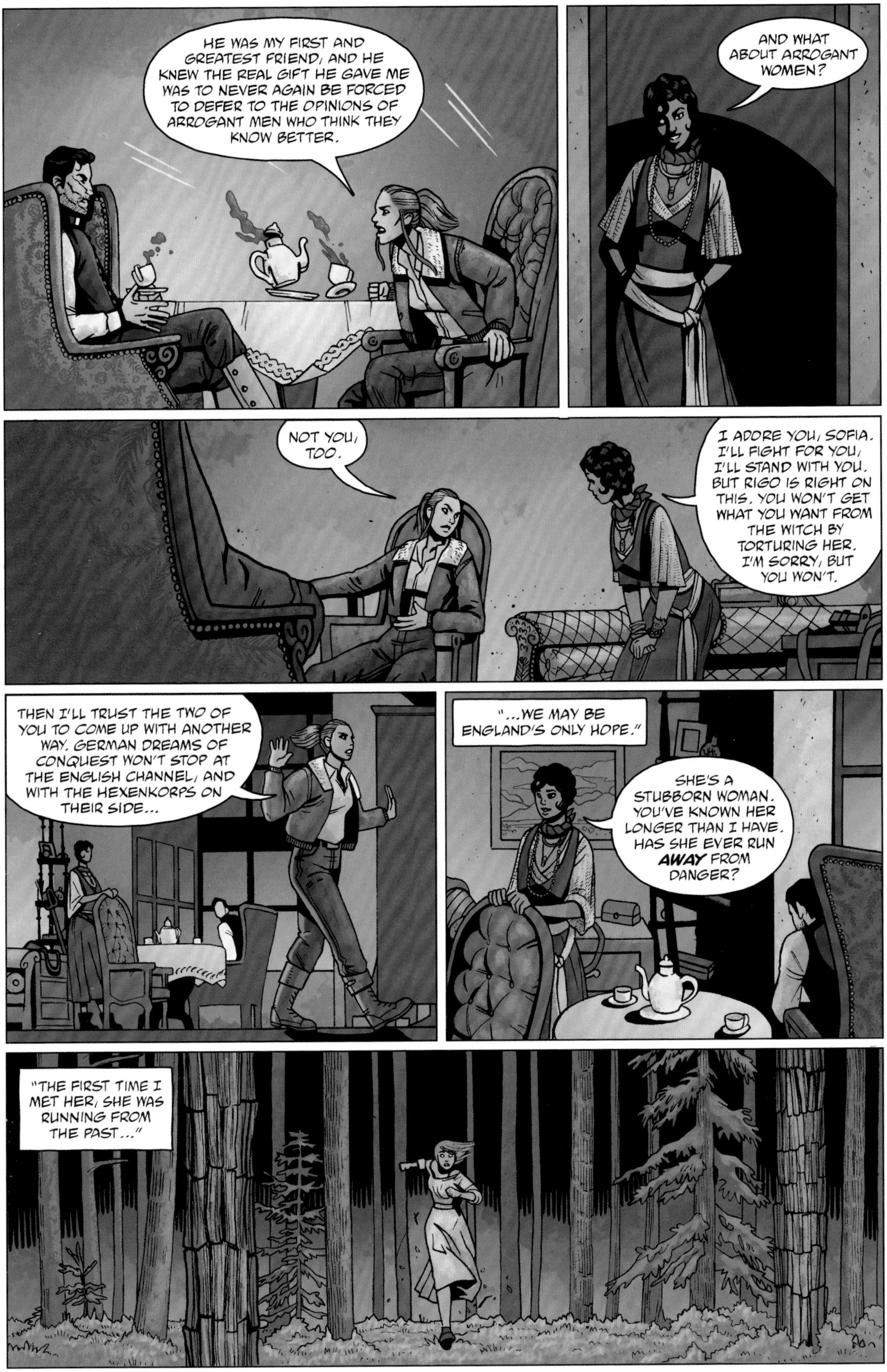
HE WAS MY FIRST AND GREATEST FRIEND, AND HE KNEW THE REAL GIFT HE GAVE ME WAS TO NEVER AGAIN BE FORCED TO DEFER TO THE OPINIONS OF ARROGANT MEN WHO THINK THEY KNOW BETTER.
AND WHAT ABOUT ARROGANT WOMEN?
NOT YOU, TOO.
I ADORE YOU, SOFIA. I'LL FIGHT FOR YOU, I'LL STAND WITH YOU. BUT RIGO IS RIGHT ON THIS. YOU WON'T GET WHAT YOU WANT FROM THE WITCH BY TORTURING HER. I'M SORRY, BUT YOU WON'T.
THEN I'LL TRUST THE TWO OF YOU TO COME UP WITH ANOTHER WAY. GERMAN DREAMS OF CONQUEST WON'T STOP AT THE ENGLISH CHANNEL, AND WITH THE HEXENKORPS ON THEIR SIDE...
"...WE MAY BE ENGLAND'S ONLY HOPE."
SHE'S A STUBBORN WOMAN. YOU'VE KNOWN HER LONGER THAN I HAVE. HAS SHE EVER RUN AWAY FROM DANGER?
"THE FIRST TIME I MET HER, SHE WAS RUNNING FROM THE PAST..."

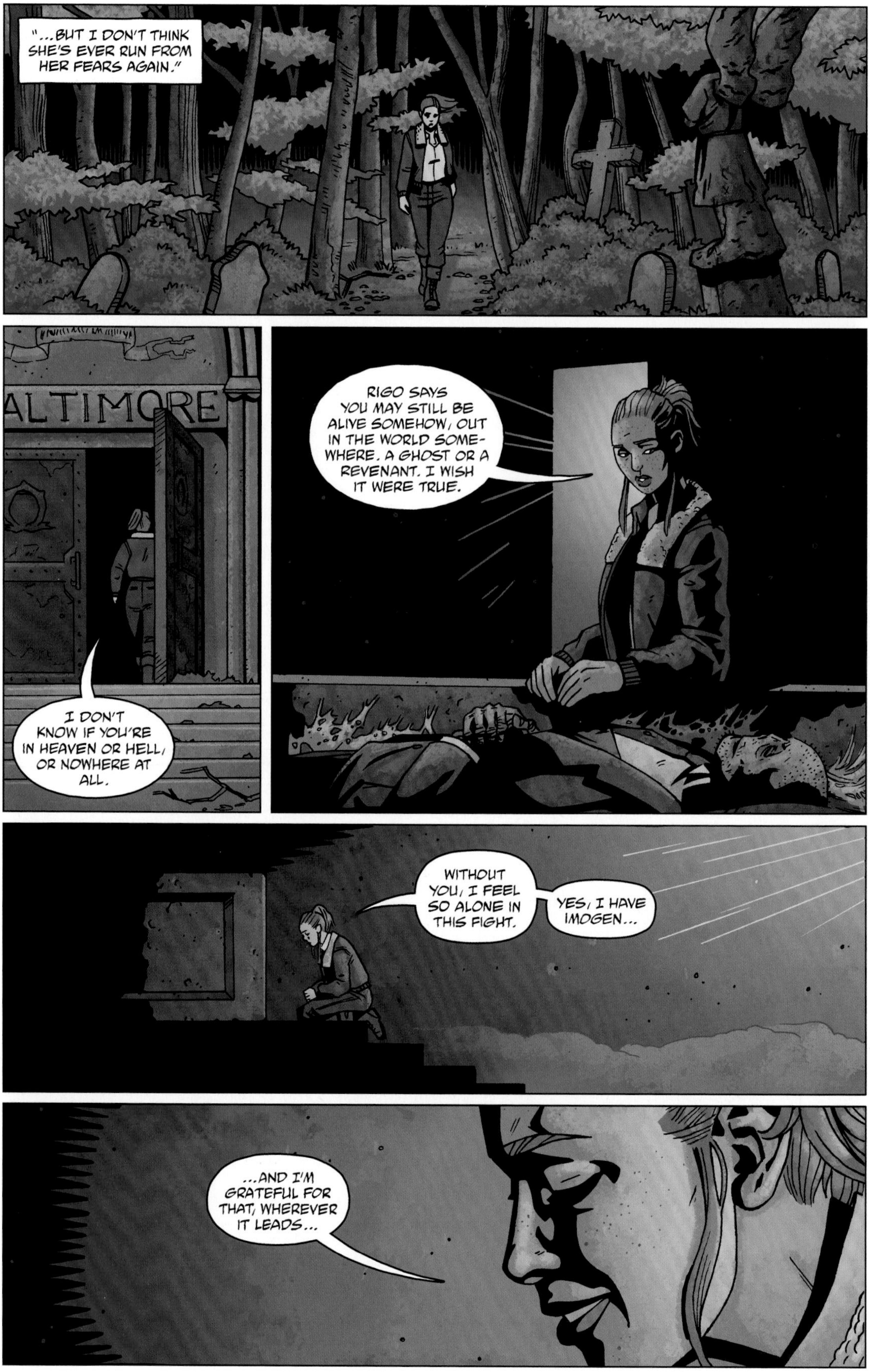
"...BUT I DON'T THINK SHE'S EVER RUN FROM HER FEARS AGAIN."
ALTIMORE
I DON'T KNOW IF YOU'RE IN HEAVEN OR HELL, OR NOWHERE AT ALL.
RIGO SAYS YOU MAY STILL BE ALIVE SOMEHOW, OUT IN THE WORLD SOMEWHERE. A GHOST OR A REVENANT. I WISH IT WERE TRUE.
WITHOUT YOU, I FEEL SO ALONE IN THIS FIGHT.
YES, I HAVE IMOGEN...
...AND I'M GRATEFUL FOR THAT, WHEREVER IT LEADS...

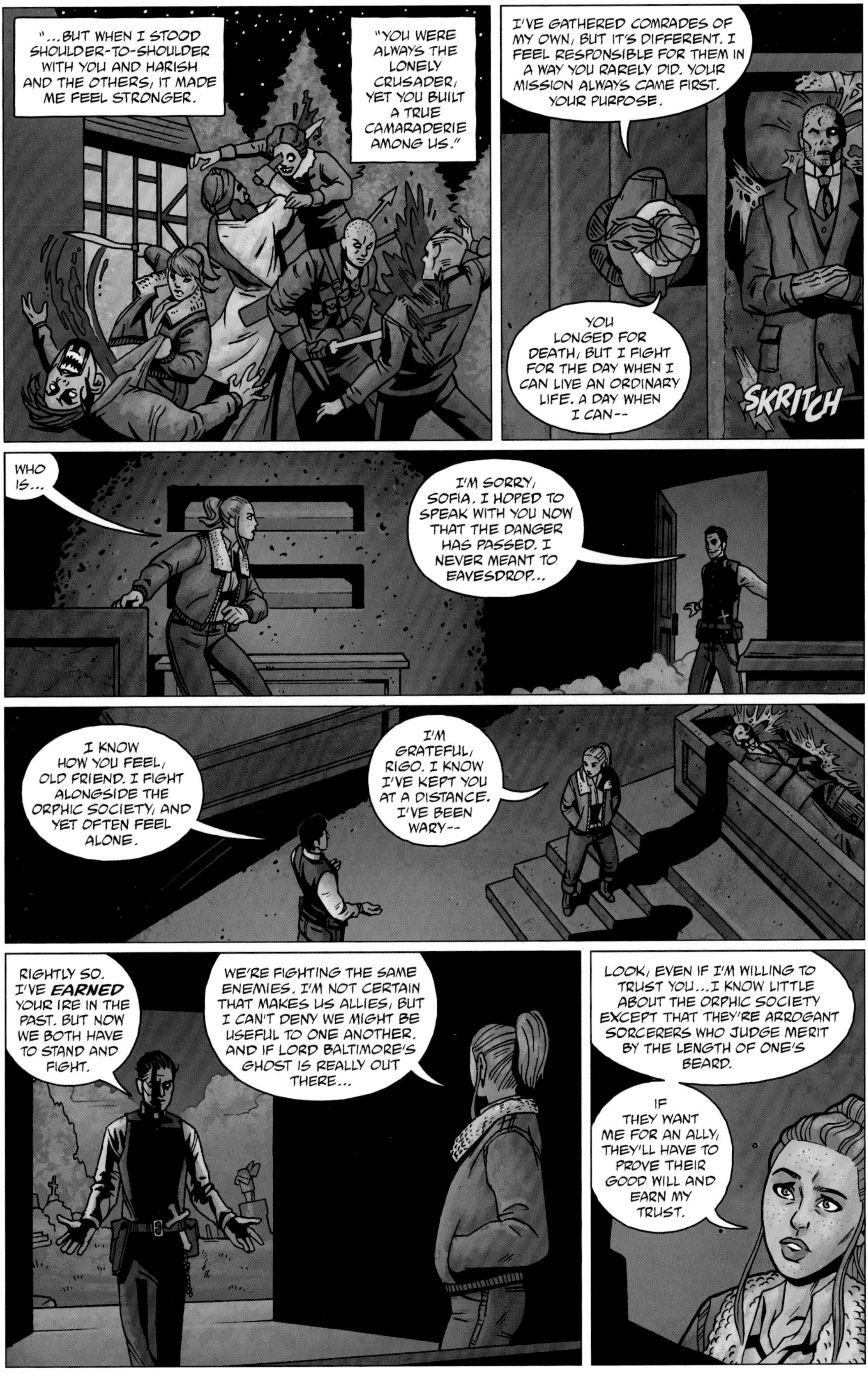
"...BUT WHEN I STOOD SHOULDER-TO-SHOULDER WITH YOU AND HARISH AND THE OTHERS, IT MADE ME FEEL STRONGER.
"YOU WERE ALWAYS THE LONELY CRUSADER, YET YOU BUILT A TRUE CAMARADERIE AMONG US."
I'VE GATHERED COMRADES OF MY OWN, BUT IT'S DIFFERENT. I FEEL RESPONSIBLE FOR THEM IN A WAY YOU RARELY DID. YOUR MISSION ALWAYS CAME FIRST. YOUR PURPOSE.
YOU LONGED FOR DEATH, BUT I FIGHT FOR THE DAY WHEN I CAN LIVE AN ORDINARY LIFE. A DAY WHEN I CAN--
SKRITCH
WHO IS...
I'M SORRY, SOFIA. I HOPED TO SPEAK WITH YOU NOW THAT THE DANGER HAS PASSED. I NEVER MEANT TO EAVESDROP...
I KNOW HOW YOU FEEL, OLD FRIEND. I FIGHT ALONGSIDE THE ORPHIC SOCIETY, AND YET OFTEN FEEL ALONE.
I'M GRATEFUL, RIGO. I KNOW I'VE KEPT YOU AT A DISTANCE. I'VE BEEN WARY--
RIGHTLY SO. I'VE EARNED YOUR IRE IN THE PAST. BUT NOW WE BOTH HAVE TO STAND AND FIGHT.
WE'RE FIGHTING THE SAME ENEMIES. I'M NOT CERTAIN THAT MAKES US ALLIES, BUT I CAN'T DENY WE MIGHT BE USEFUL TO ONE ANOTHER. AND IF LORD BALTIMORE'S GHOST IS REALLY OUT THERE...
LOOK, EVEN IF I'M WILLING TO TRUST YOU...I KNOW LITTLE ABOUT THE ORPHIC SOCIETY EXCEPT THAT THEY'RE ARROGANT SORCERERS WHO JUDGE MERIT BY THE LENGTH OF ONE'S BEARD.
IF THEY WANT ME FOR AN ALLY, THEY'LL HAVE TO PROVE THEIR GOOD WILL AND EARN MY TRUST.

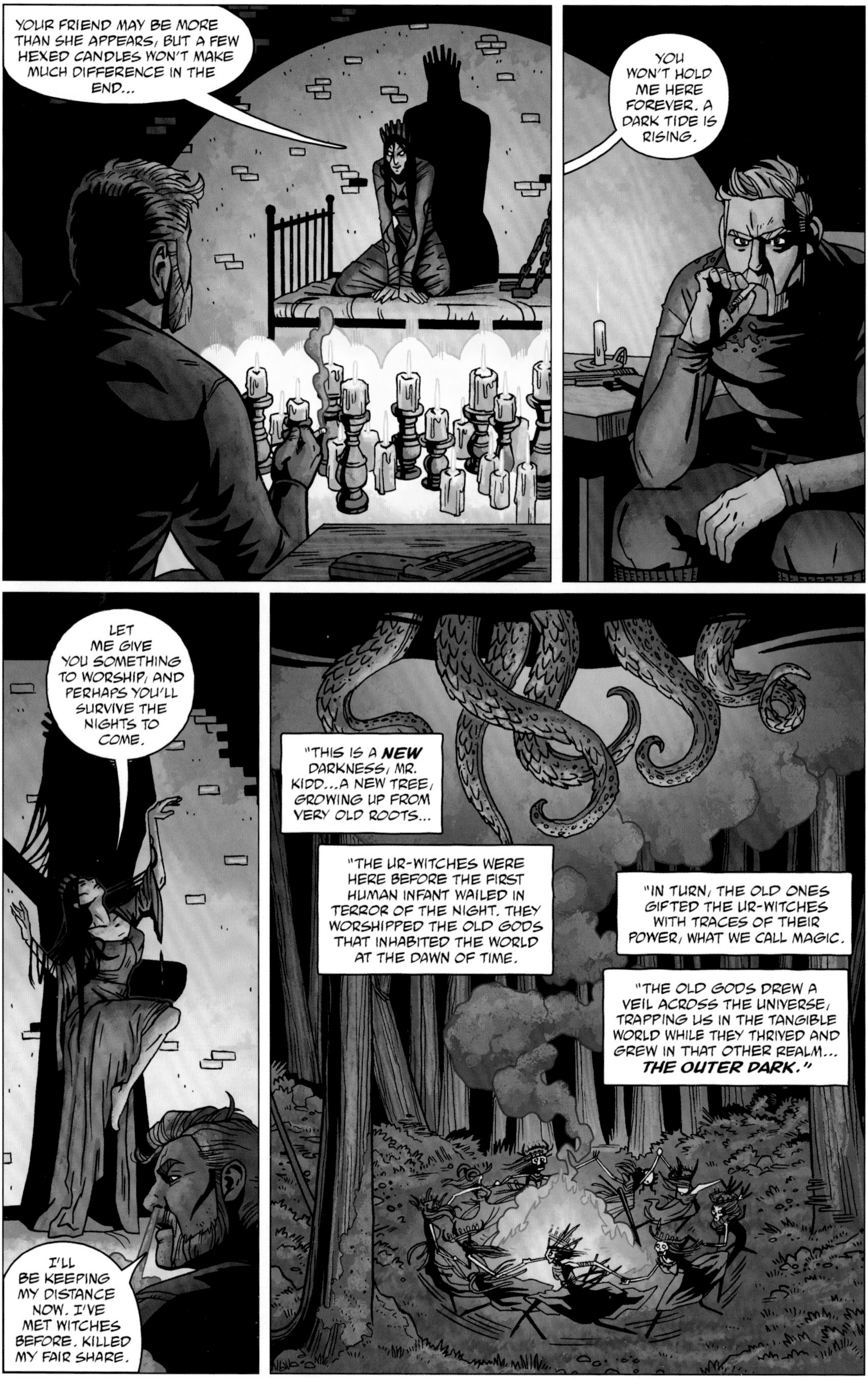
YOUR FRIEND MAY BE MORE THAN SHE APPEARS, BUT A FEW HEXED CANDLES WON'T MAKE MUCH DIFFERENCE IN THE END...
YOU WON'T HOLD ME HERE FOREVER. A DARK TIDE IS RISING.
LET ME GIVE YOU SOMETHING TO WORSHIP, AND PERHAPS YOU'LL SURVIVE THE NIGHTS TO COME.
I'LL BE KEEPING MY DISTANCE NOW. I'VE MET WITCHES BEFORE. KILLED MY FAIR SHARE.
"THIS IS A NEW DARKNESS, MR. KIDD...A NEW TREE, GROWING UP FROM VERY OLD ROOTS...
"THE UR-WITCHES WERE HERE BEFORE THE FIRST HUMAN INFANT WAILED IN TERROR OF THE NIGHT. THEY WORSHIPPED THE OLD GODS THAT INHABITED THE WORLD AT THE DAWN OF TIME.
"IN TURN, THE OLD ONES GIFTED THE UR-WITCHES WITH TRACES OF THEIR POWER, WHAT WE CALL MAGIC.
"THE OLD GODS DREW A VEIL ACROSS THE UNIVERSE, TRAPPING US IN THE TANGIBLE WORLD WHILE THEY THRIVED AND GREW IN THAT OTHER REALM... THE OUTER DARK."

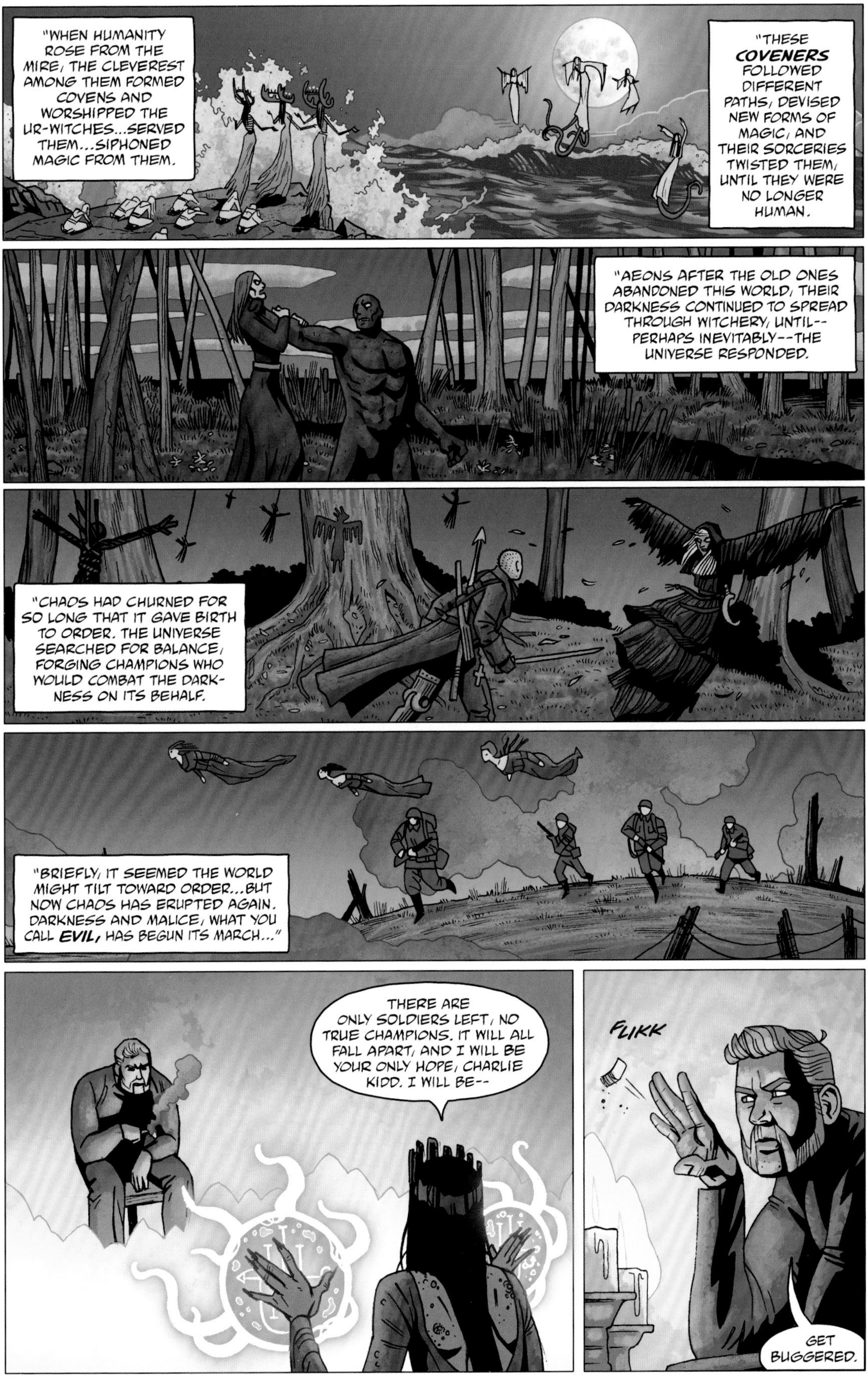
"WHEN HUMANITY ROSE FROM THE MIRE, THE CLEVEREST AMONG THEM FORMED COVENS AND WORSHIPPED THE UR-WITCHES...SERVED THEM...SIPHONED MAGIC FROM THEM.
"THESE COVENERS FOLLOWED DIFFERENT PATHS, DEVISED NEW FORMS OF MAGIC, AND THEIR SORCERIES TWISTED THEM, UNTIL THEY WERE NO LONGER HUMAN.
"AEONS AFTER THE OLD ONES ABANDONED THIS WORLD, THEIR DARKNESS CONTINUED TO SPREAD THROUGH WITCHERY, UNTIL--PERHAPS INEVITABLY--THE UNIVERSE RESPONDED.
"CHAOS HAD CHURNED FOR SO LONG THAT IT GAVE BIRTH TO ORDER. THE UNIVERSE SEARCHED FOR BALANCE, FORGING CHAMPIONS WHO WOULD COMBAT THE DARKNESS ON ITS BEHALF.
"BRIEFLY, IT SEEMED THE WORLD MIGHT TILT TOWARD ORDER...BUT NOW CHAOS HAS ERUPTED AGAIN. DARKNESS AND MALICE, WHAT YOU CALL EVIL, HAS BEGUN ITS MARCH..."
THERE ARE ONLY SOLDIERS LEFT, NO TRUE CHAMPIONS. IT WILL ALL FALL APART, AND I WILL BE YOUR ONLY HOPE, CHARLIE KIDD. I WILL BE--
FLIKK
GET BUGGERED.

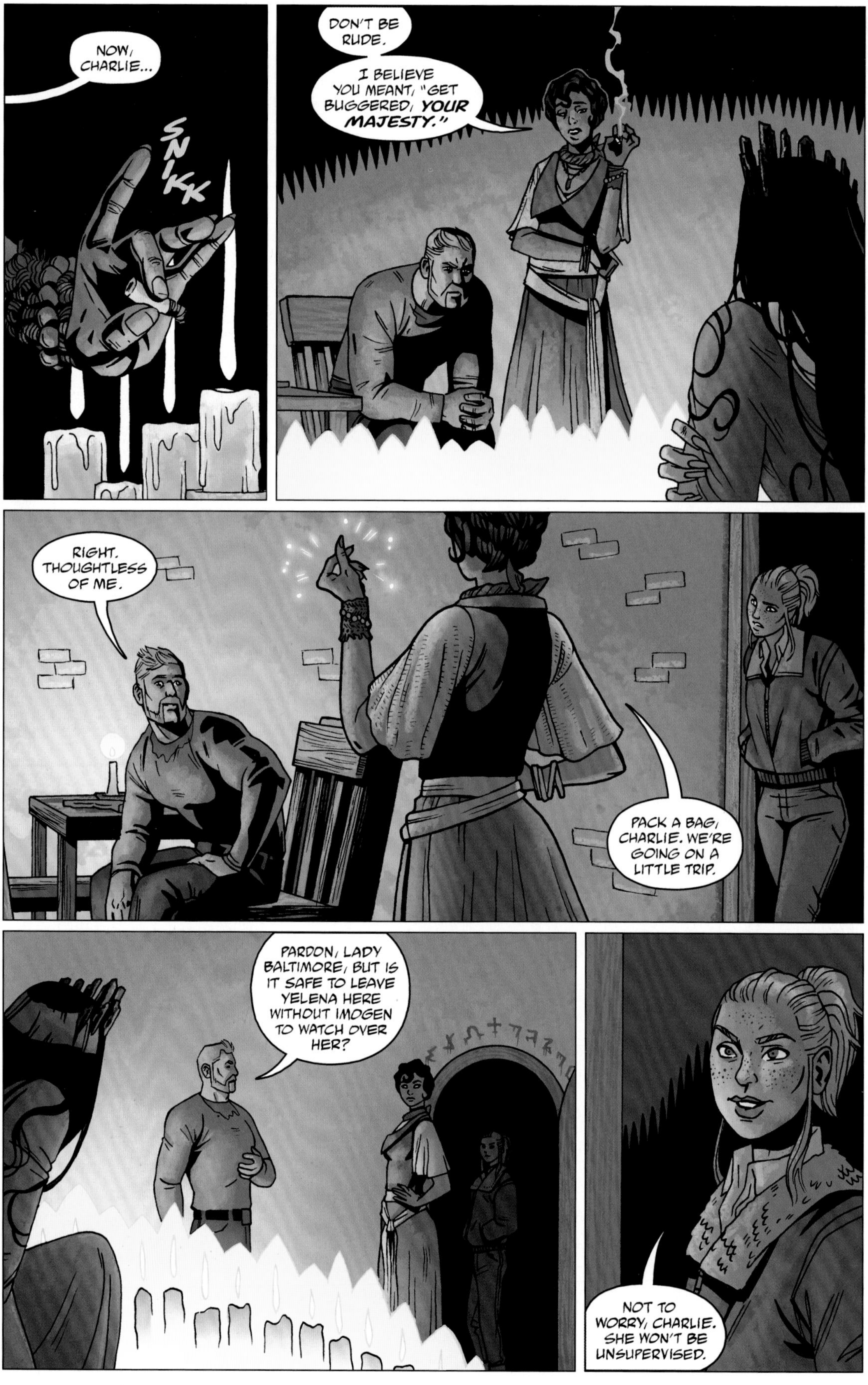
NOW, CHARLIE...
SNIKK
DON'T BE RUDE.
I BELIEVE YOU MEANT, "GET BUGGERED, YOUR MAJESTY."
RIGHT. THOUGHTLESS OF ME.
PACK A BAG, CHARLIE. WE'RE GOING ON A LITTLE TRIP.
PARDON, LADY BALTIMORE, BUT IS IT SAFE TO LEAVE YELENA HERE WITHOUT IMOGEN TO WATCH OVER HER?
NOT TO WORRY, CHARLIE. SHE WON'T BE UNSUPERVISED.

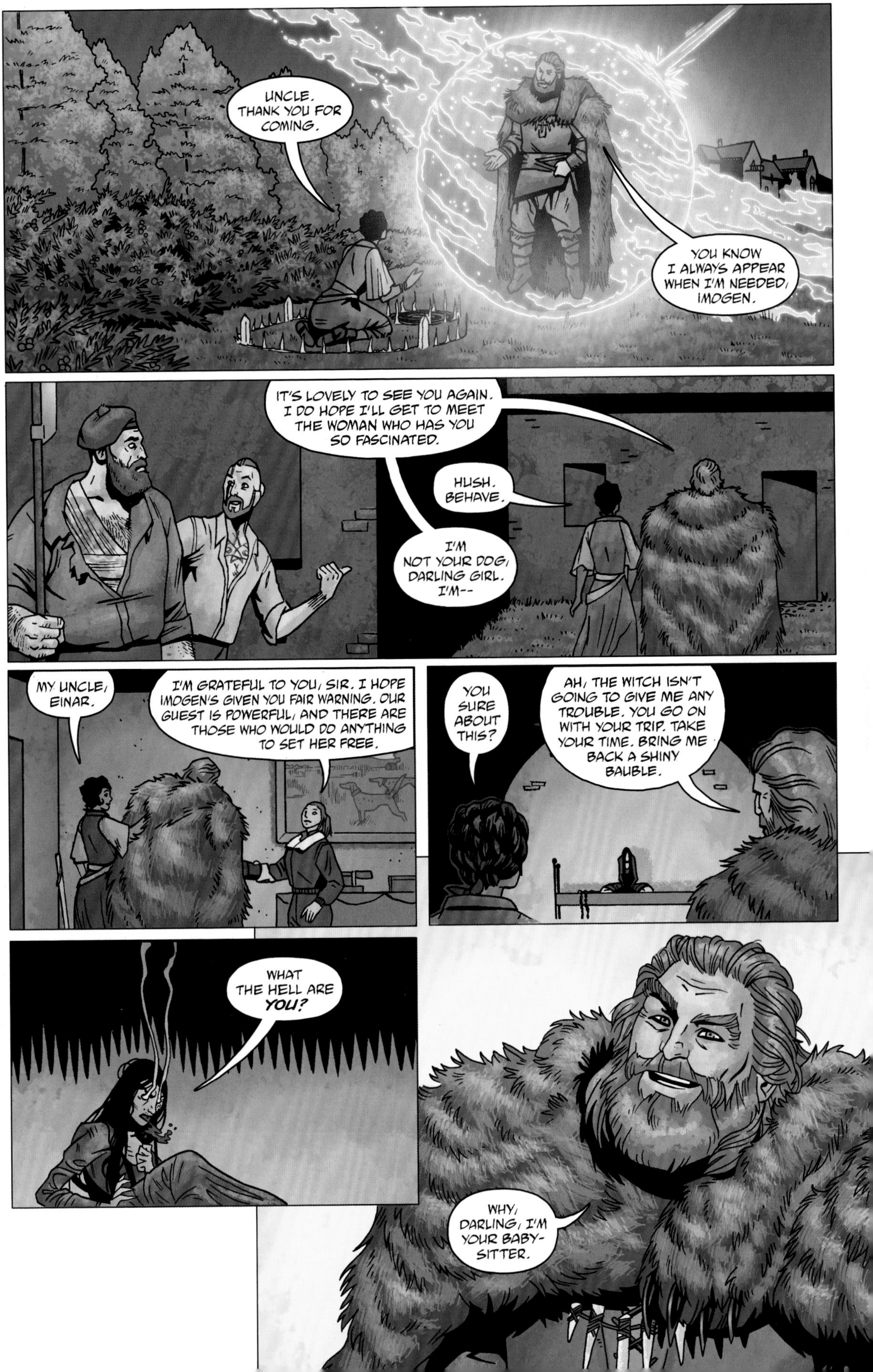
UNCLE. THANK YOU FOR COMING.
YOU KNOW I ALWAYS APPEAR WHEN I'M NEEDED, IMOGEN.
IT'S LOVELY TO SEE YOU AGAIN. I DO HOPE I'LL GET TO MEET THE WOMAN WHO HAS YOU SO FASCINATED.
HUSH. BEHAVE.
I'M NOT YOUR DOG, DARLING GIRL. I'M--
MY UNCLE, EINAR.
I'M GRATEFUL TO YOU, SIR. I HOPE IMOGEN'S GIVEN YOU FAIR WARNING. OUR GUEST IS POWERFUL, AND THERE ARE THOSE WHO WOULD DO ANYTHING TO SET HER FREE.
YOU SURE ABOUT THIS?
AH, THE WITCH ISN'T GOING TO GIVE ME ANY TROUBLE. YOU GO ON WITH YOUR TRIP. TAKE YOUR TIME. BRING ME BACK A SHINY BAUBLE.
WHAT THE HELL ARE *YOU?*
WHY, DARLING, I'M YOUR BABY-SITTER.

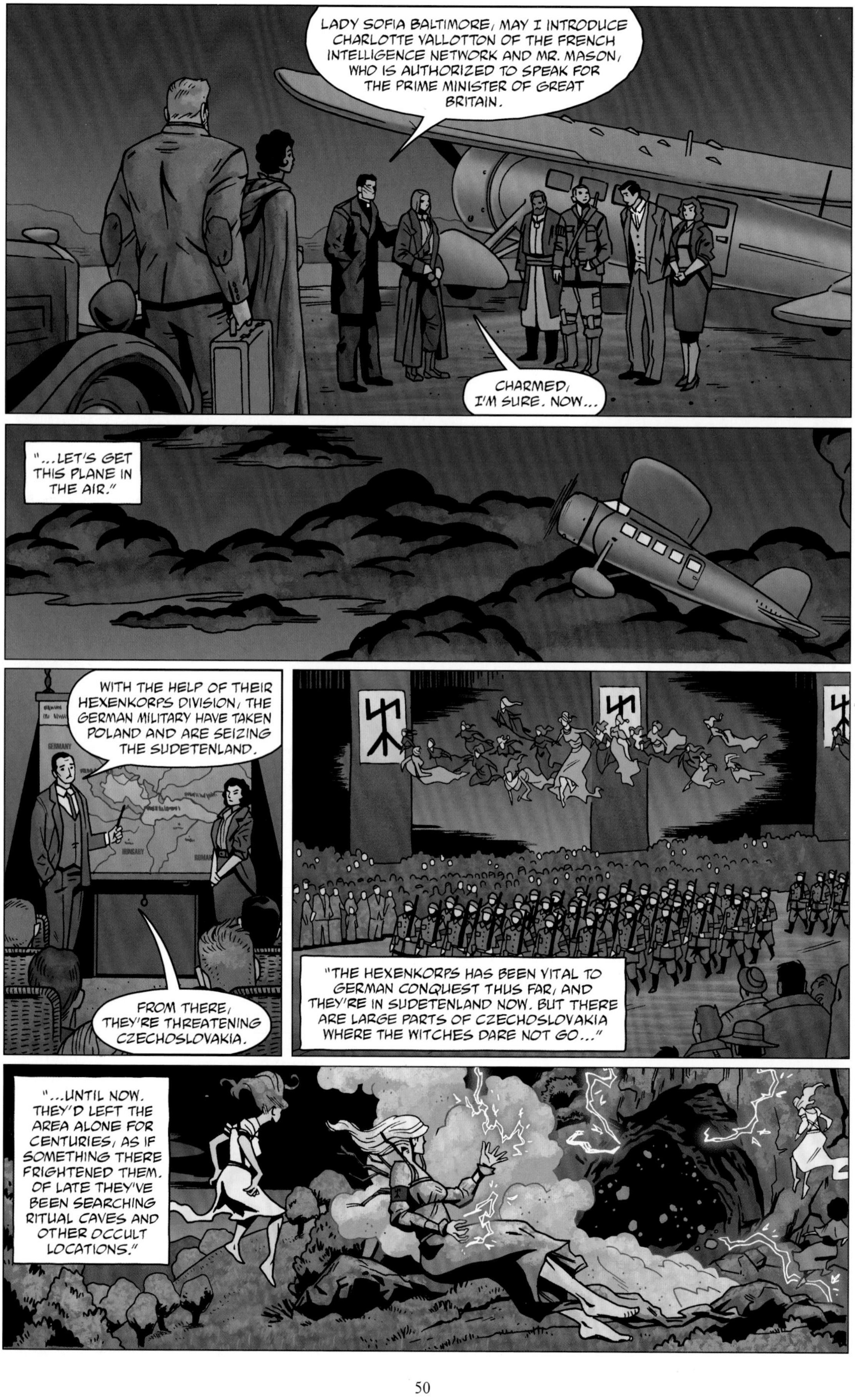
LADY SOFIA BALTIMORE, MAY I INTRODUCE CHARLOTTE VALLOTTON OF THE FRENCH INTELLIGENCE NETWORK AND MR. MASON, WHO IS AUTHORIZED TO SPEAK FOR THE PRIME MINISTER OF GREAT BRITAIN.
CHARMED, I'M SURE. NOW...
"...LET'S GET THIS PLANE IN THE AIR."
WITH THE HELP OF THEIR HEXENKORPS DIVISION, THE GERMAN MILITARY HAVE TAKEN POLAND AND ARE SEIZING THE SUDETENLAND.
GERMANY
HUNGARY
FROM THERE, THEY'RE THREATENING CZECHOSLOVAKIA.
"THE HEXENKORPS HAS BEEN VITAL TO GERMAN CONQUEST THUS FAR, AND THEY'RE IN SUDETENLAND NOW. BUT THERE ARE LARGE PARTS OF CZECHOSLOVAKIA WHERE THE WITCHES DARE NOT GO..."
"...UNTIL NOW. THEY'D LEFT THE AREA ALONE FOR CENTURIES, AS IF SOMETHING THERE FRIGHTENED THEM. OF LATE THEY'VE BEEN SEARCHING RITUAL CAVES AND OTHER OCCULT LOCATIONS."

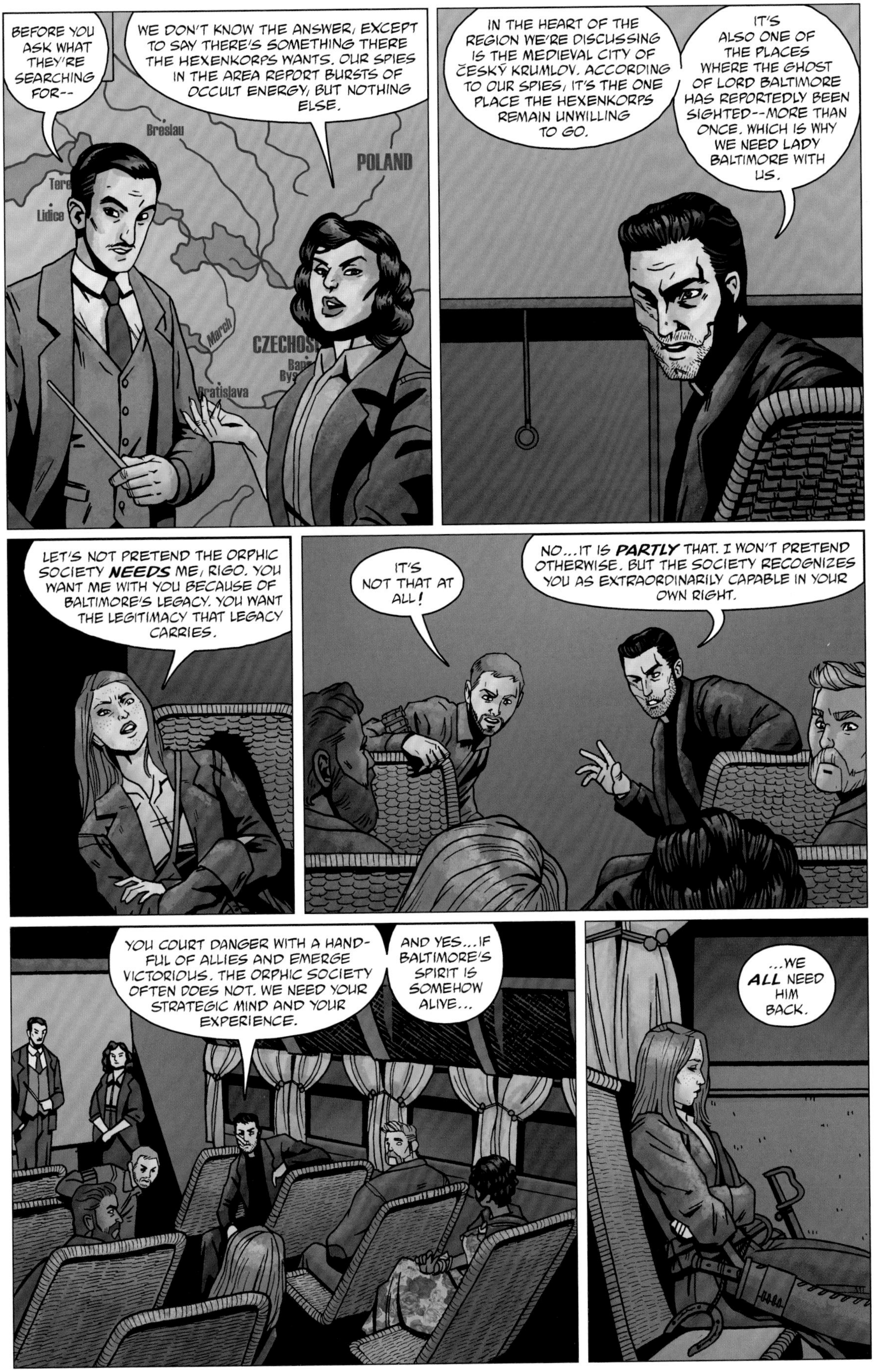
BEFORE YOU ASK WHAT THEY'RE SEARCHING FOR--
WE DON'T KNOW THE ANSWER, EXCEPT TO SAY THERE'S SOMETHING THERE THE HEXENKORPS WANTS. OUR SPIES IN THE AREA REPORT BURSTS OF OCCULT ENERGY, BUT NOTHING ELSE.
Breslau
POLAND
Lidice
March
Bratislava
IN THE HEART OF THE REGION WE'RE DISCUSSING IS THE MEDIEVAL CITY OF ČESKÝ KRUMLOV. ACCORDING TO OUR SPIES, IT'S THE ONE PLACE THE HEXENKORPS REMAIN UNWILLING TO GO.
IT'S ALSO ONE OF THE PLACES WHERE THE GHOST OF LORD BALTIMORE HAS REPORTEDLY BEEN SIGHTED--MORE THAN ONCE. WHICH IS WHY WE NEED LADY BALTIMORE WITH US.
LET'S NOT PRETEND THE ORPHIC SOCIETY NEEDS ME, RIGO. YOU WANT ME WITH YOU BECAUSE OF BALTIMORE'S LEGACY. YOU WANT THE LEGITIMACY THAT LEGACY CARRIES.
IT'S NOT THAT AT ALL!
NO...IT IS PARTLY THAT. I WON'T PRETEND OTHERWISE. BUT THE SOCIETY RECOGNIZES YOU AS EXTRAORDINARILY CAPABLE IN YOUR OWN RIGHT.
YOU COURT DANGER WITH A HANDFUL OF ALLIES AND EMERGE VICTORIOUS. THE ORPHIC SOCIETY OFTEN DOES NOT. WE NEED YOUR STRATEGIC MIND AND YOUR EXPERIENCE.
AND YES...IF BALTIMORE'S SPIRIT IS SOMEHOW ALIVE...
...WE ALL NEED HIM BACK.

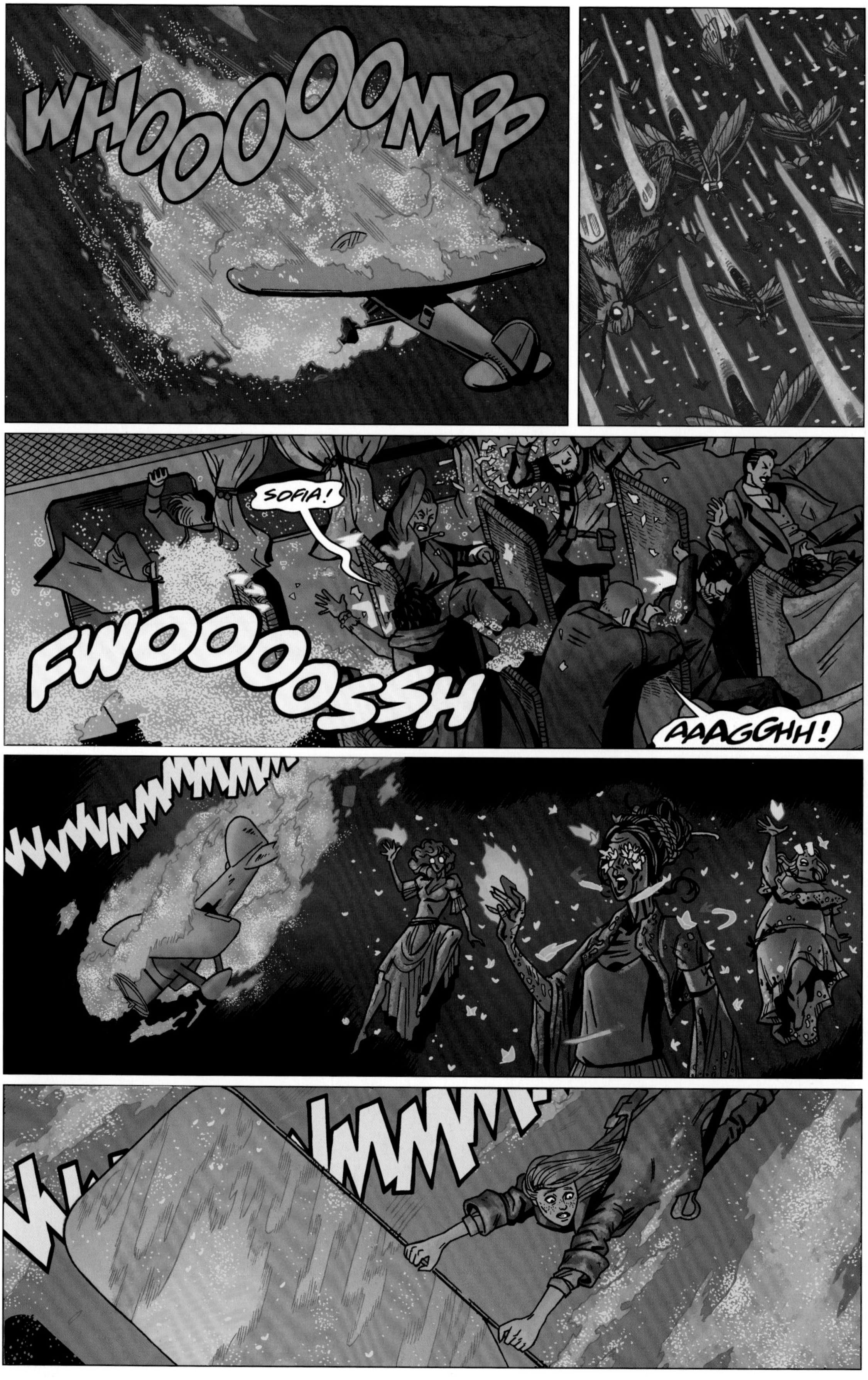
WHOOOOOOMPP
SOFIA!
FWOOOOOSSH
AAAGGHH!

CHAPTER THREE

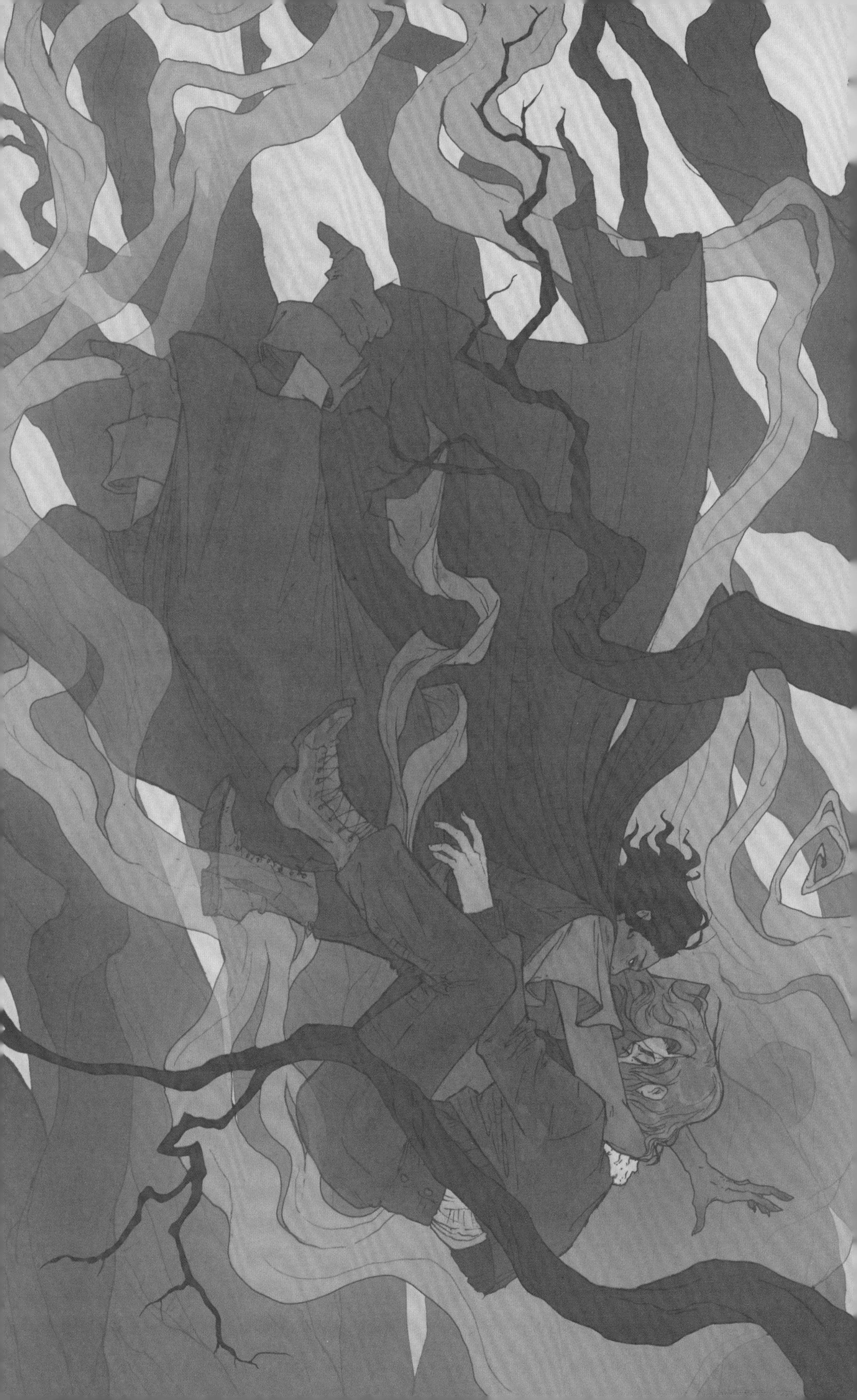

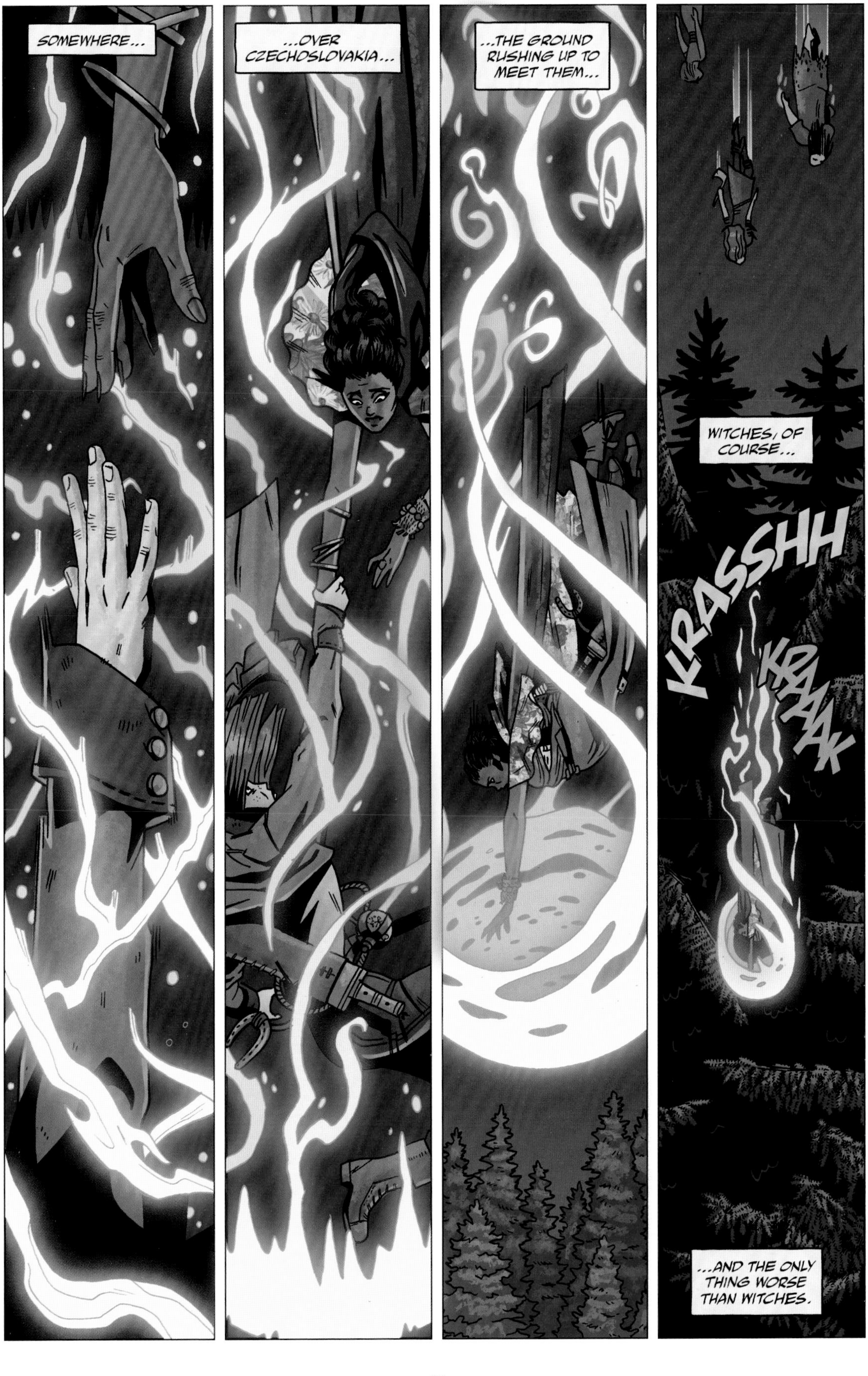
SOMEWHERE...
...OVER CZECHOSLOVAKIA...
...THE GROUND RUSHING UP TO MEET THEM...
WITCHES, OF COURSE...
KRASSHH
KRAAAK
...AND THE ONLY THING WORSE THAN WITCHES.

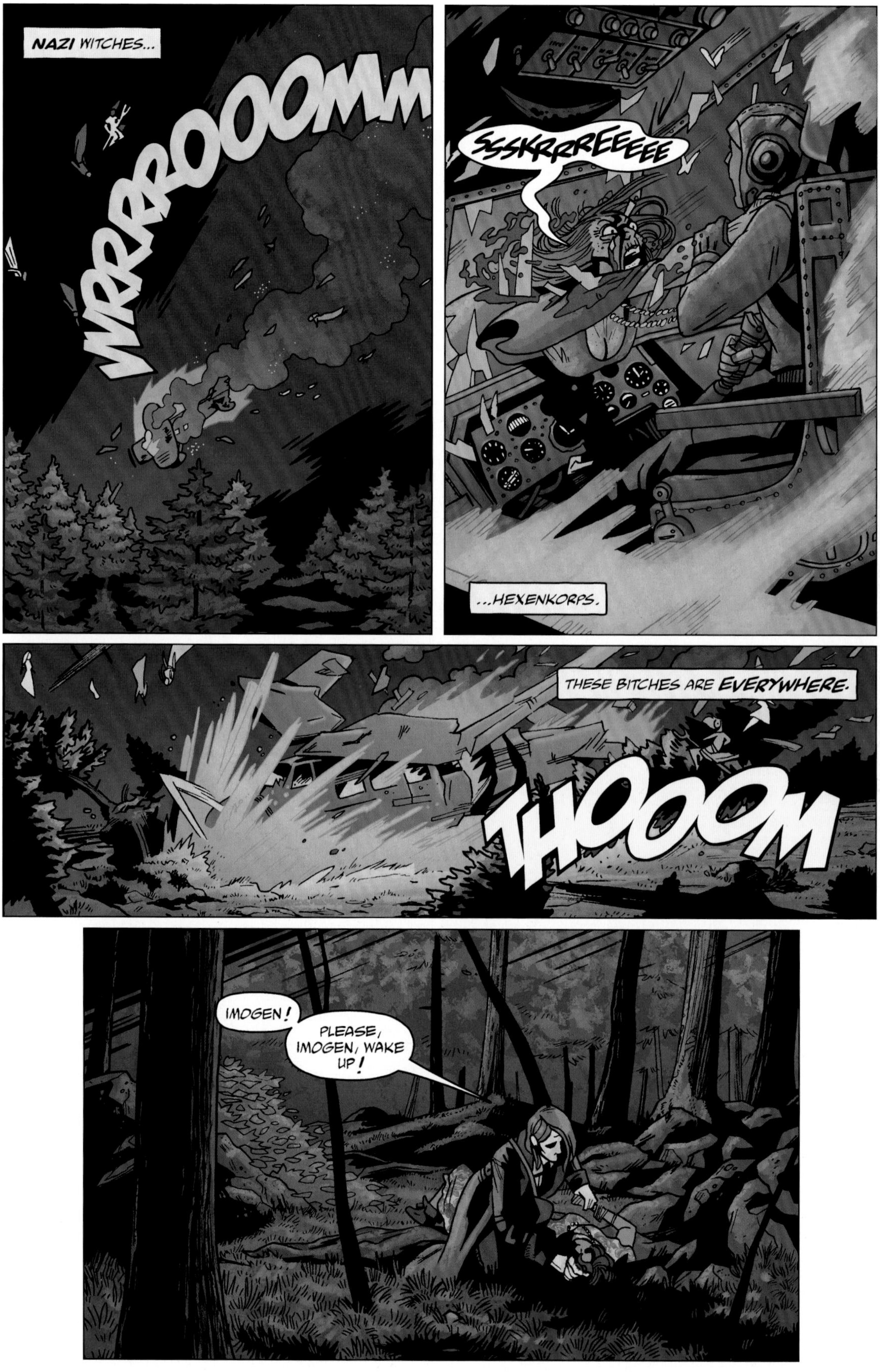
NAZI WITCHES...
WRRRROOOMM
SSSKRRREEEEEE
...HEXENKORPS.
THESE BITCHES ARE EVERYWHERE.
THOOOM
IMOGEN!
PLEASE, IMOGEN, WAKE UP!

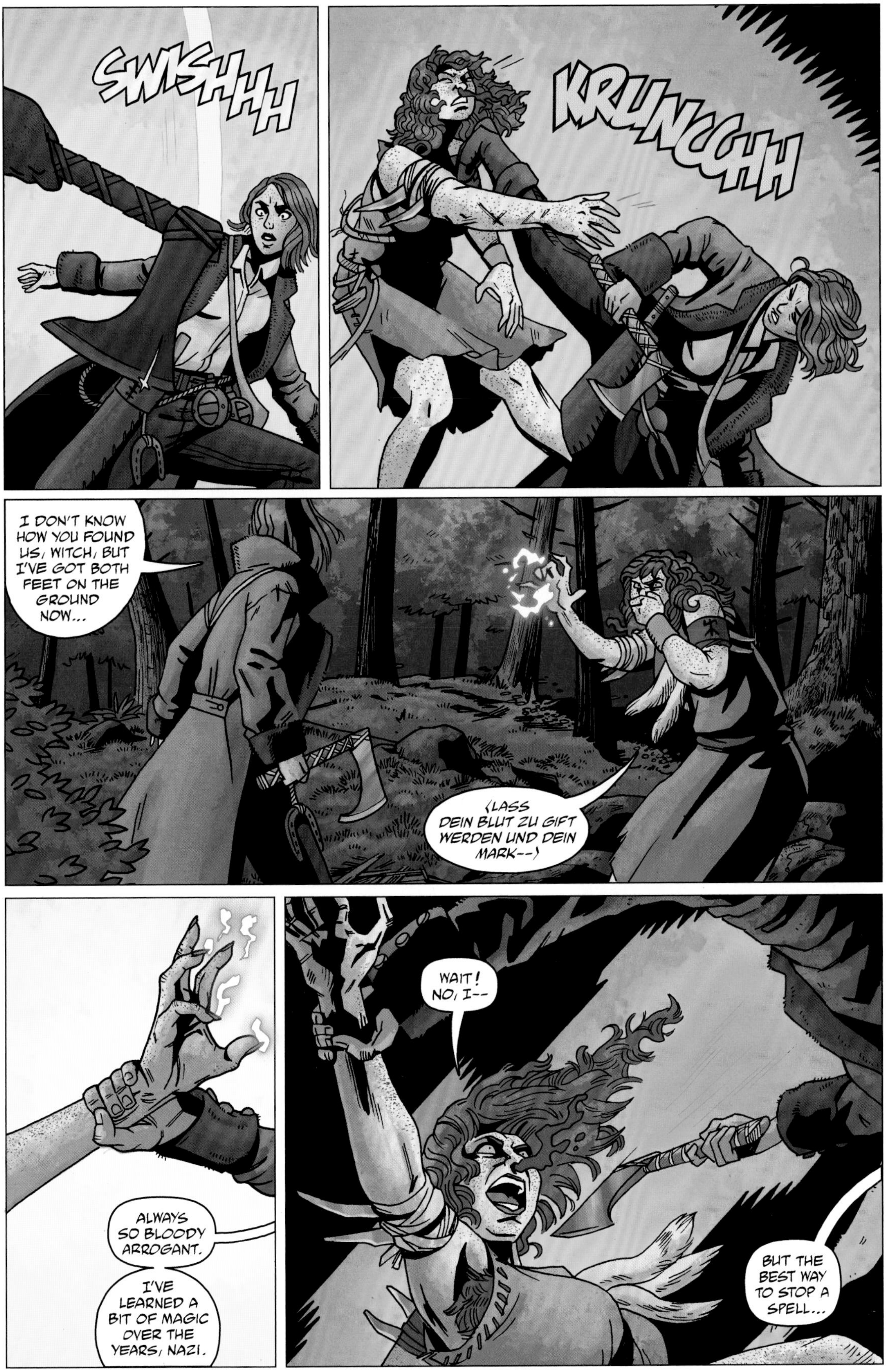
SWISHHH
KRUNCHH
I DON'T KNOW HOW YOU FOUND US, WITCH, BUT I'VE GOT BOTH FEET ON THE GROUND NOW...
‹LASS DEIN BLUT ZU GIFT WERDEN UND DEIN MARK--›
ALWAYS SO BLOODY ARROGANT.
I'VE LEARNED A BIT OF MAGIC OVER THE YEARS, NAZI.
WAIT! NO, I--
BUT THE BEST WAY TO STOP A SPELL...

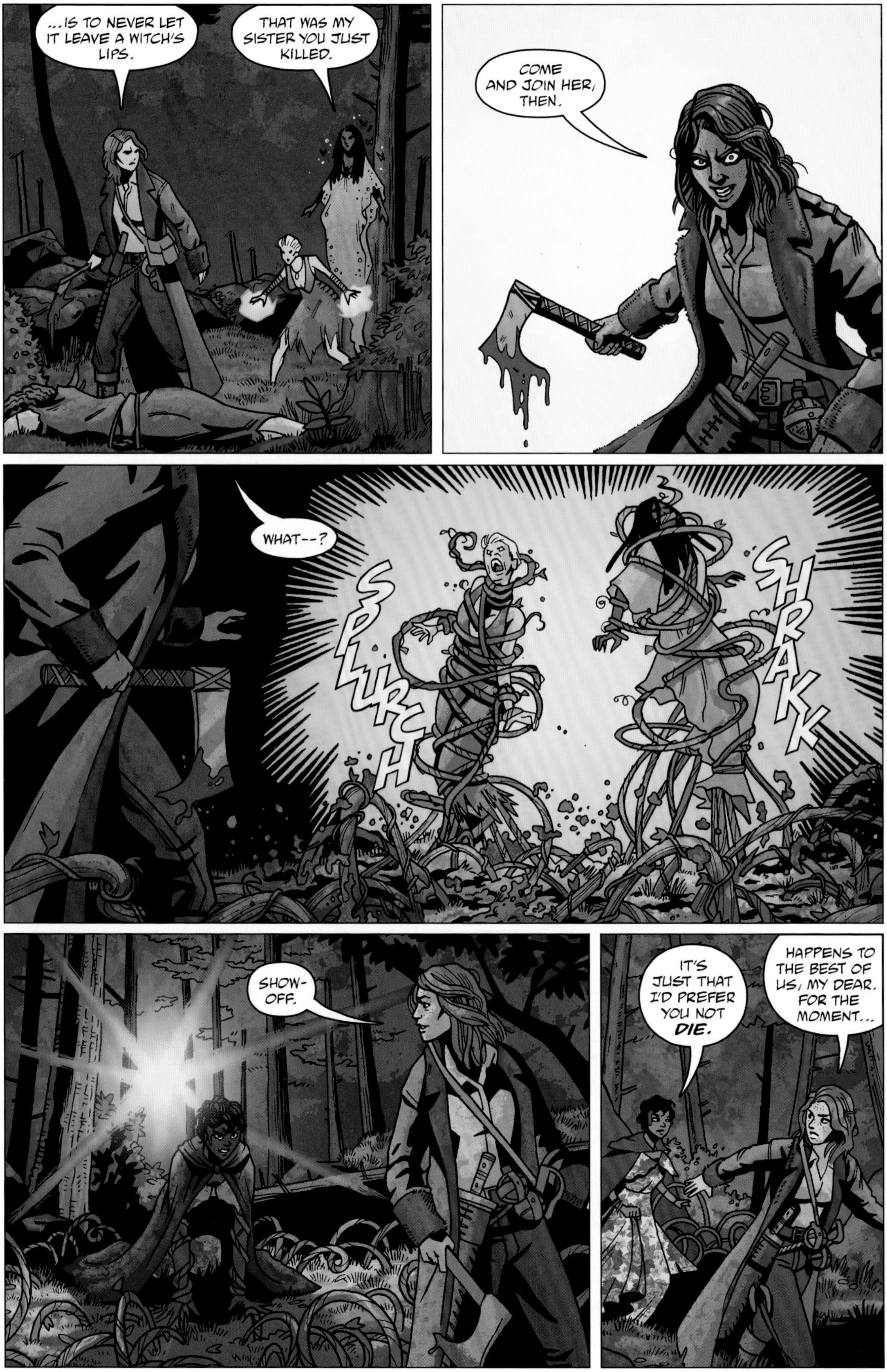
...IS TO NEVER LET IT LEAVE A WITCH'S LIPS.
THAT WAS MY SISTER YOU JUST KILLED.
COME AND JOIN HER, THEN.
WHAT--?
SPLURCH
SHRAKK
SHOW-OFF.
IT'S JUST THAT I'D PREFER YOU NOT DIE.
HAPPENS TO THE BEST OF US, MY DEAR. FOR THE MOMENT...

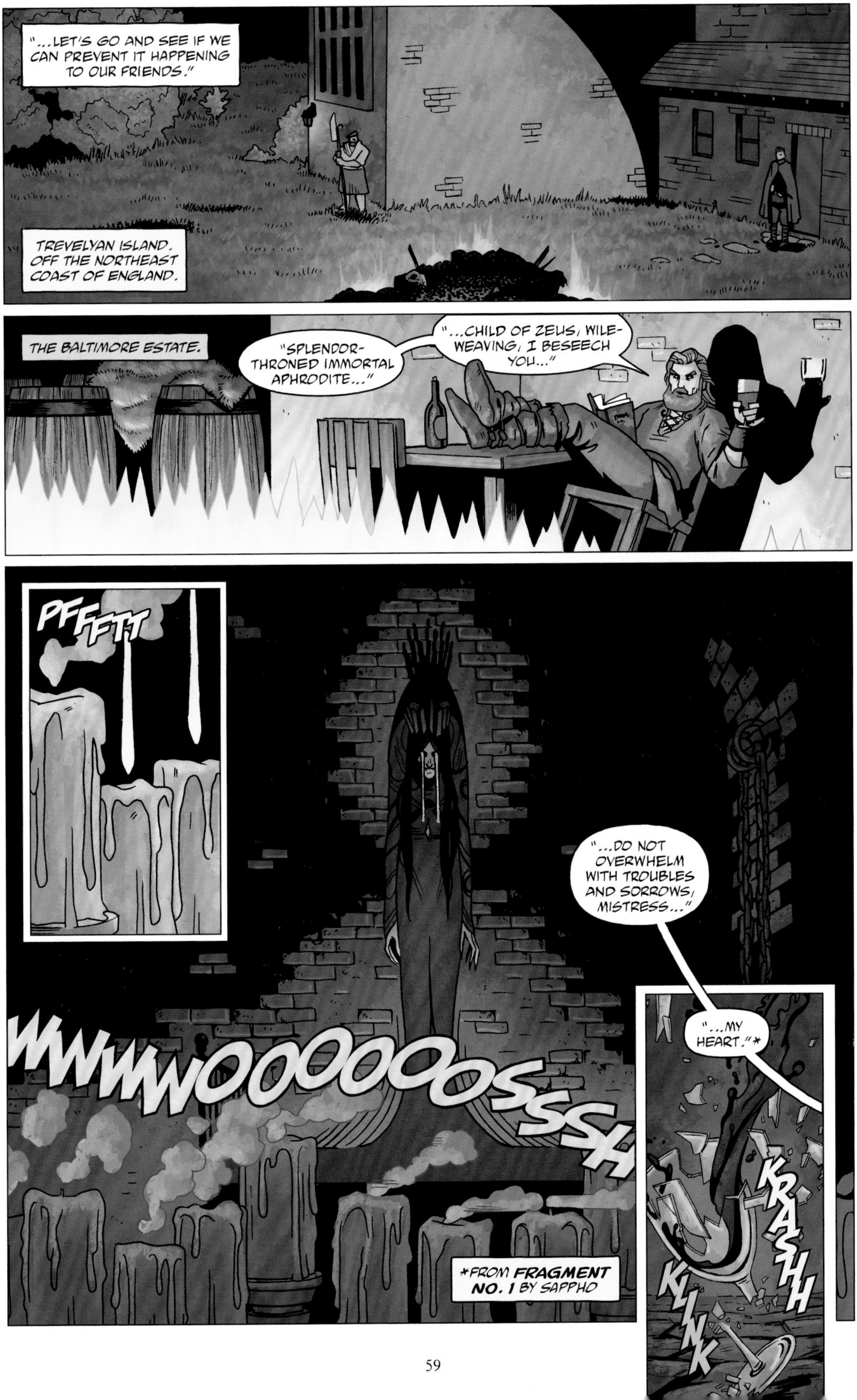
"...LET'S GO AND SEE IF WE CAN PREVENT IT HAPPENING TO OUR FRIENDS."
TREVELYAN ISLAND. OFF THE NORTHEAST COAST OF ENGLAND.
THE BALTIMORE ESTATE.
"SPLENDOR-THRONED IMMORTAL APHRODITE..."
"...CHILD OF ZEUS, WILE-WEAVING, I BESEECH YOU..."
PFFFTT
"...DO NOT OVERWHELM WITH TROUBLES AND SORROWS, MISTRESS..."
"...MY HEART."*
WWWWOOOOOOSSSH
KRASHH
KLINK
*FROM **FRAGMENT NO. 1** BY SAPPHO

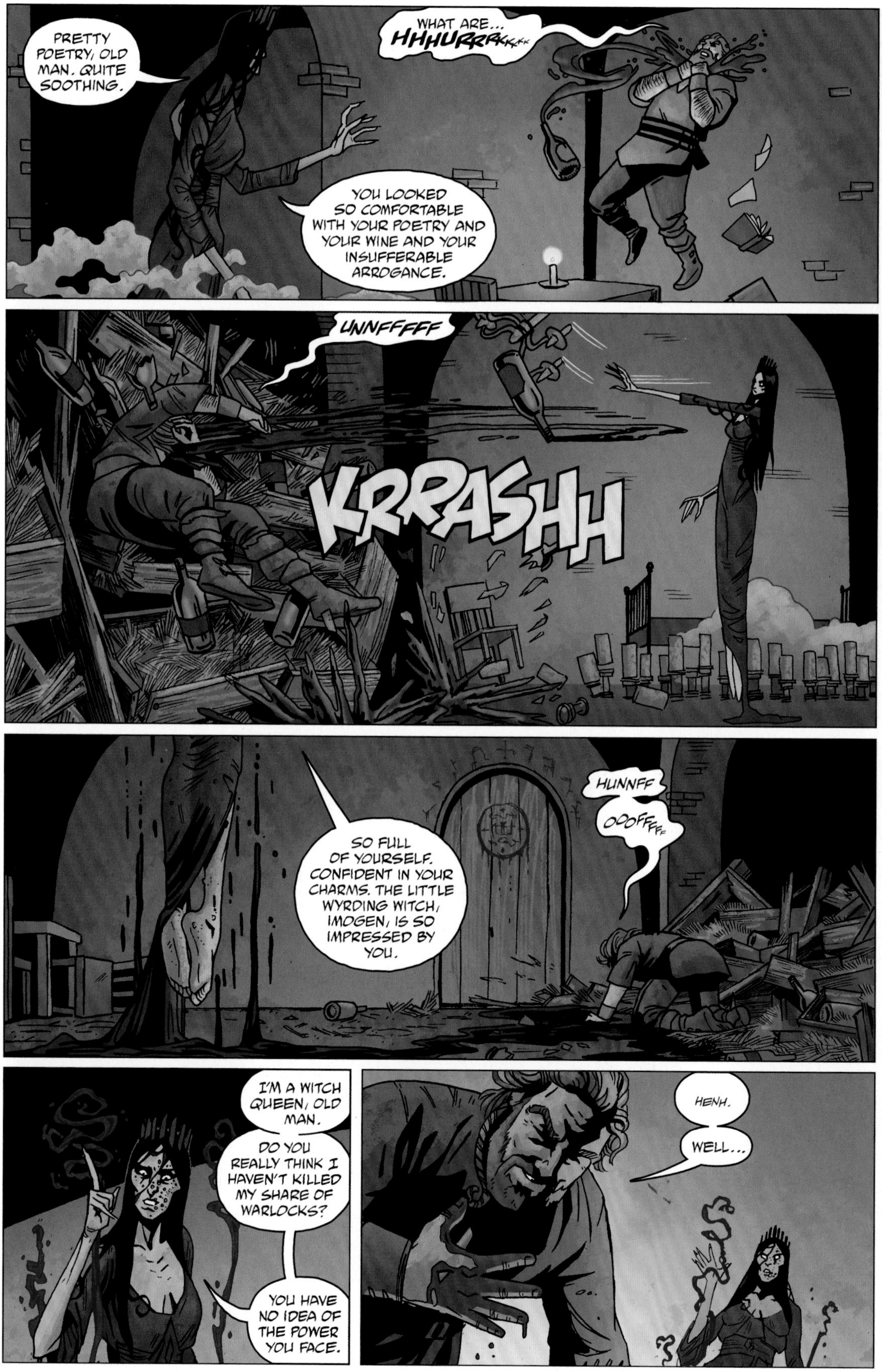
PRETTY POETRY, OLD MAN. QUITE SOOTHING.
WHAT ARE... HHHURRRKKKK
YOU LOOKED SO COMFORTABLE WITH YOUR POETRY AND YOUR WINE AND YOUR INSUFFERABLE ARROGANCE.
UNNFFFFF
KRRASHH
HUNNFF
OOOFFFFF
SO FULL OF YOURSELF. CONFIDENT IN YOUR CHARMS. THE LITTLE WYRDING WITCH, IMOGEN, IS SO IMPRESSED BY YOU.
I'M A WITCH QUEEN, OLD MAN.
DO YOU REALLY THINK I HAVEN'T KILLED MY SHARE OF WARLOCKS?
YOU HAVE NO IDEA OF THE POWER YOU FACE.
HENH.
WELL...

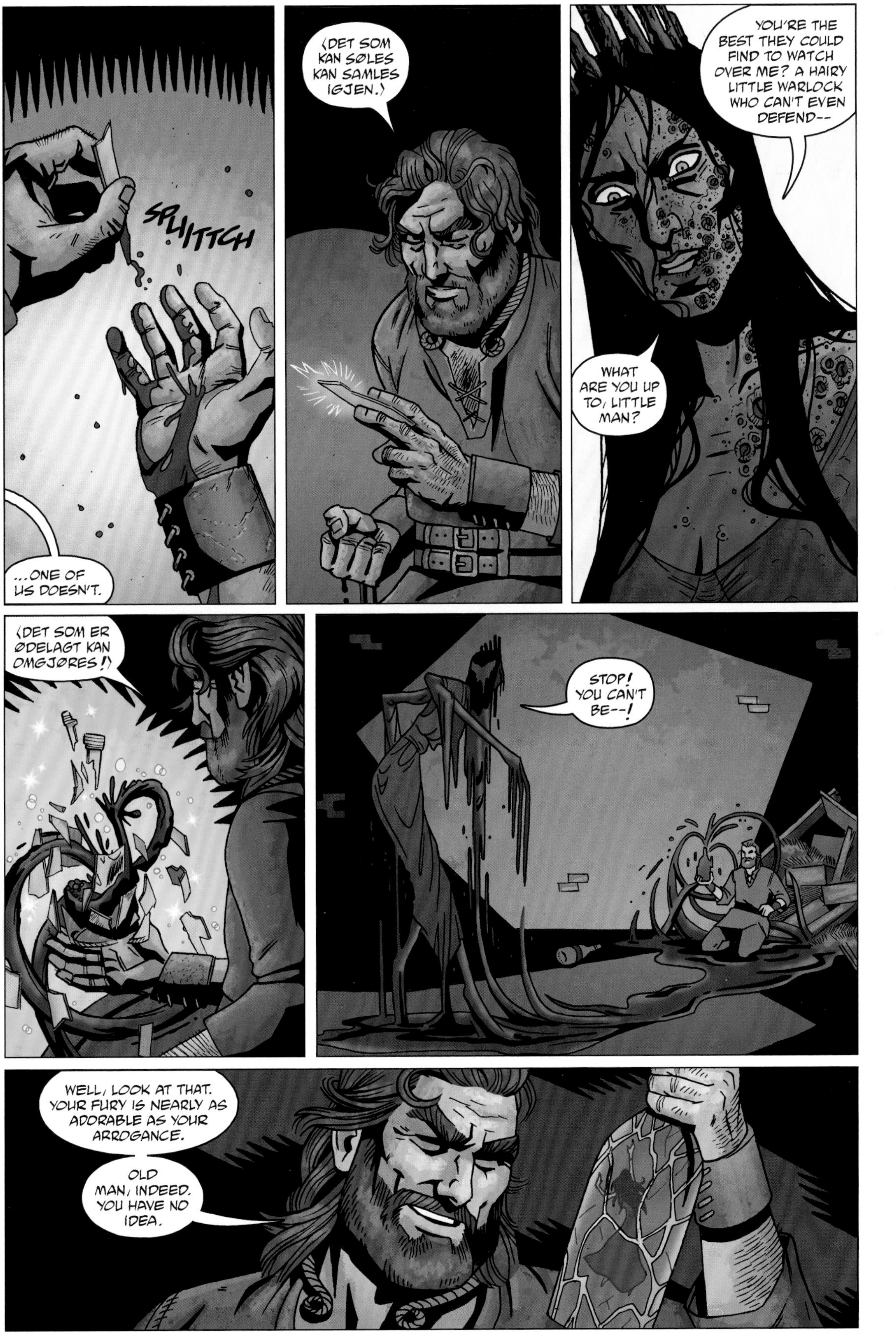
SPLITTCH
...ONE OF US DOESN'T.
⟨DET SOM KAN SØLES KAN SAMLES IGJEN.⟩
YOU'RE THE BEST THEY COULD FIND TO WATCH OVER ME? A HAIRY LITTLE WARLOCK WHO CAN'T EVEN DEFEND--
WHAT ARE YOU UP TO, LITTLE MAN?
⟨DET SOM ER ØDELAGT KAN OMGJØRES!⟩
STOP! YOU CAN'T BE--!
WELL, LOOK AT THAT. YOUR FURY IS NEARLY AS ADORABLE AS YOUR ARROGANCE.
OLD MAN, INDEED. YOU HAVE NO IDEA.

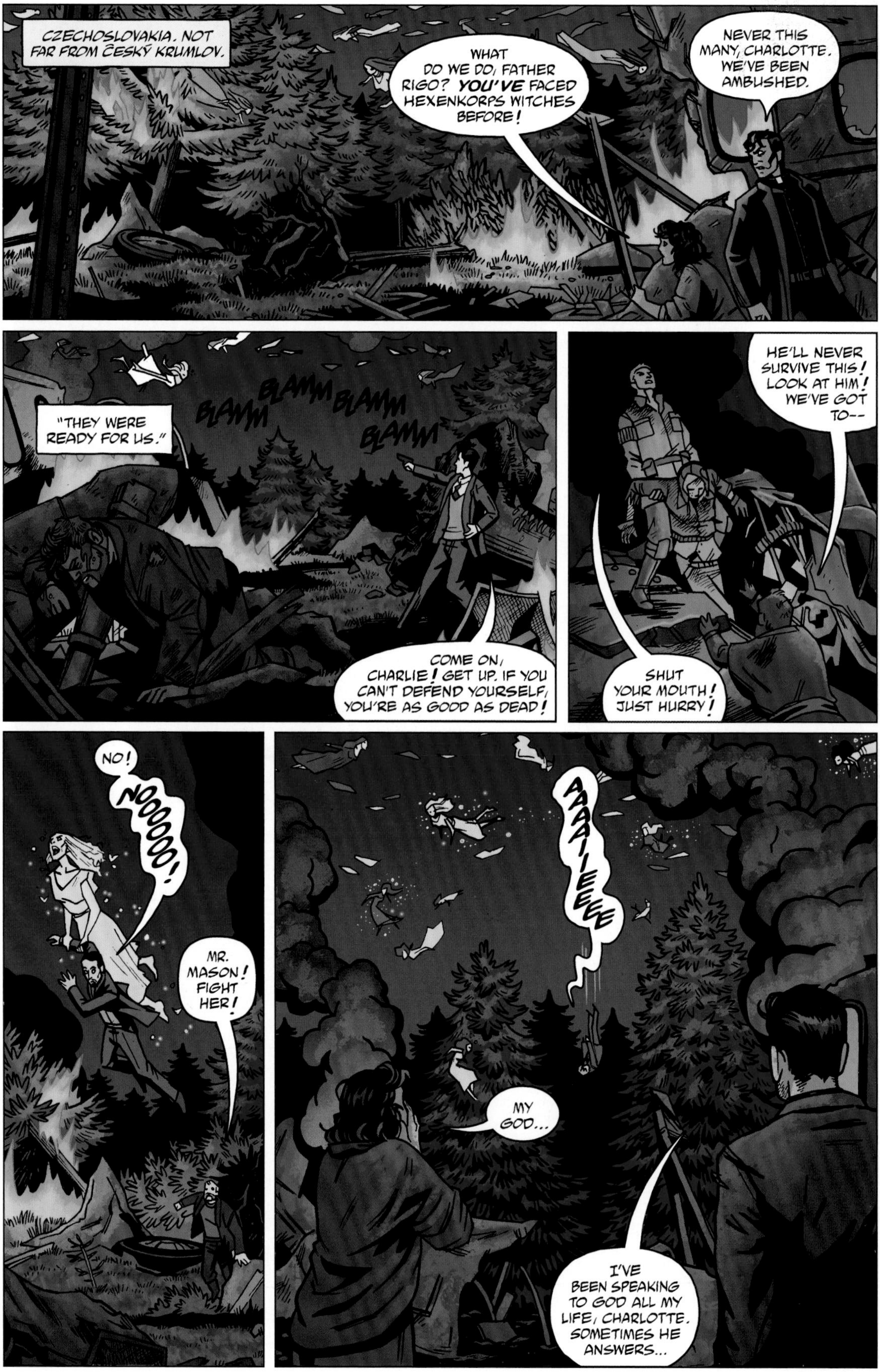
CZECHOSLOVAKIA. NOT FAR FROM ČESKÝ KRUMLOV.
WHAT DO WE DO, FATHER RIGO? YOU'VE FACED HEXENKORPS WITCHES BEFORE!
NEVER THIS MANY, CHARLOTTE. WE'VE BEEN AMBUSHED.
"THEY WERE READY FOR US."
BLAMM BLAMM BLAMM BLAMM
COME ON, CHARLIE! GET UP. IF YOU CAN'T DEFEND YOURSELF, YOU'RE AS GOOD AS DEAD!
HE'LL NEVER SURVIVE THIS! LOOK AT HIM! WE'VE GOT TO--
SHUT YOUR MOUTH! JUST HURRY!
NO!
NOOOOOO!
MR. MASON! FIGHT HER!
AAAAIEEEE
MY GOD...
I'VE BEEN SPEAKING TO GOD ALL MY LIFE, CHARLOTTE. SOMETIMES HE ANSWERS...

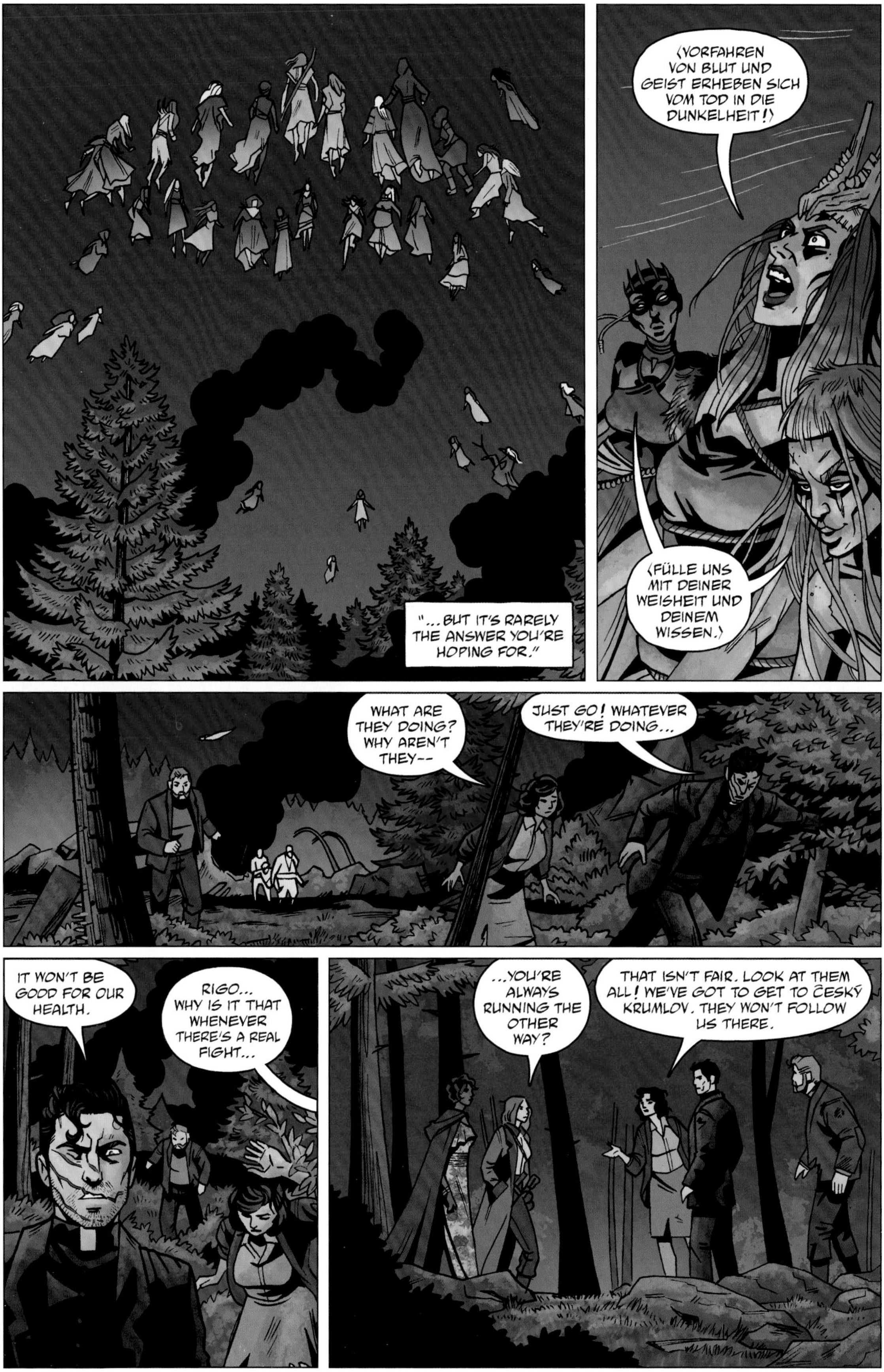
"...BUT IT'S RARELY THE ANSWER YOU'RE HOPING FOR."
⟨VORFAHREN VON BLUT UND GEIST ERHEBEN SICH VOM TOD IN DIE DUNKELHEIT!⟩
⟨FÜLLE UNS MIT DEINER WEISHEIT UND DEINEM WISSEN.⟩
WHAT ARE THEY DOING? WHY AREN'T THEY--
JUST GO! WHATEVER THEY'RE DOING...
IT WON'T BE GOOD FOR OUR HEALTH.
RIGO... WHY IS IT THAT WHENEVER THERE'S A REAL FIGHT...
...YOU'RE ALWAYS RUNNING THE OTHER WAY?
THAT ISN'T FAIR. LOOK AT THEM ALL! WE'VE GOT TO GET TO ČESKÝ KRUMLOV. THEY WON'T FOLLOW US THERE.

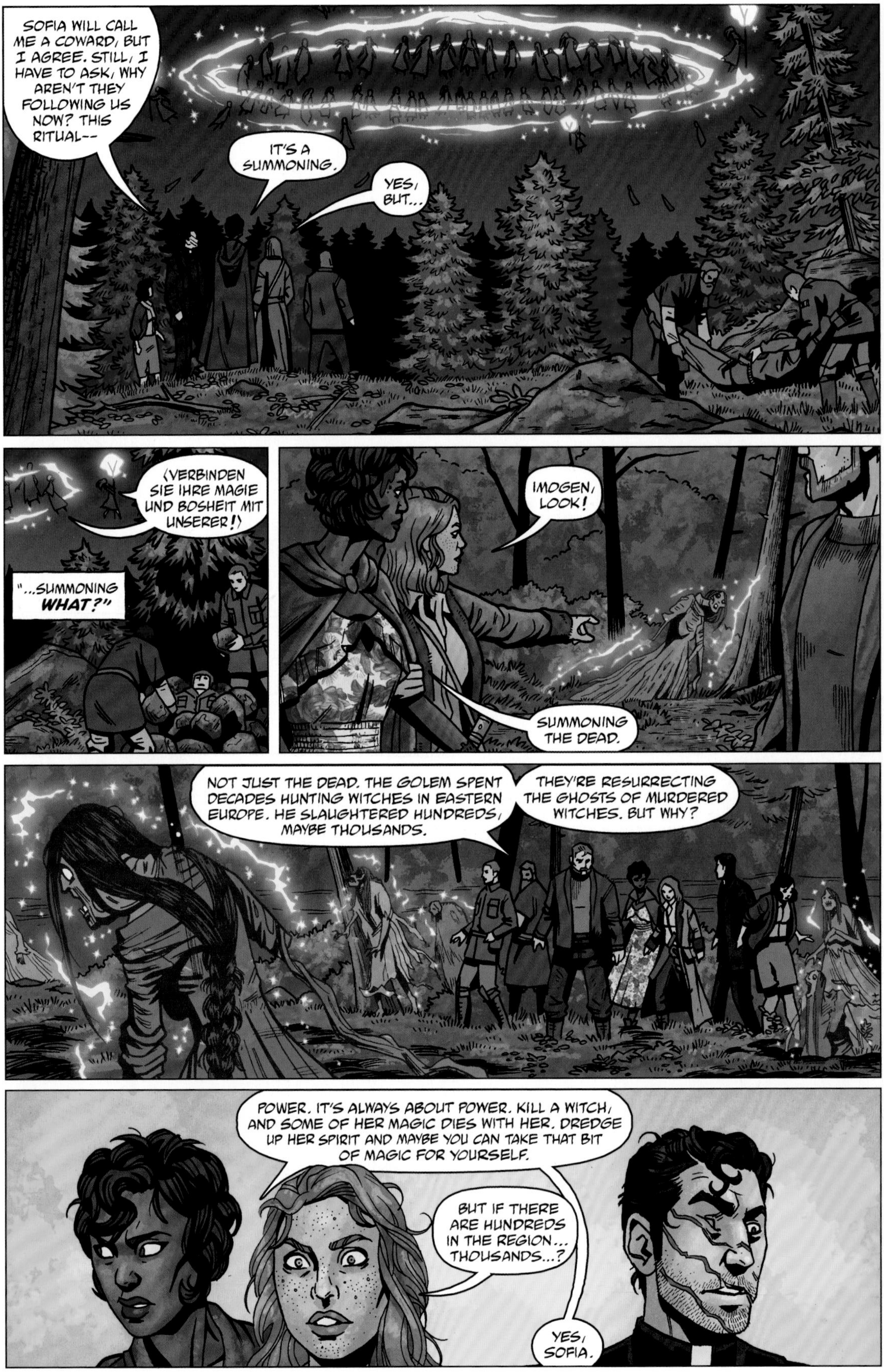
SOFIA WILL CALL ME A COWARD, BUT I AGREE. STILL, I HAVE TO ASK, WHY AREN'T THEY FOLLOWING US NOW? THIS RITUAL--
IT'S A SUMMONING.
YES, BUT...
(VERBINDEN SIE IHRE MAGIE UND BOSHEIT MIT UNSERER!)
"...SUMMONING WHAT?"
IMOGEN, LOOK!
SUMMONING THE DEAD.
NOT JUST THE DEAD. THE GOLEM SPENT DECADES HUNTING WITCHES IN EASTERN EUROPE. HE SLAUGHTERED HUNDREDS, MAYBE THOUSANDS.
THEY'RE RESURRECTING THE GHOSTS OF MURDERED WITCHES. BUT WHY?
POWER. IT'S ALWAYS ABOUT POWER. KILL A WITCH, AND SOME OF HER MAGIC DIES WITH HER. DREDGE UP HER SPIRIT AND MAYBE YOU CAN TAKE THAT BIT OF MAGIC FOR YOURSELF.
BUT IF THERE ARE HUNDREDS IN THE REGION... THOUSANDS...?
YES, SOFIA.

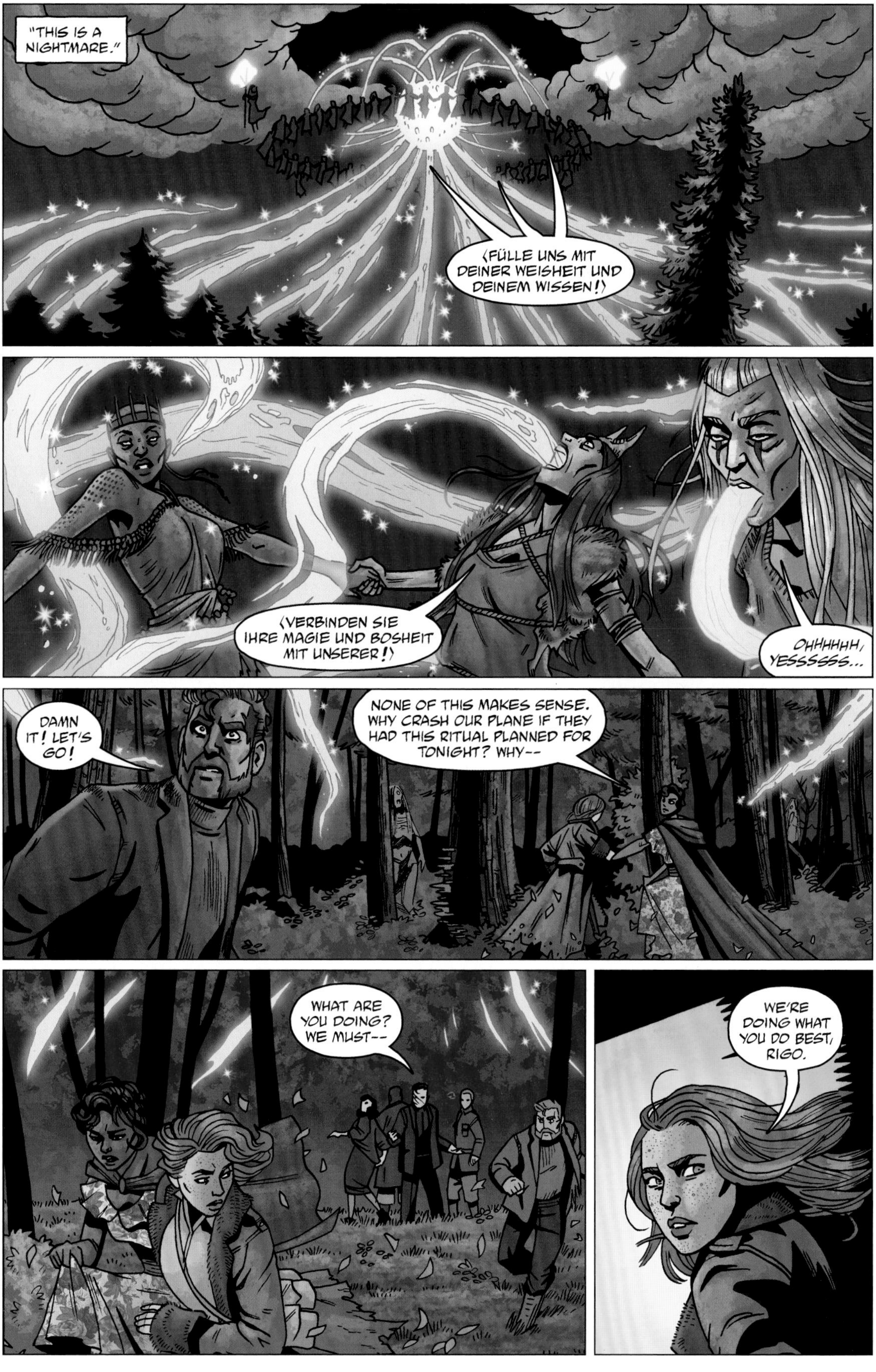
"THIS IS A NIGHTMARE."
⟨FÜLLE UNS MIT DEINER WEISHEIT UND DEINEM WISSEN!⟩
⟨VERBINDEN SIE IHRE MAGIE UND BOSHEIT MIT UNSERER!⟩
OHHHHHH, YESSSSSS...
DAMN IT! LET'S GO!
NONE OF THIS MAKES SENSE. WHY CRASH OUR PLANE IF THEY HAD THIS RITUAL PLANNED FOR TONIGHT? WHY--
WHAT ARE YOU DOING? WE MUST--
WE'RE DOING WHAT YOU DO BEST, RIGO.

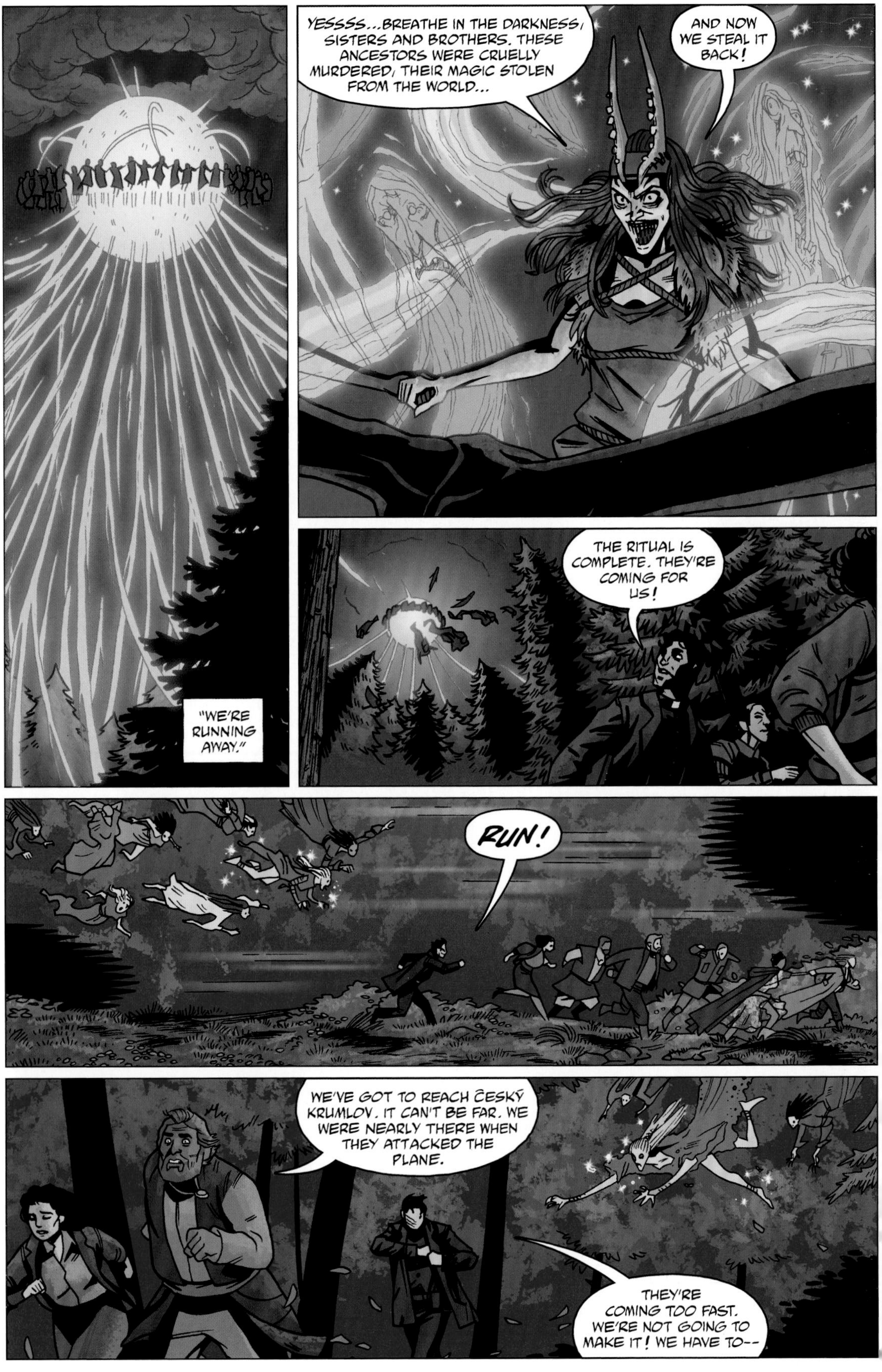
YESSSS...BREATHE IN THE DARKNESS, SISTERS AND BROTHERS. THESE ANCESTORS WERE CRUELLY MURDERED, THEIR MAGIC STOLEN FROM THE WORLD...
AND NOW WE STEAL IT BACK!
"WE'RE RUNNING AWAY."
THE RITUAL IS COMPLETE. THEY'RE COMING FOR US!
RUN!
WE'VE GOT TO REACH ČESKÝ KRUMLOV. IT CAN'T BE FAR. WE WERE NEARLY THERE WHEN THEY ATTACKED THE PLANE.
THEY'RE COMING TOO FAST. WE'RE NOT GOING TO MAKE IT! WE HAVE TO--

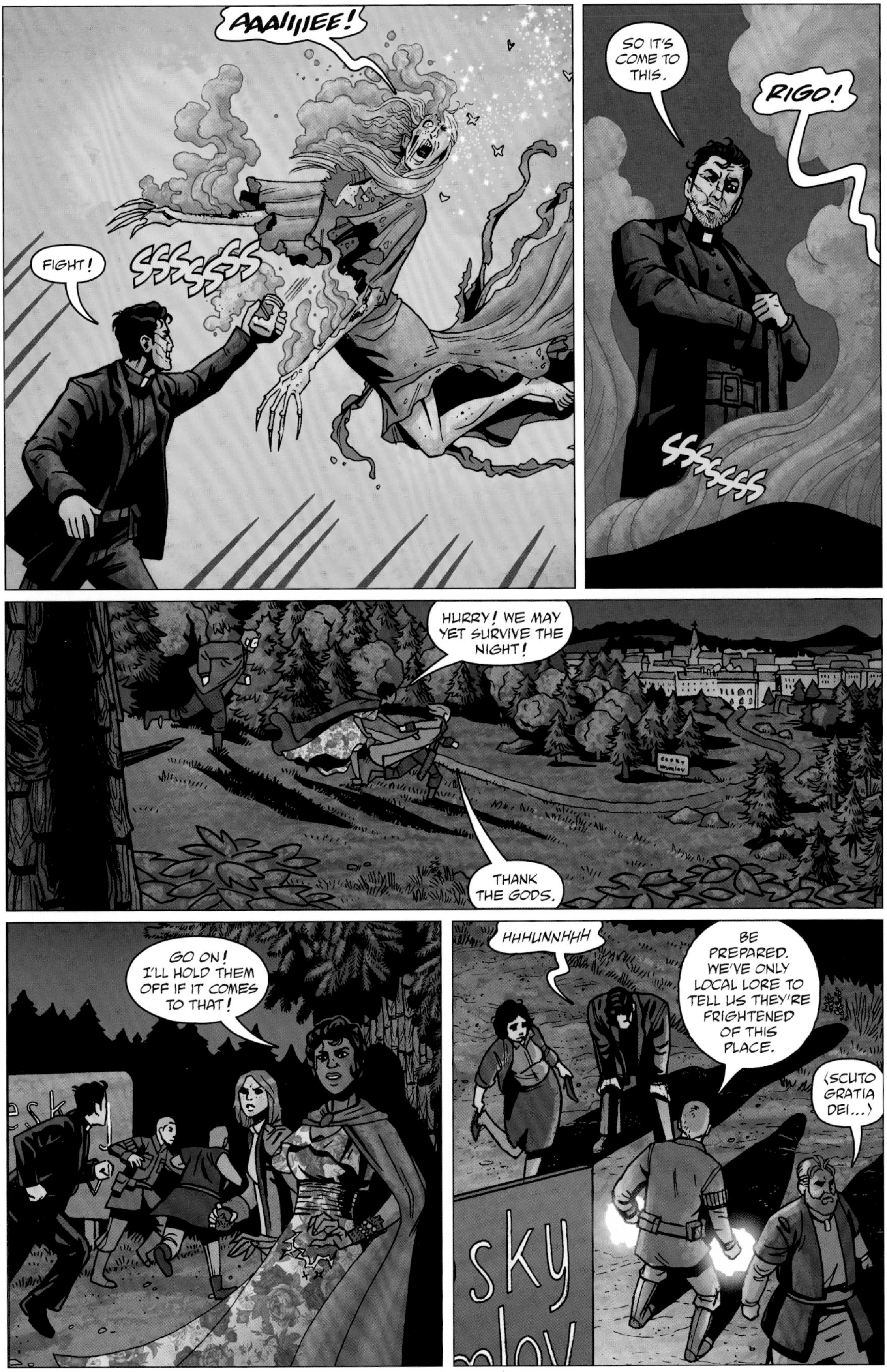

AAAIIIIEE!
FIGHT!
SSSSSS
SO IT'S COME TO THIS.
RIGO!
SSSSSS
HURRY! WE MAY YET SURVIVE THE NIGHT!
THANK THE GODS.
GO ON! I'LL HOLD THEM OFF IF IT COMES TO THAT!
HHHUNNHHH
BE PREPARED. WE'VE ONLY LOCAL LORE TO TELL US THEY'RE FRIGHTENED OF THIS PLACE.
‹SCUTO GRATIA DEI...›

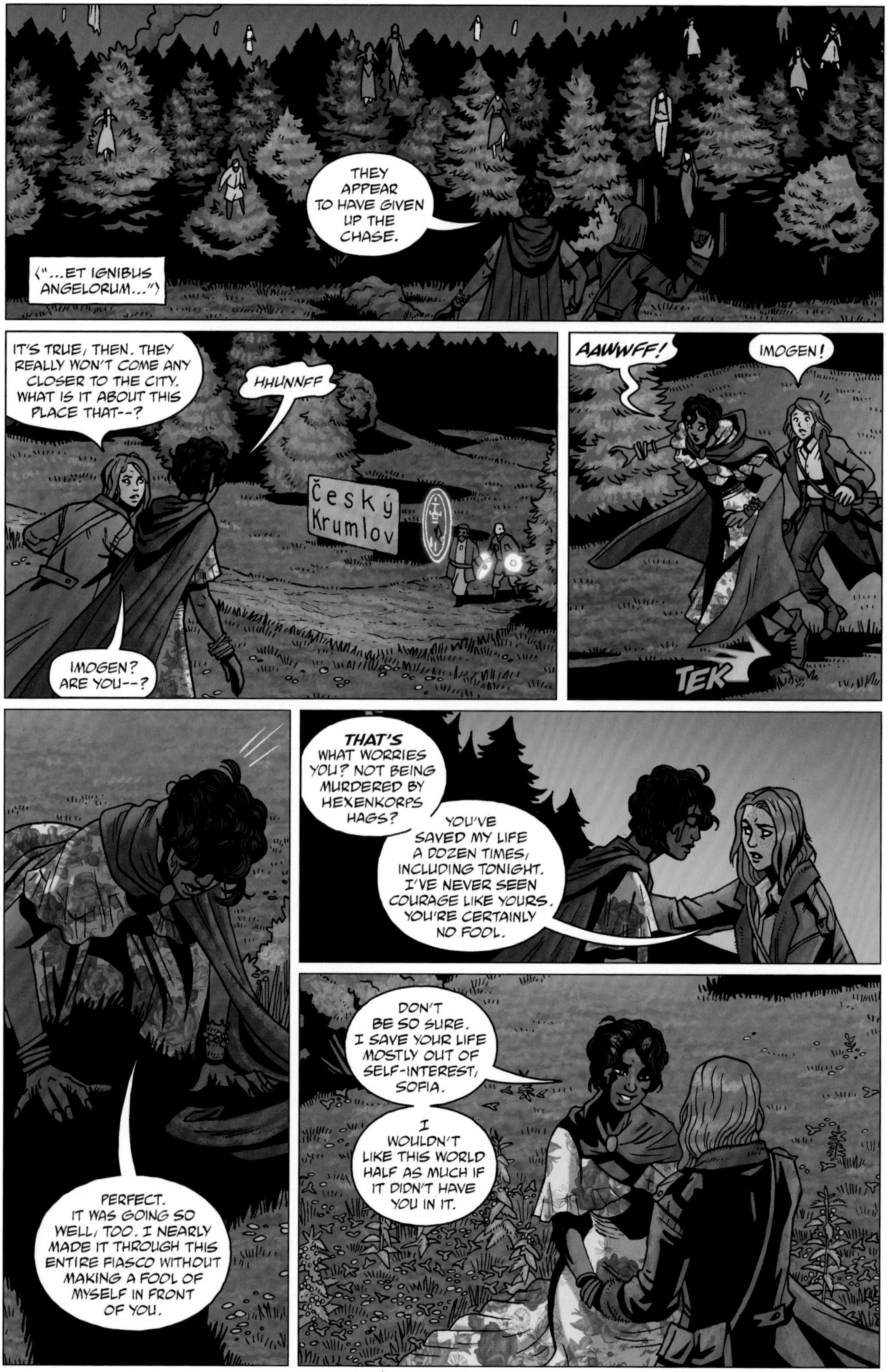
("...ET IGNIBUS ANGELORUM...")
THEY APPEAR TO HAVE GIVEN UP THE CHASE.
IT'S TRUE, THEN. THEY REALLY WON'T COME ANY CLOSER TO THE CITY. WHAT IS IT ABOUT THIS PLACE THAT--?
HHUNNFF
Český Krumlov
IMOGEN? ARE YOU--?
AAWWFF!
IMOGEN!
TEK
PERFECT. IT WAS GOING SO WELL, TOO. I NEARLY MADE IT THROUGH THIS ENTIRE FIASCO WITHOUT MAKING A FOOL OF MYSELF IN FRONT OF YOU.
THAT'S WHAT WORRIES YOU? NOT BEING MURDERED BY HEXENKORPS HAGS?
YOU'VE SAVED MY LIFE A DOZEN TIMES, INCLUDING TONIGHT. I'VE NEVER SEEN COURAGE LIKE YOURS. YOU'RE CERTAINLY NO FOOL.
DON'T BE SO SURE. I SAVE YOUR LIFE MOSTLY OUT OF SELF-INTEREST, SOFIA.
I WOULDN'T LIKE THIS WORLD HALF AS MUCH IF IT DIDN'T HAVE YOU IN IT.

YOU...YOU ARE SO DEAR TO ME. THERE'S NO ONE I TRUST MORE... NO ONE WITH WHOM I FEEL SO...

IMOGEN.

YOU CAN KEEP PRETENDING WHAT YOU FEEL ISN'T LOVE, SOFIA...BUT IF THIS *ISN'T* LOVE, WHAT *IS* IT?

I'M HONESTLY NOT SURE I'M...CAPABLE...OF LOVING *ANYONE*.

MMMMFFF

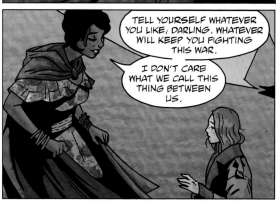

TELL YOURSELF WHATEVER YOU LIKE, DARLING. WHATEVER WILL KEEP YOU FIGHTING THIS WAR.

I DON'T CARE WHAT WE CALL THIS THING BETWEEN US.

I ONLY CARE HOW IT FEELS.

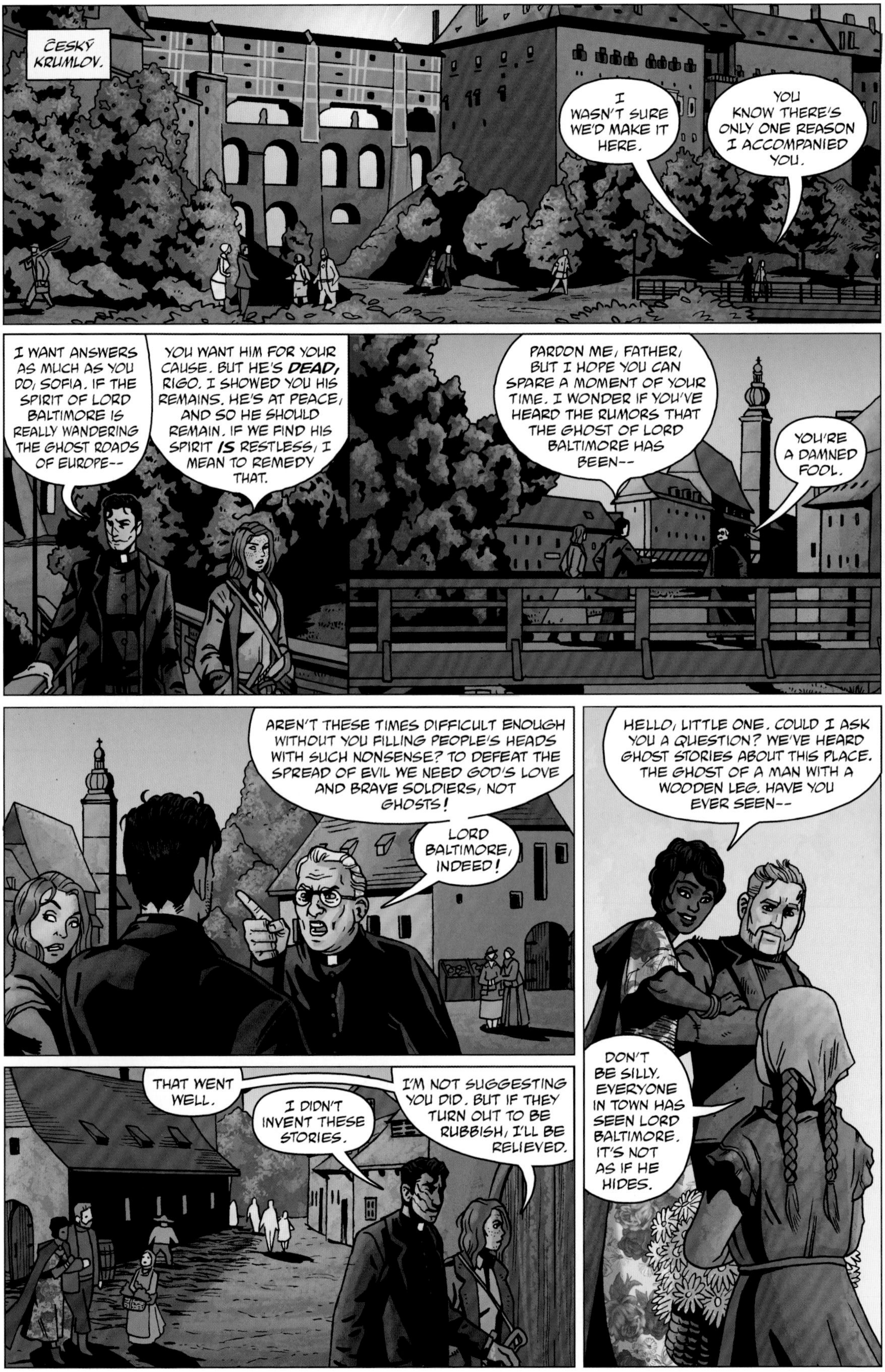
ČESKÝ KRUMLOV.
I WASN'T SURE WE'D MAKE IT HERE.
YOU KNOW THERE'S ONLY ONE REASON I ACCOMPANIED YOU.
I WANT ANSWERS AS MUCH AS YOU DO, SOFIA. IF THE SPIRIT OF LORD BALTIMORE IS REALLY WANDERING THE GHOST ROADS OF EUROPE--
YOU WANT HIM FOR YOUR CAUSE. BUT HE'S DEAD, RIGO. I SHOWED YOU HIS REMAINS. HE'S AT PEACE, AND SO HE SHOULD REMAIN. IF WE FIND HIS SPIRIT IS RESTLESS, I MEAN TO REMEDY THAT.
PARDON ME, FATHER, BUT I HOPE YOU CAN SPARE A MOMENT OF YOUR TIME. I WONDER IF YOU'VE HEARD THE RUMORS THAT THE GHOST OF LORD BALTIMORE HAS BEEN--
YOU'RE A DAMNED FOOL.
AREN'T THESE TIMES DIFFICULT ENOUGH WITHOUT YOU FILLING PEOPLE'S HEADS WITH SUCH NONSENSE? TO DEFEAT THE SPREAD OF EVIL WE NEED GOD'S LOVE AND BRAVE SOLDIERS, NOT GHOSTS!
LORD BALTIMORE, INDEED!
HELLO, LITTLE ONE. COULD I ASK YOU A QUESTION? WE'VE HEARD GHOST STORIES ABOUT THIS PLACE. THE GHOST OF A MAN WITH A WOODEN LEG. HAVE YOU EVER SEEN--
DON'T BE SILLY. EVERYONE IN TOWN HAS SEEN LORD BALTIMORE. IT'S NOT AS IF HE HIDES.
THAT WENT WELL.
I DIDN'T INVENT THESE STORIES.
I'M NOT SUGGESTING YOU DID. BUT IF THEY TURN OUT TO BE RUBBISH, I'LL BE RELIEVED.

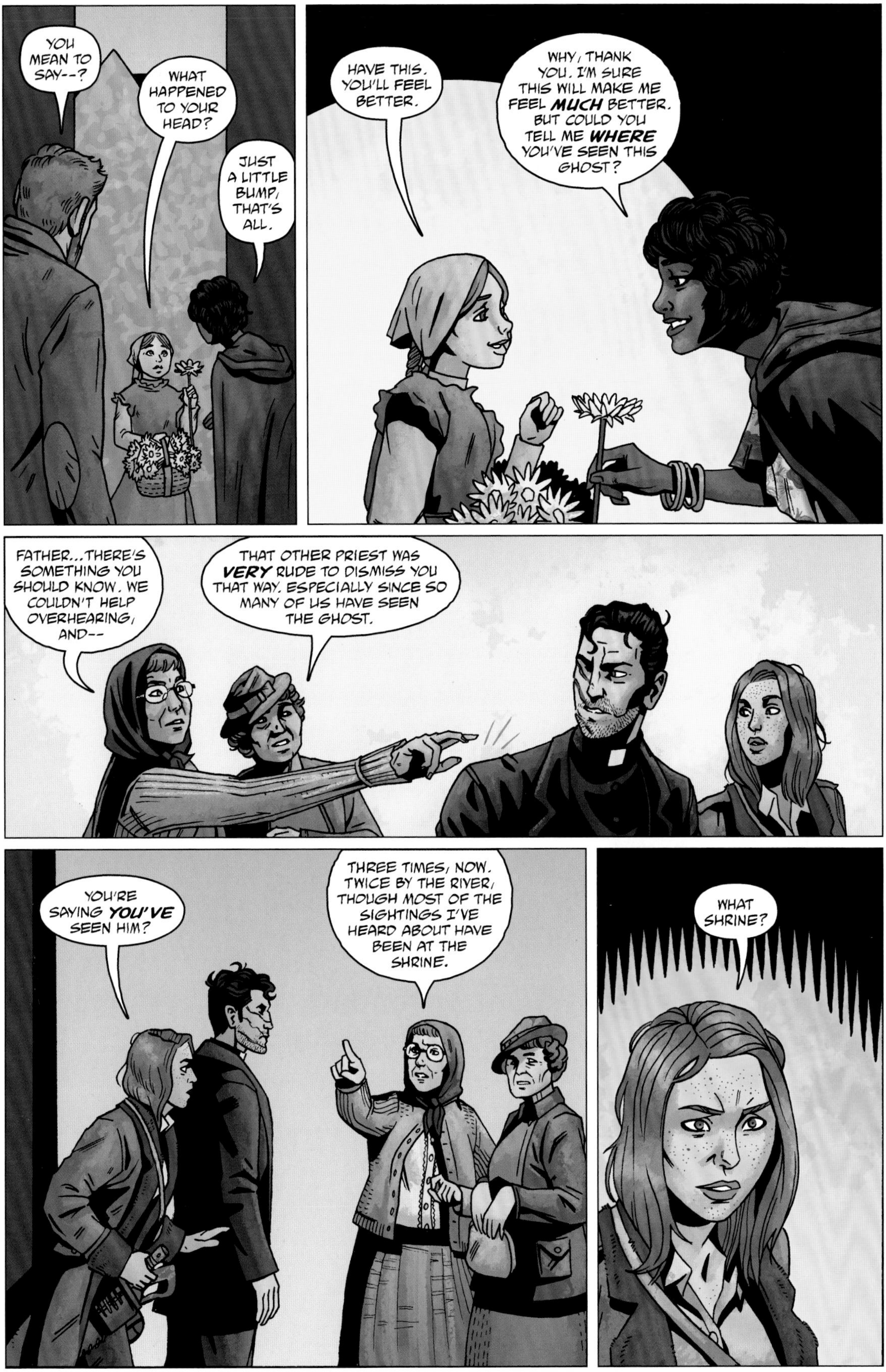
YOU MEAN TO SAY--?
WHAT HAPPENED TO YOUR HEAD?
JUST A LITTLE BUMP, THAT'S ALL.
HAVE THIS. YOU'LL FEEL BETTER.
WHY, THANK YOU. I'M SURE THIS WILL MAKE ME FEEL MUCH BETTER. BUT COULD YOU TELL ME WHERE YOU'VE SEEN THIS GHOST?
FATHER...THERE'S SOMETHING YOU SHOULD KNOW. WE COULDN'T HELP OVERHEARING, AND--
THAT OTHER PRIEST WAS VERY RUDE TO DISMISS YOU THAT WAY. ESPECIALLY SINCE SO MANY OF US HAVE SEEN THE GHOST.
YOU'RE SAYING YOU'VE SEEN HIM?
THREE TIMES, NOW. TWICE BY THE RIVER, THOUGH MOST OF THE SIGHTINGS I'VE HEARD ABOUT HAVE BEEN AT THE SHRINE.
WHAT SHRINE?

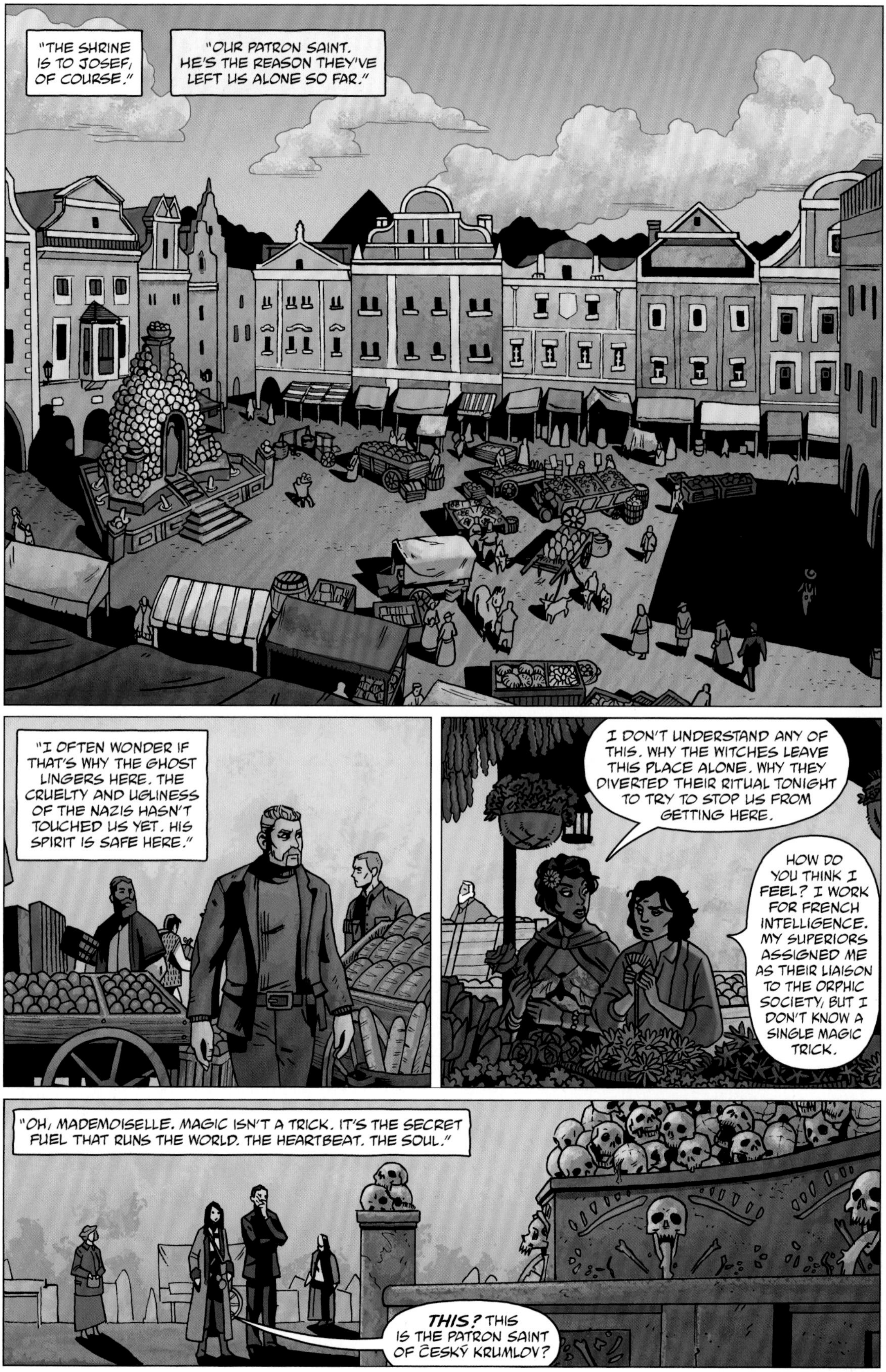
"THE SHRINE IS TO JOSEF, OF COURSE."
"OUR PATRON SAINT. HE'S THE REASON THEY'VE LEFT US ALONE SO FAR."
"I OFTEN WONDER IF THAT'S WHY THE GHOST LINGERS HERE. THE CRUELTY AND UGLINESS OF THE NAZIS HASN'T TOUCHED US YET. HIS SPIRIT IS SAFE HERE."
I DON'T UNDERSTAND ANY OF THIS. WHY THE WITCHES LEAVE THIS PLACE ALONE. WHY THEY DIVERTED THEIR RITUAL TONIGHT TO TRY TO STOP US FROM GETTING HERE.
HOW DO YOU THINK I FEEL? I WORK FOR FRENCH INTELLIGENCE. MY SUPERIORS ASSIGNED ME AS THEIR LIAISON TO THE ORPHIC SOCIETY, BUT I DON'T KNOW A SINGLE MAGIC TRICK.
"OH, MADEMOISELLE. MAGIC ISN'T A TRICK. IT'S THE SECRET FUEL THAT RUNS THE WORLD. THE HEARTBEAT. THE SOUL."
THIS? THIS IS THE PATRON SAINT OF ČESKÝ KRUMLOV?

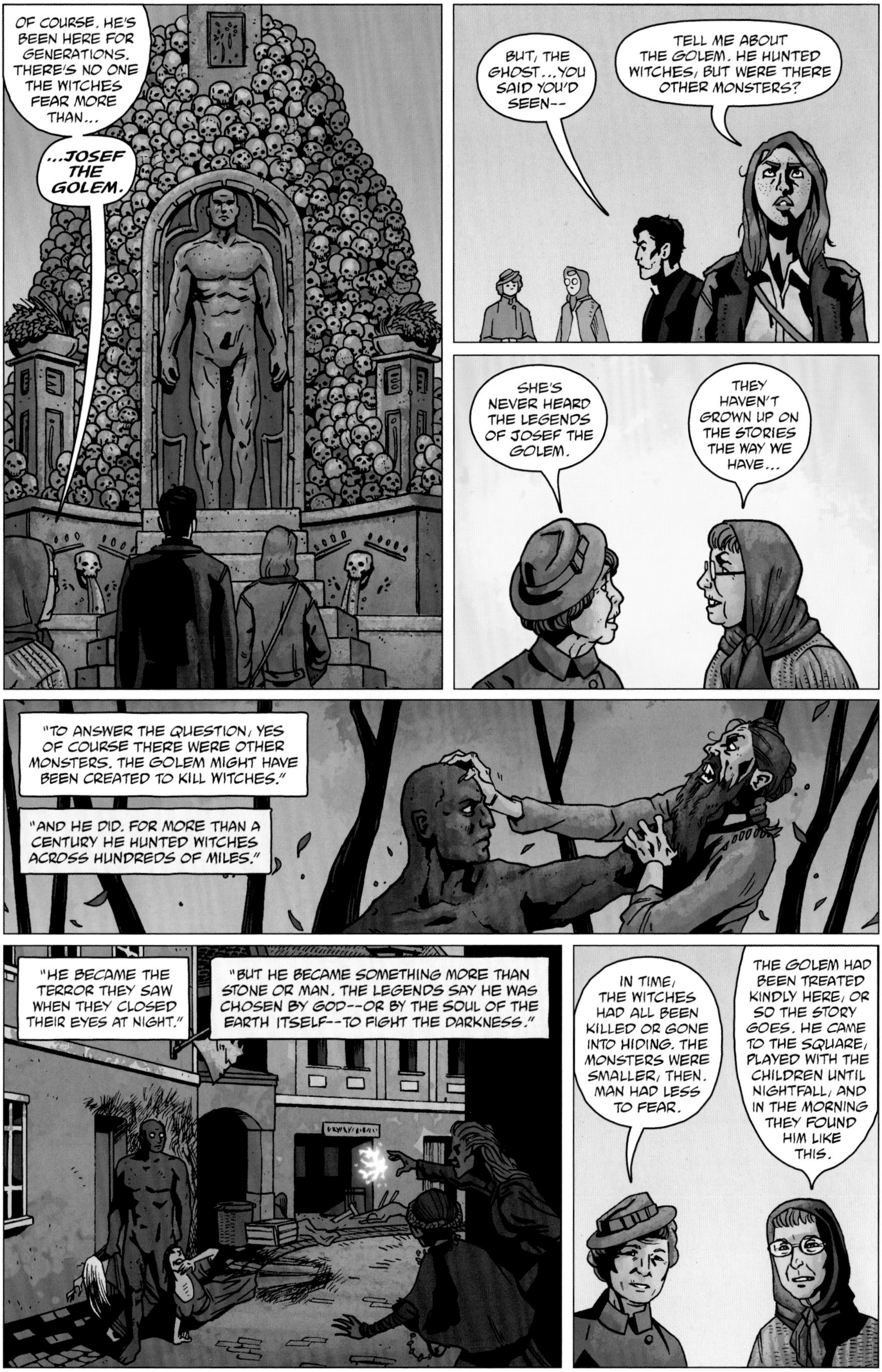
OF COURSE. HE'S BEEN HERE FOR GENERATIONS. THERE'S NO ONE THE WITCHES FEAR MORE THAN...
...JOSEF THE GOLEM.
TELL ME ABOUT THE GOLEM. HE HUNTED WITCHES, BUT WERE THERE OTHER MONSTERS?
BUT, THE GHOST...YOU SAID YOU'D SEEN--
SHE'S NEVER HEARD THE LEGENDS OF JOSEF THE GOLEM.
THEY HAVEN'T GROWN UP ON THE STORIES THE WAY WE HAVE...
"TO ANSWER THE QUESTION, YES OF COURSE THERE WERE OTHER MONSTERS. THE GOLEM MIGHT HAVE BEEN CREATED TO KILL WITCHES."
"AND HE DID. FOR MORE THAN A CENTURY HE HUNTED WITCHES ACROSS HUNDREDS OF MILES."
"HE BECAME THE TERROR THEY SAW WHEN THEY CLOSED THEIR EYES AT NIGHT."
"BUT HE BECAME SOMETHING MORE THAN STONE OR MAN. THE LEGENDS SAY HE WAS CHOSEN BY GOD--OR BY THE SOUL OF THE EARTH ITSELF--TO FIGHT THE DARKNESS."
IN TIME, THE WITCHES HAD ALL BEEN KILLED OR GONE INTO HIDING. THE MONSTERS WERE SMALLER, THEN. MAN HAD LESS TO FEAR.
THE GOLEM HAD BEEN TREATED KINDLY HERE, OR SO THE STORY GOES. HE CAME TO THE SQUARE, PLAYED WITH THE CHILDREN UNTIL NIGHTFALL, AND IN THE MORNING THEY FOUND HIM LIKE THIS.

HE THOUGHT HIS JOB WAS DONE.

BUT IT ISN'T REALLY DONE AT ALL.

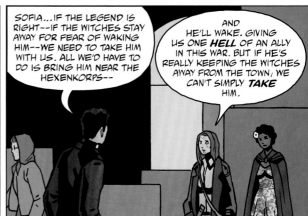

SOFIA...IF THE LEGEND IS RIGHT--IF THE WITCHES STAY AWAY FOR FEAR OF WAKING HIM--WE NEED TO TAKE HIM WITH US. ALL WE'D HAVE TO DO IS BRING HIM NEAR THE HEXENKORPS--

AND HE'LL WAKE. GIVING US ONE *HELL* OF AN ALLY IN THIS WAR. BUT IF HE'S REALLY KEEPING THE WITCHES AWAY FROM THE TOWN, WE CAN'T SIMPLY *TAKE* HIM.

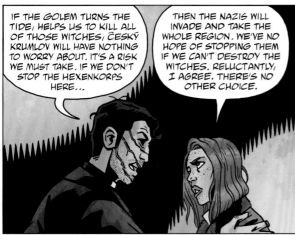

IF THE GOLEM TURNS THE TIDE, HELPS US TO KILL ALL OF THOSE WITCHES, ČESKÝ KRUMLOV WILL HAVE NOTHING TO WORRY ABOUT. IT'S A RISK WE MUST TAKE. IF WE DON'T STOP THE HEXENKORPS HERE...

THEN THE NAZIS WILL INVADE AND TAKE THE WHOLE REGION. WE'VE NO HOPE OF STOPPING THEM IF WE CAN'T DESTROY THE WITCHES. RELUCTANTLY, I AGREE. THERE'S NO OTHER CHOICE.

THE TWO OF YOU, FIND A TRUCK AND BRING IT HERE. QUICK AS YOU CAN.

RIGHT AWAY, BROTHER.

THIS IS ABSURD. YOU'RE GOING TO DESTROY THIS PUBLIC SHRINE BASED ON SOME RIDICULOUS LEGEND?

YOU MAY NOT BELIEVE THE STONE MAN IS PROTECTING THE CITY FROM THE WITCHES...

"...BUT SOMEBODY SEEMS *VERY* DETERMINED NOT TO LET US TAKE HIM AWAY."

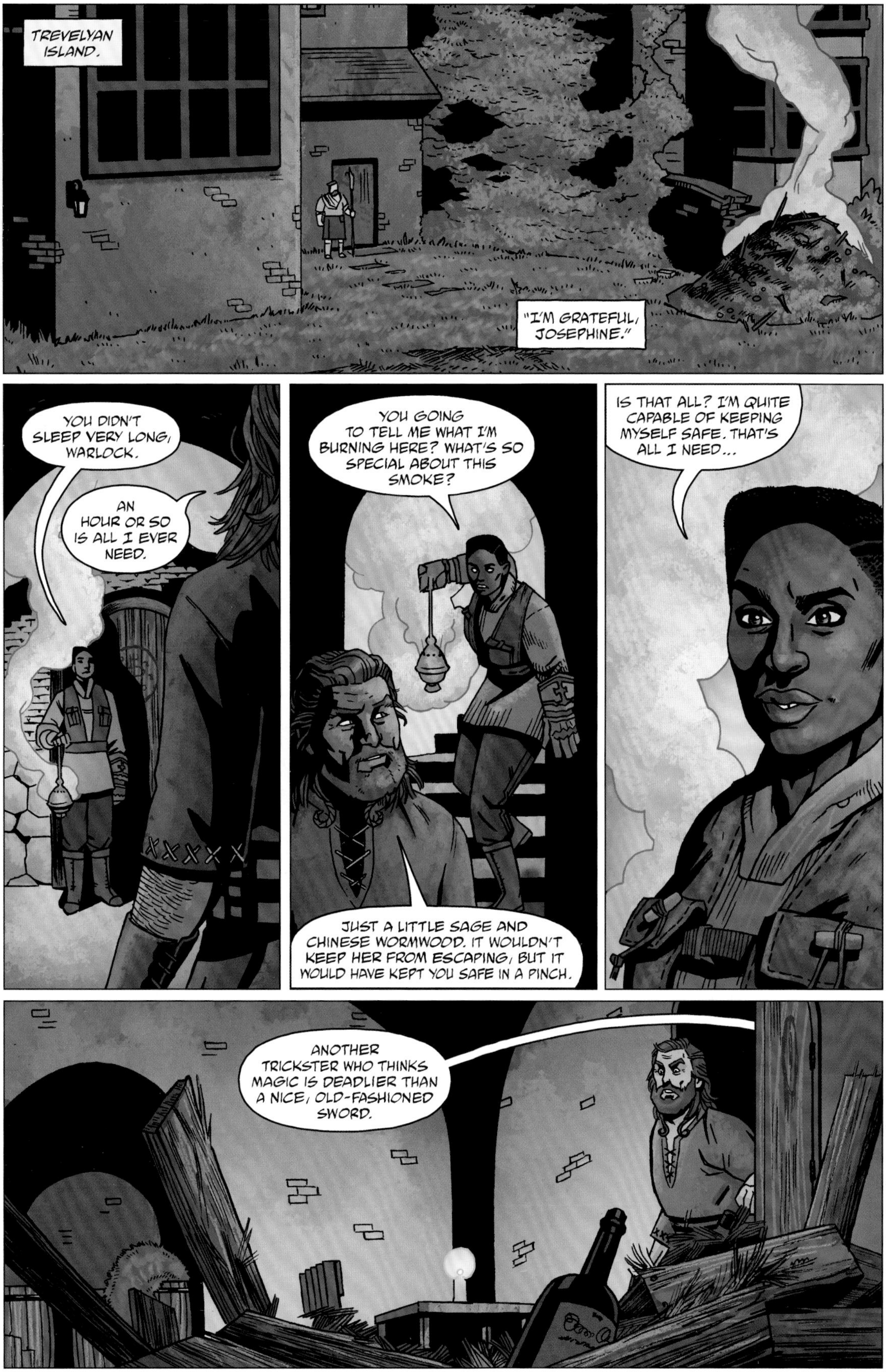
TREVELYAN ISLAND.
"I'M GRATEFUL, JOSEPHINE."
YOU DIDN'T SLEEP VERY LONG, WARLOCK.
AN HOUR OR SO IS ALL I EVER NEED.
YOU GOING TO TELL ME WHAT I'M BURNING HERE? WHAT'S SO SPECIAL ABOUT THIS SMOKE?
JUST A LITTLE SAGE AND CHINESE WORMWOOD. IT WOULDN'T KEEP HER FROM ESCAPING, BUT IT WOULD HAVE KEPT YOU SAFE IN A PINCH.
IS THAT ALL? I'M QUITE CAPABLE OF KEEPING MYSELF SAFE. THAT'S ALL I NEED...
ANOTHER TRICKSTER WHO THINKS MAGIC IS DEADLIER THAN A NICE, OLD-FASHIONED SWORD.

HELLO, WARLOCK.

HOW...?

KRASSH

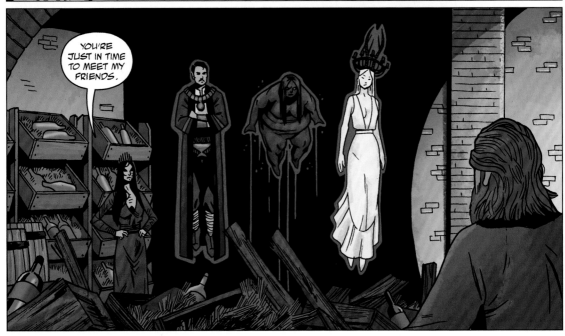

YOU'RE JUST IN TIME TO MEET MY FRIENDS.

CHAPTER FOUR

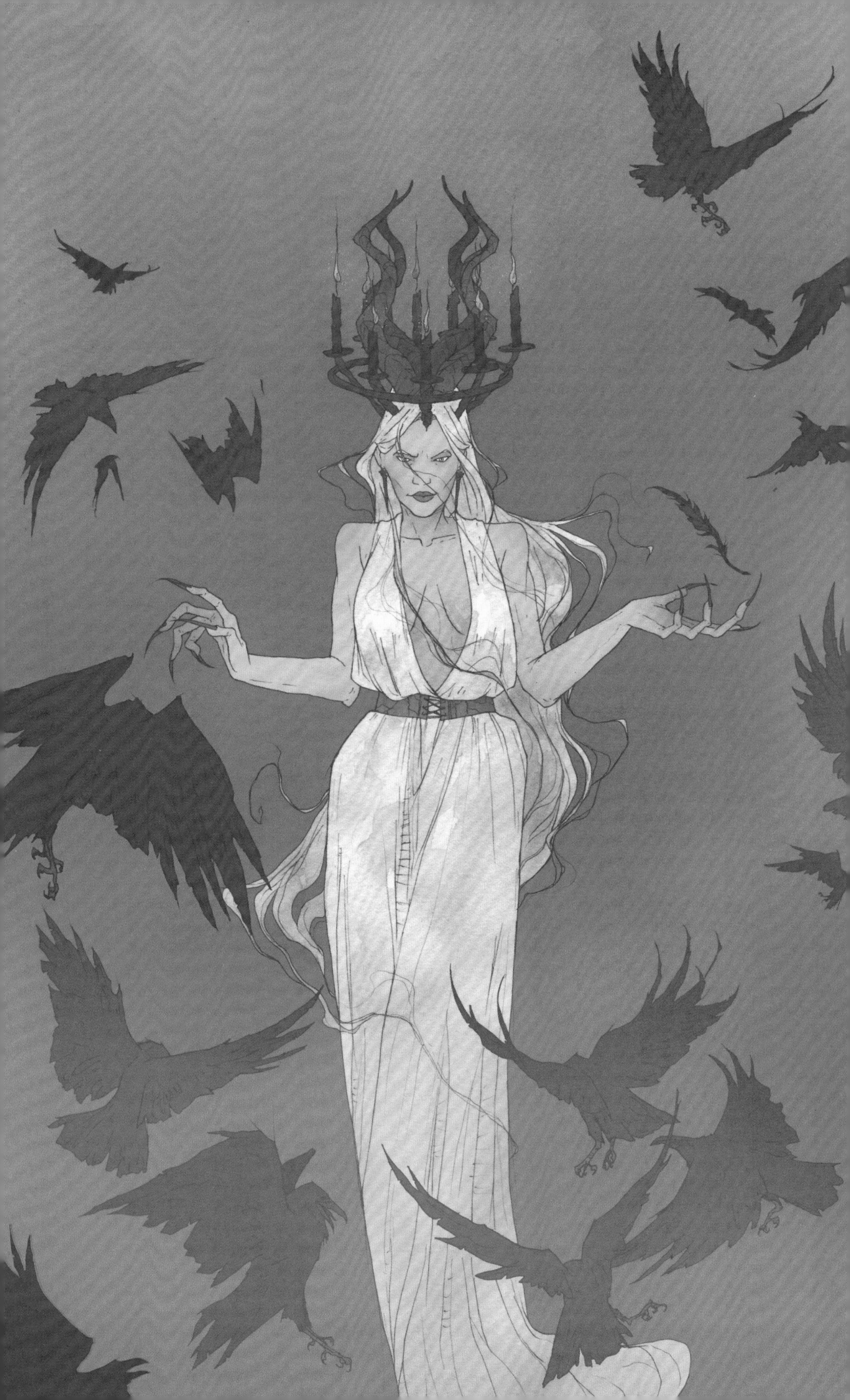

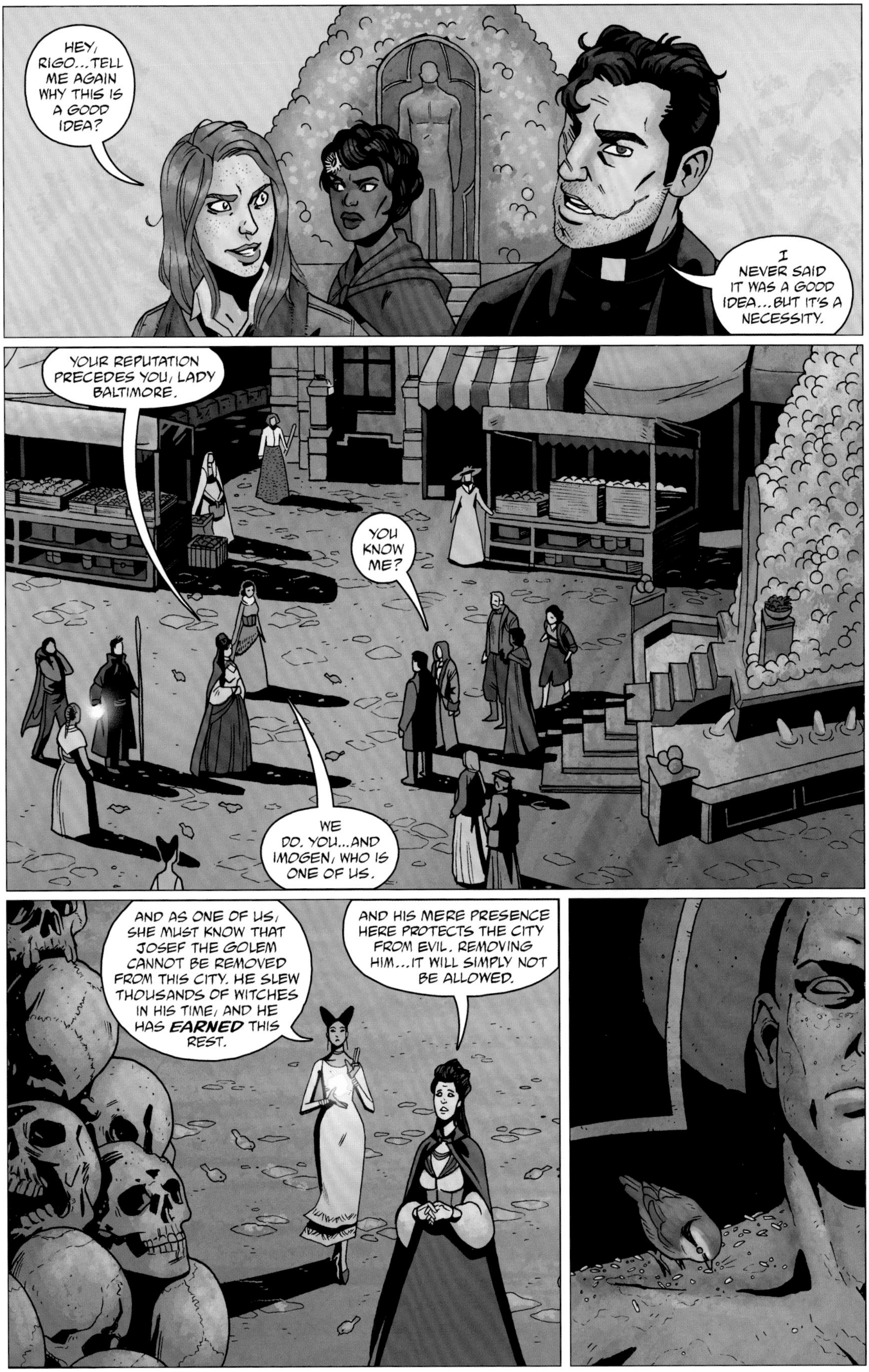
HEY, RIGO...TELL ME AGAIN WHY THIS IS A GOOD IDEA?
I NEVER SAID IT WAS A GOOD IDEA...BUT IT'S A NECESSITY.
YOUR REPUTATION PRECEDES YOU, LADY BALTIMORE.
YOU KNOW ME?
WE DO. YOU...AND IMOGEN, WHO IS ONE OF US.
AND AS ONE OF US, SHE MUST KNOW THAT JOSEF THE GOLEM CANNOT BE REMOVED FROM THIS CITY. HE SLEW THOUSANDS OF WITCHES IN HIS TIME, AND HE HAS EARNED THIS REST.
AND HIS MERE PRESENCE HERE PROTECTS THE CITY FROM EVIL. REMOVING HIM...IT WILL SIMPLY NOT BE ALLOWED.

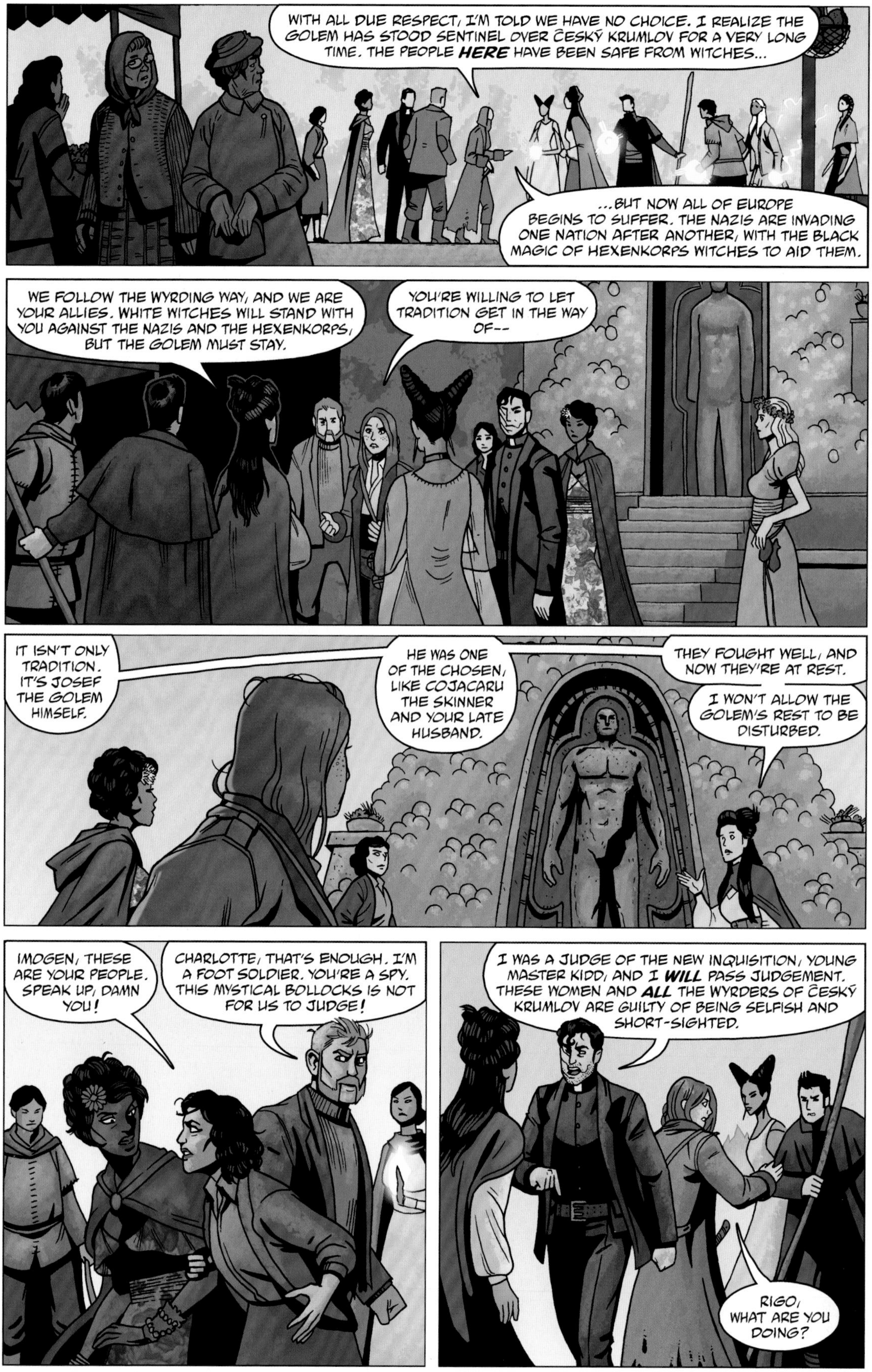
WITH ALL DUE RESPECT, I'M TOLD WE HAVE NO CHOICE. I REALIZE THE GOLEM HAS STOOD SENTINEL OVER ČESKÝ KRUMLOV FOR A VERY LONG TIME. THE PEOPLE **HERE** HAVE BEEN SAFE FROM WITCHES...
...BUT NOW ALL OF EUROPE BEGINS TO SUFFER. THE NAZIS ARE INVADING ONE NATION AFTER ANOTHER, WITH THE BLACK MAGIC OF HEXENKORPS WITCHES TO AID THEM.
WE FOLLOW THE WYRDING WAY, AND WE ARE YOUR ALLIES. WHITE WITCHES WILL STAND WITH YOU AGAINST THE NAZIS AND THE HEXENKORPS, BUT THE GOLEM MUST STAY.
YOU'RE WILLING TO LET TRADITION GET IN THE WAY OF--
IT ISN'T ONLY TRADITION. IT'S JOSEF THE GOLEM HIMSELF.
HE WAS ONE OF THE CHOSEN, LIKE COJACARU THE SKINNER AND YOUR LATE HUSBAND.
THEY FOUGHT WELL, AND NOW THEY'RE AT REST.
I WON'T ALLOW THE GOLEM'S REST TO BE DISTURBED.
IMOGEN, THESE ARE YOUR PEOPLE. SPEAK UP, DAMN YOU!
CHARLOTTE, THAT'S ENOUGH. I'M A FOOT SOLDIER. YOU'RE A SPY. THIS MYSTICAL BOLLOCKS IS NOT FOR US TO JUDGE!
I WAS A JUDGE OF THE NEW INQUISITION, YOUNG MASTER KIDD, AND I **WILL** PASS JUDGEMENT. THESE WOMEN AND **ALL** THE WYRDERS OF ČESKÝ KRUMLOV ARE GUILTY OF BEING SELFISH AND SHORT-SIGHTED.
RIGO, WHAT ARE YOU DOING?

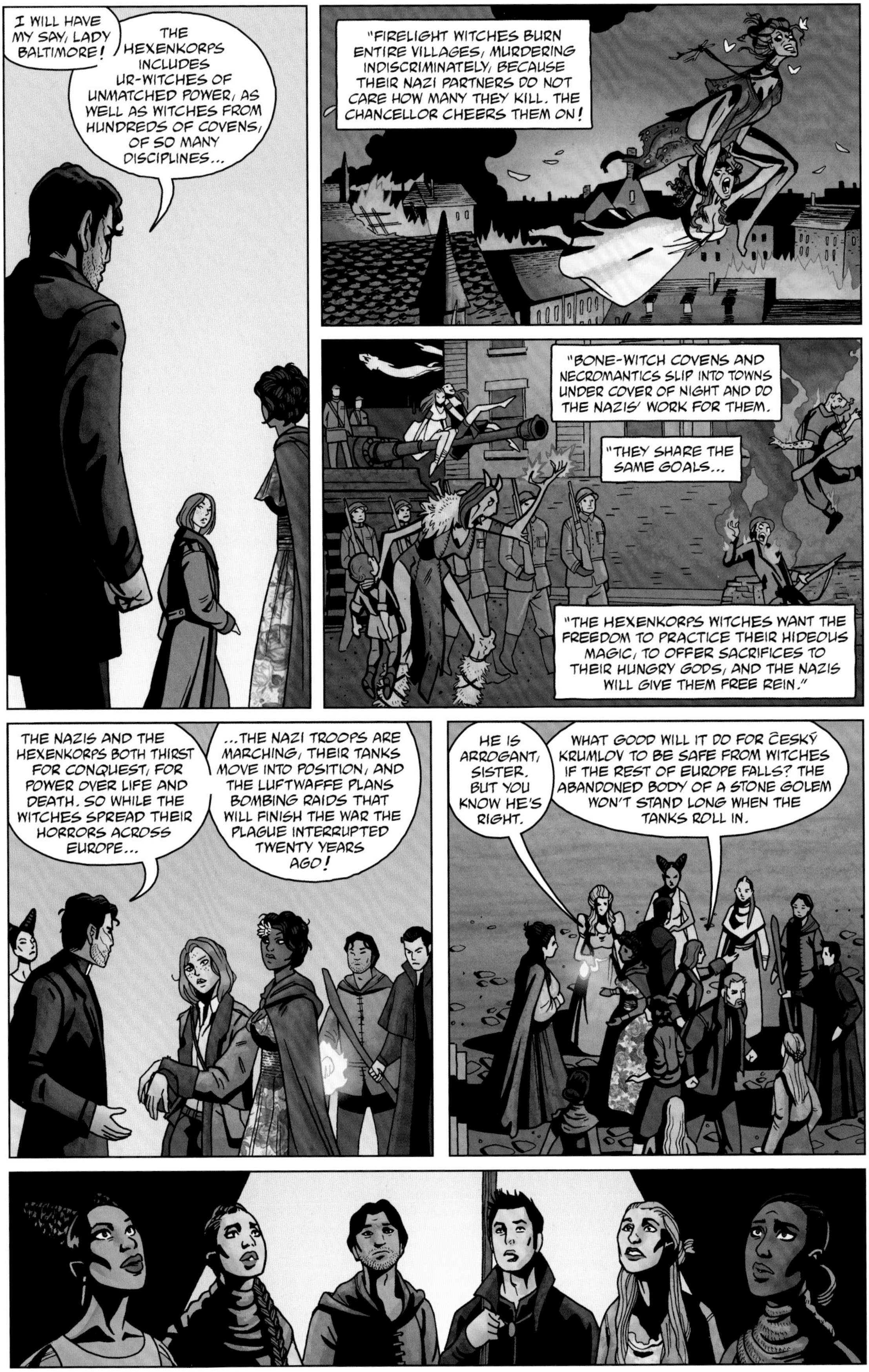

I WILL HAVE MY SAY, LADY BALTIMORE!
THE HEXENKORPS INCLUDES UR-WITCHES OF UNMATCHED POWER, AS WELL AS WITCHES FROM HUNDREDS OF COVENS, OF SO MANY DISCIPLINES...
"FIRELIGHT WITCHES BURN ENTIRE VILLAGES, MURDERING INDISCRIMINATELY, BECAUSE THEIR NAZI PARTNERS DO NOT CARE HOW MANY THEY KILL. THE CHANCELLOR CHEERS THEM ON!
"BONE-WITCH COVENS AND NECROMANTICS SLIP INTO TOWNS UNDER COVER OF NIGHT AND DO THE NAZIS' WORK FOR THEM.
"THEY SHARE THE SAME GOALS...
"THE HEXENKORPS WITCHES WANT THE FREEDOM TO PRACTICE THEIR HIDEOUS MAGIC, TO OFFER SACRIFICES TO THEIR HUNGRY GODS, AND THE NAZIS WILL GIVE THEM FREE REIN."
THE NAZIS AND THE HEXENKORPS BOTH THIRST FOR CONQUEST, FOR POWER OVER LIFE AND DEATH. SO WHILE THE WITCHES SPREAD THEIR HORRORS ACROSS EUROPE...
...THE NAZI TROOPS ARE MARCHING, THEIR TANKS MOVE INTO POSITION, AND THE LUFTWAFFE PLANS BOMBING RAIDS THAT WILL FINISH THE WAR THE PLAGUE INTERRUPTED TWENTY YEARS AGO!
HE IS ARROGANT, SISTER. BUT YOU KNOW HE'S RIGHT.
WHAT GOOD WILL IT DO FOR ČESKÝ KRUMLOV TO BE SAFE FROM WITCHES IF THE REST OF EUROPE FALLS? THE ABANDONED BODY OF A STONE GOLEM WON'T STAND LONG WHEN THE TANKS ROLL IN.

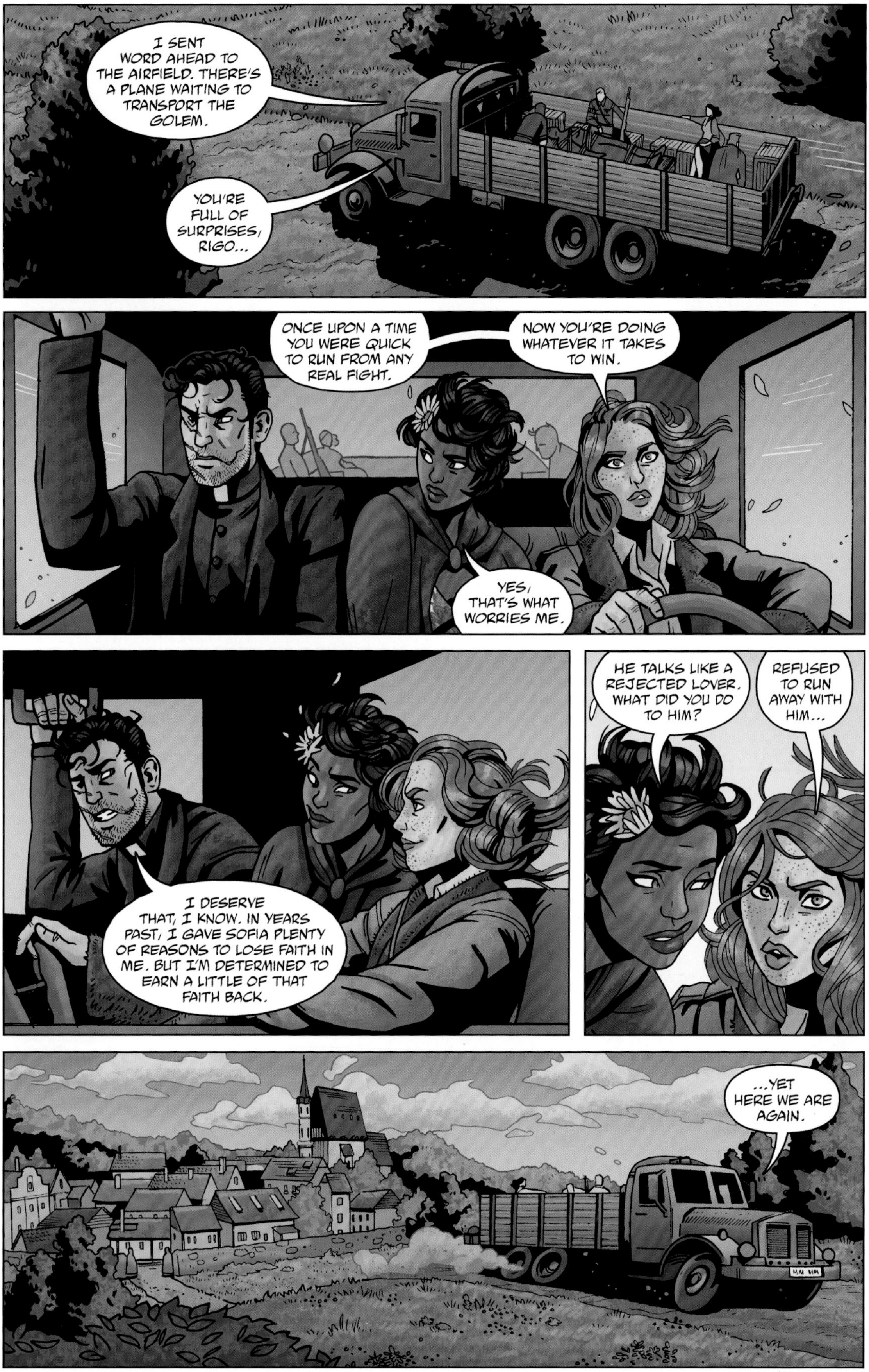
I SENT WORD AHEAD TO THE AIRFIELD. THERE'S A PLANE WAITING TO TRANSPORT THE GOLEM.
YOU'RE FULL OF SURPRISES, RIGO...
ONCE UPON A TIME YOU WERE QUICK TO RUN FROM ANY REAL FIGHT.
NOW YOU'RE DOING WHATEVER IT TAKES TO WIN.
YES, THAT'S WHAT WORRIES ME.
I DESERVE THAT, I KNOW. IN YEARS PAST, I GAVE SOFIA PLENTY OF REASONS TO LOSE FAITH IN ME. BUT I'M DETERMINED TO EARN A LITTLE OF THAT FAITH BACK.
HE TALKS LIKE A REJECTED LOVER. WHAT DID YOU DO TO HIM?
REFUSED TO RUN AWAY WITH HIM...
...YET HERE WE ARE AGAIN.

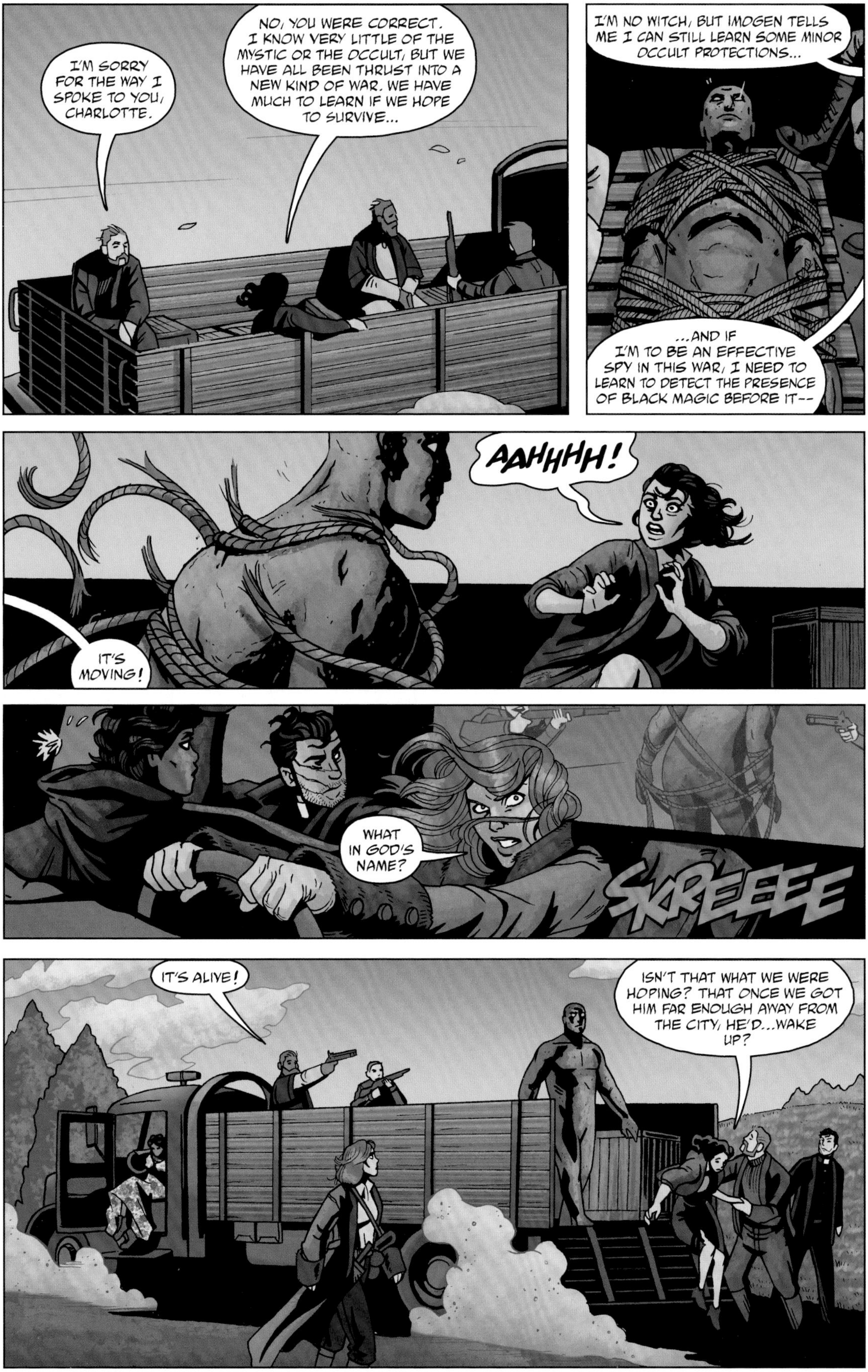
I'M SORRY FOR THE WAY I SPOKE TO YOU, CHARLOTTE.
NO, YOU WERE CORRECT. I KNOW VERY LITTLE OF THE MYSTIC OR THE OCCULT, BUT WE HAVE ALL BEEN THRUST INTO A NEW KIND OF WAR. WE HAVE MUCH TO LEARN IF WE HOPE TO SURVIVE...
I'M NO WITCH, BUT IMOGEN TELLS ME I CAN STILL LEARN SOME MINOR OCCULT PROTECTIONS...
...AND IF I'M TO BE AN EFFECTIVE SPY IN THIS WAR, I NEED TO LEARN TO DETECT THE PRESENCE OF BLACK MAGIC BEFORE IT--
AAHHHH!
IT'S MOVING!
WHAT IN GOD'S NAME?
SKREEEEE
IT'S ALIVE!
ISN'T THAT WHAT WE WERE HOPING? THAT ONCE WE GOT HIM FAR ENOUGH AWAY FROM THE CITY, HE'D...WAKE UP?

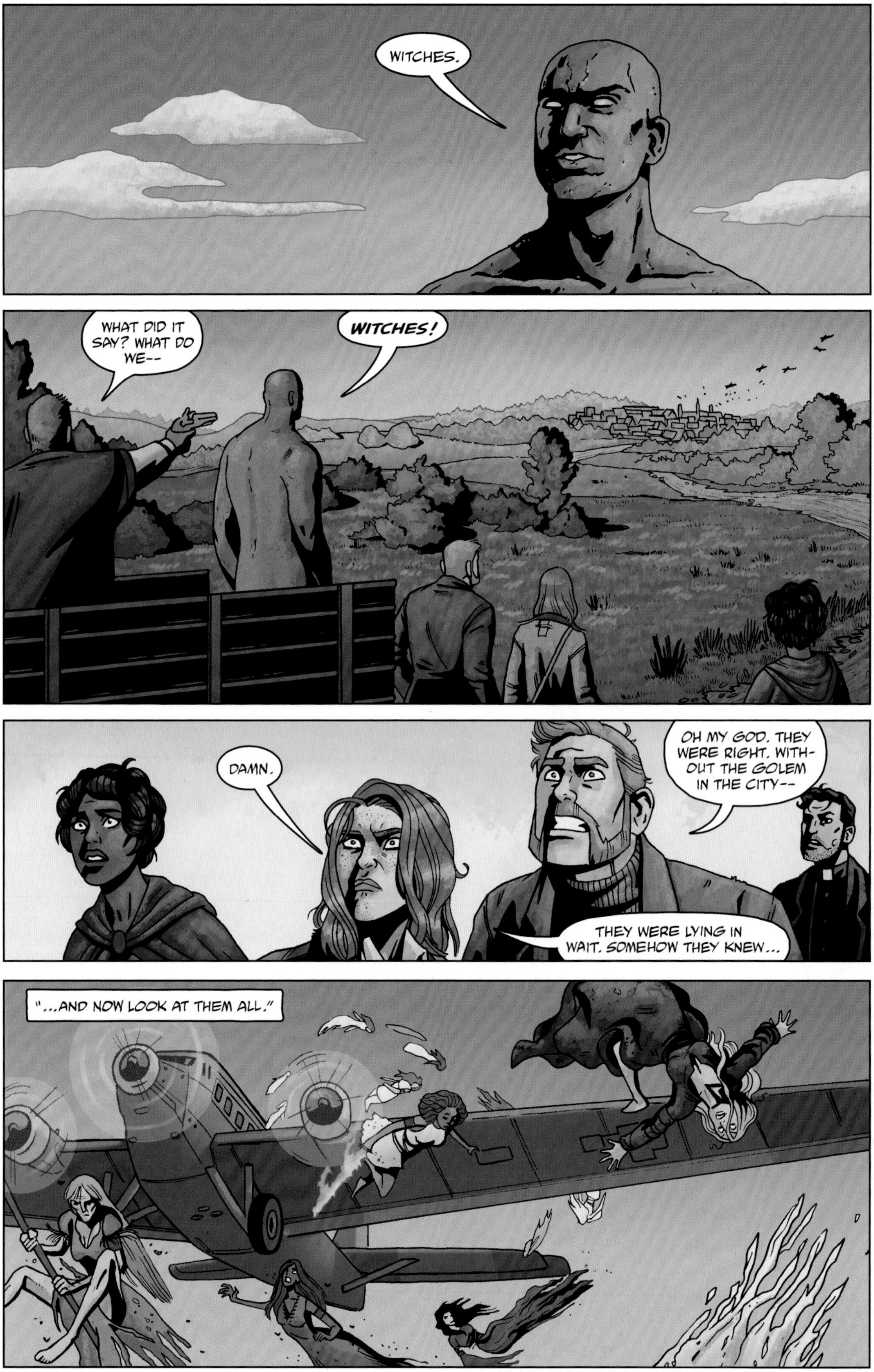
WITCHES.
WHAT DID IT SAY? WHAT DO WE--
WITCHES!
DAMN.
OH MY GOD. THEY WERE RIGHT. WITHOUT THE GOLEM IN THE CITY--
THEY WERE LYING IN WAIT. SOMEHOW THEY KNEW...
"...AND NOW LOOK AT THEM ALL."

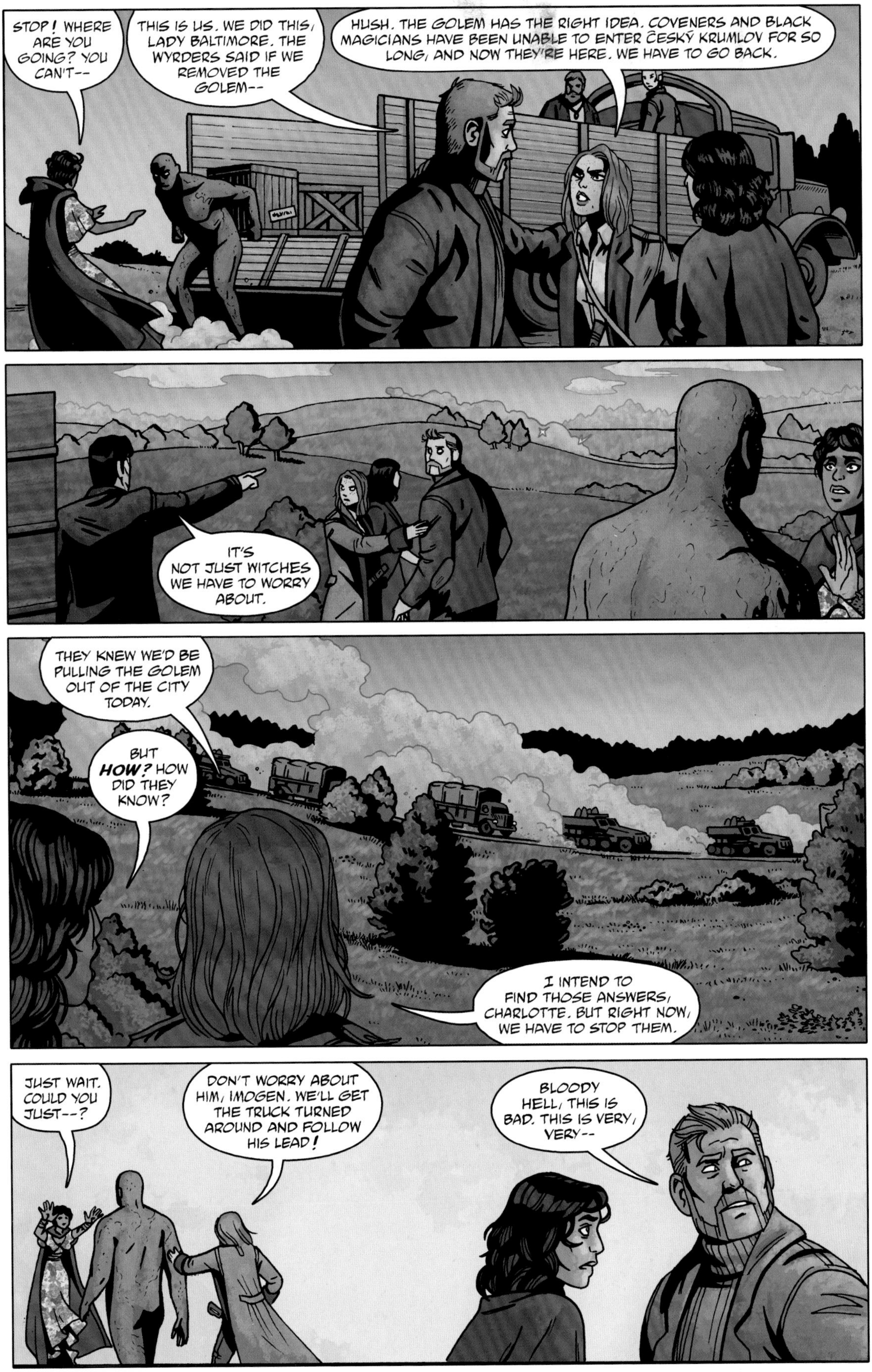
STOP! WHERE ARE YOU GOING? YOU CAN'T--
THIS IS US. WE DID THIS, LADY BALTIMORE. THE WYRDERS SAID IF WE REMOVED THE GOLEM--
HUSH. THE GOLEM HAS THE RIGHT IDEA. COVENERS AND BLACK MAGICIANS HAVE BEEN UNABLE TO ENTER ČESKÝ KRUMLOV FOR SO LONG, AND NOW THEY'RE HERE. WE HAVE TO GO BACK.
IT'S NOT JUST WITCHES WE HAVE TO WORRY ABOUT.
THEY KNEW WE'D BE PULLING THE GOLEM OUT OF THE CITY TODAY.
BUT HOW? HOW DID THEY KNOW?
I INTEND TO FIND THOSE ANSWERS, CHARLOTTE. BUT RIGHT NOW, WE HAVE TO STOP THEM.
JUST WAIT. COULD YOU JUST--?
DON'T WORRY ABOUT HIM, IMOGEN. WE'LL GET THE TRUCK TURNED AROUND AND FOLLOW HIS LEAD!
BLOODY HELL, THIS IS BAD. THIS IS VERY, VERY--

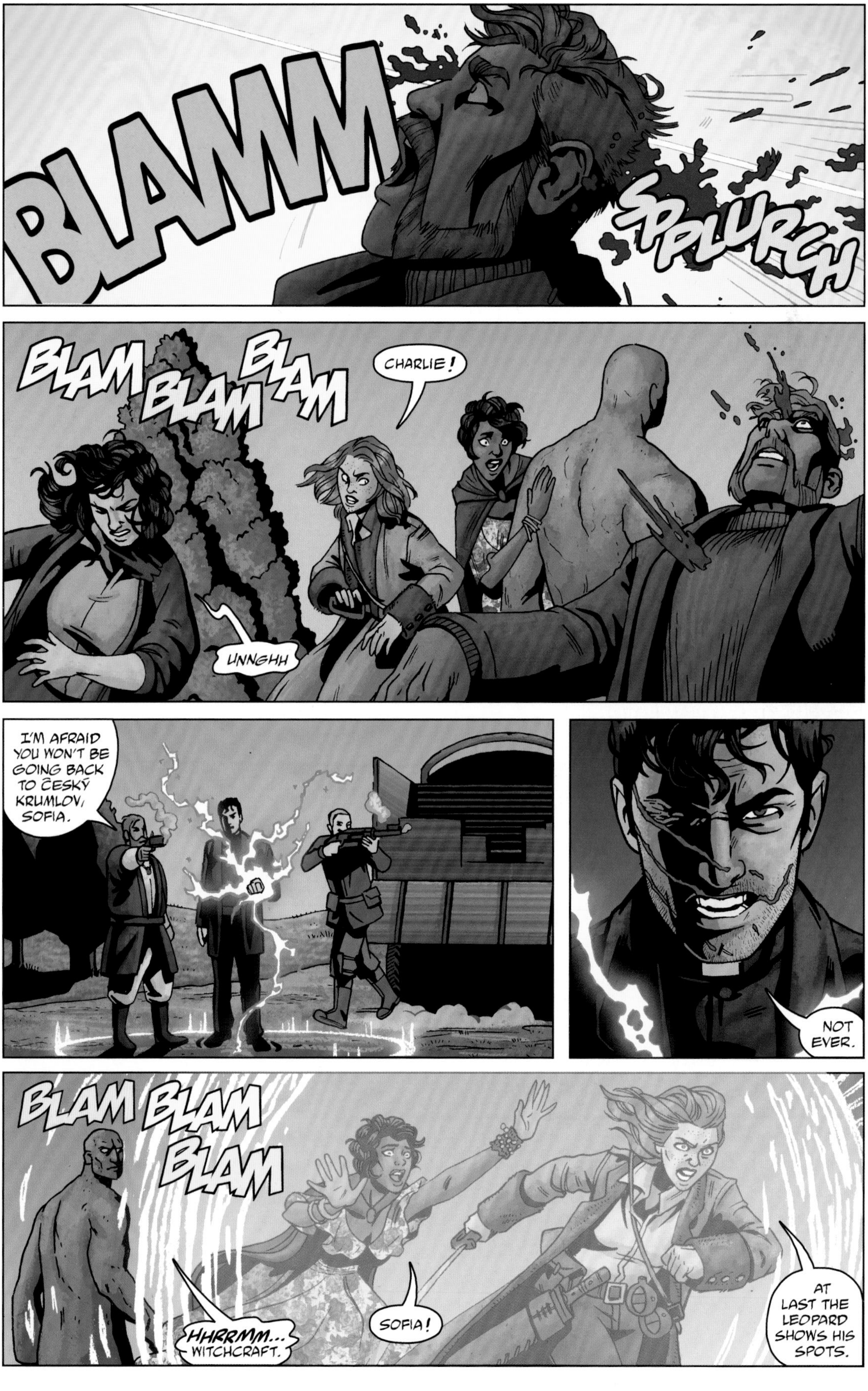
BLAMM
SPPLURCH
BLAM BLAM BLAM
CHARLIE!
UNNGHH
I'M AFRAID YOU WON'T BE GOING BACK TO ČESKÝ KRUMLOV, SOFIA.
NOT EVER.
BLAM BLAM BLAM
HHRRMM... WITCHCRAFT.
SOFIA!
AT LAST THE LEOPARD SHOWS HIS SPOTS.

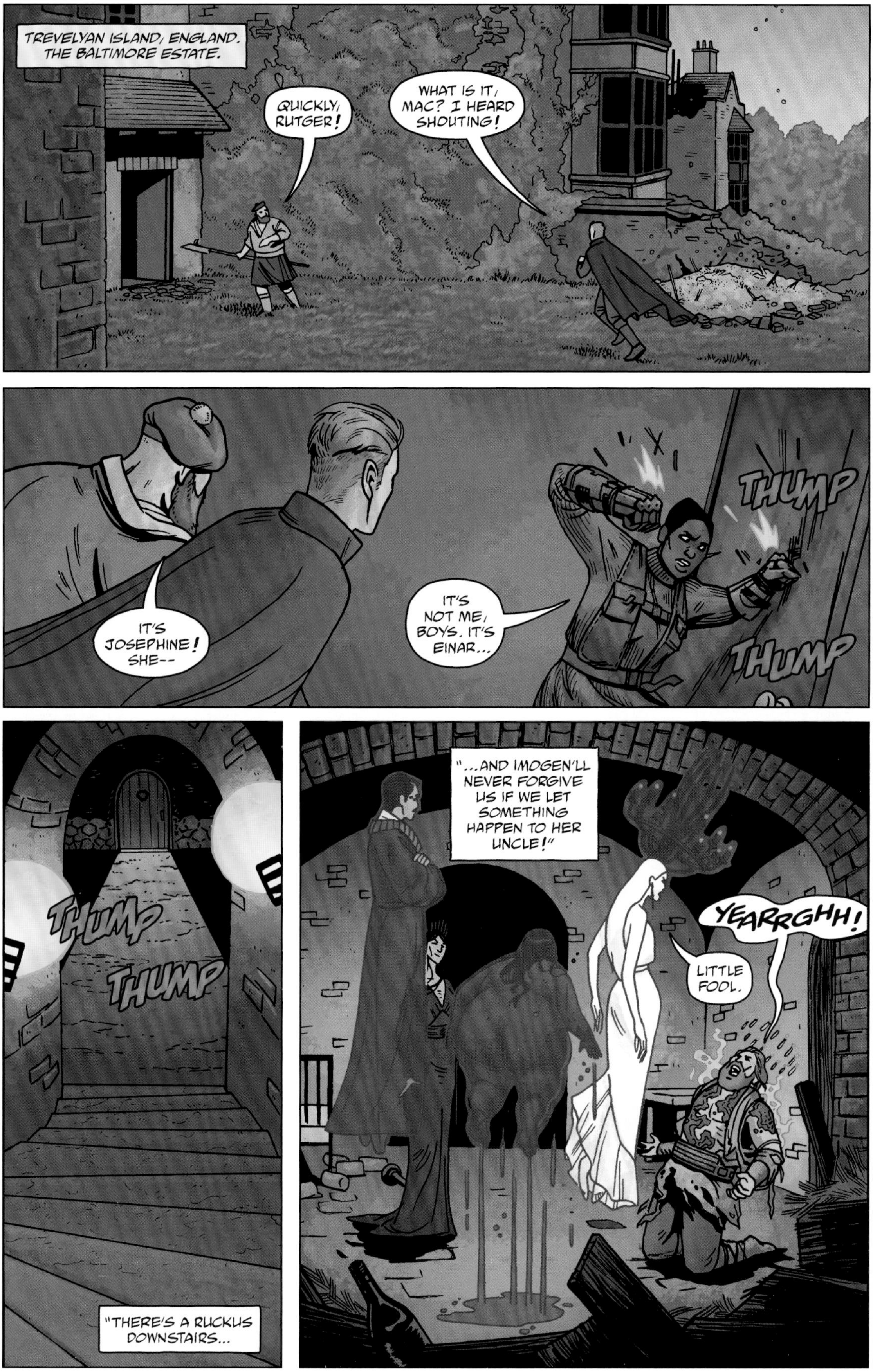
TREVELYAN ISLAND, ENGLAND. THE BALTIMORE ESTATE.
QUICKLY, RUTGER!
WHAT IS IT, MAC? I HEARD SHOUTING!
IT'S JOSEPHINE! SHE--
IT'S NOT ME, BOYS. IT'S EINAR...
THUMP
THUMP
THUMP
THUMP
"THERE'S A RUCKUS DOWNSTAIRS...
"...AND IMOGEN'LL NEVER FORGIVE US IF WE LET SOMETHING HAPPEN TO HER UNCLE!"
YEARRGHH!
LITTLE FOOL.

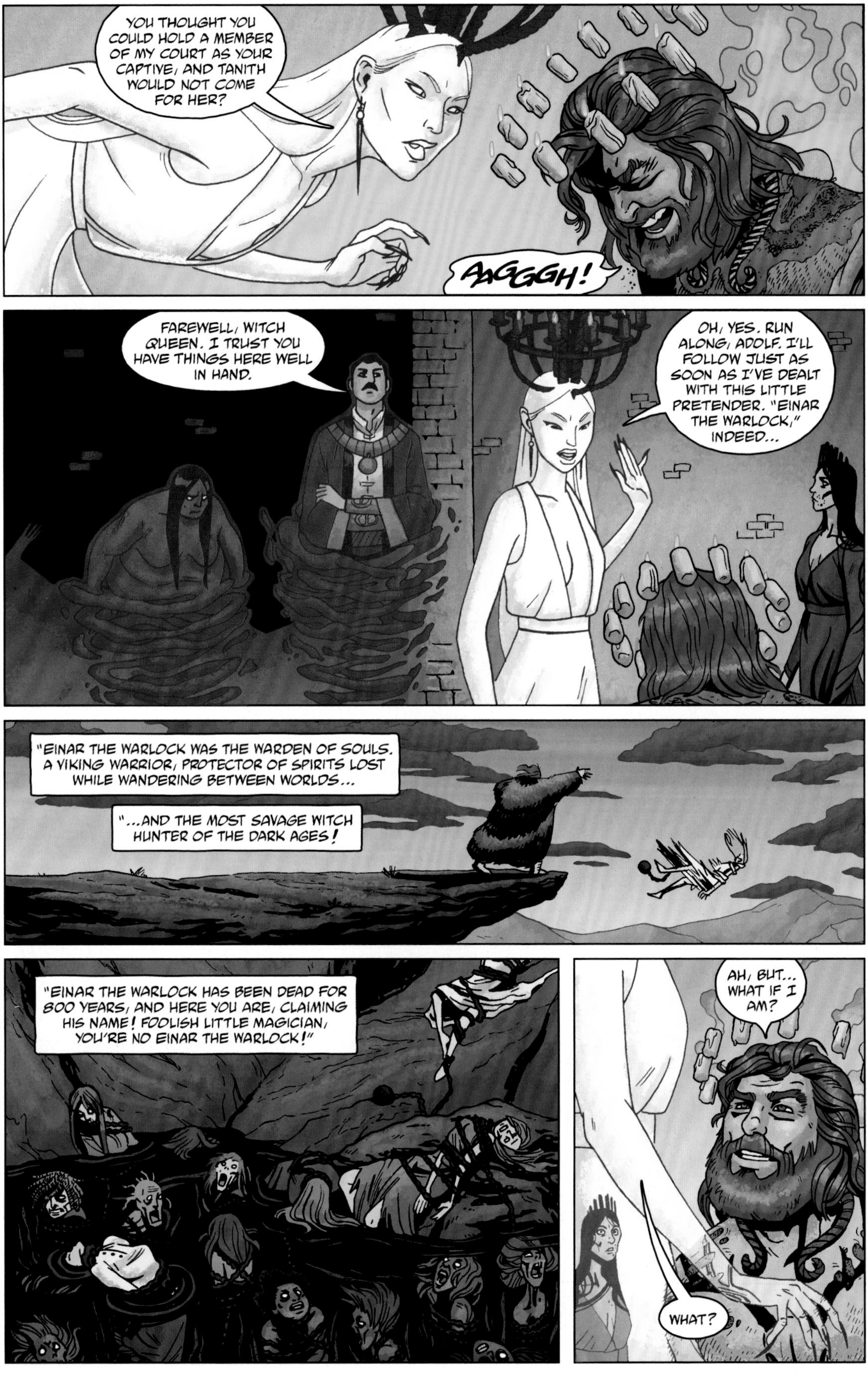
YOU THOUGHT YOU COULD HOLD A MEMBER OF MY COURT AS YOUR CAPTIVE, AND TANITH WOULD NOT COME FOR HER?
AAGGGH!
FAREWELL, WITCH QUEEN. I TRUST YOU HAVE THINGS HERE WELL IN HAND.
OH, YES. RUN ALONG, ADOLF. I'LL FOLLOW JUST AS SOON AS I'VE DEALT WITH THIS LITTLE PRETENDER. "EINAR THE WARLOCK," INDEED...
"EINAR THE WARLOCK WAS THE WARDEN OF SOULS. A VIKING WARRIOR, PROTECTOR OF SPIRITS LOST WHILE WANDERING BETWEEN WORLDS...
"...AND THE MOST SAVAGE WITCH HUNTER OF THE DARK AGES!
"EINAR THE WARLOCK HAS BEEN DEAD FOR 800 YEARS, AND HERE YOU ARE, CLAIMING HIS NAME! FOOLISH LITTLE MAGICIAN, YOU'RE NO EINAR THE WARLOCK!"
AH, BUT... WHAT IF I AM?
WHAT?

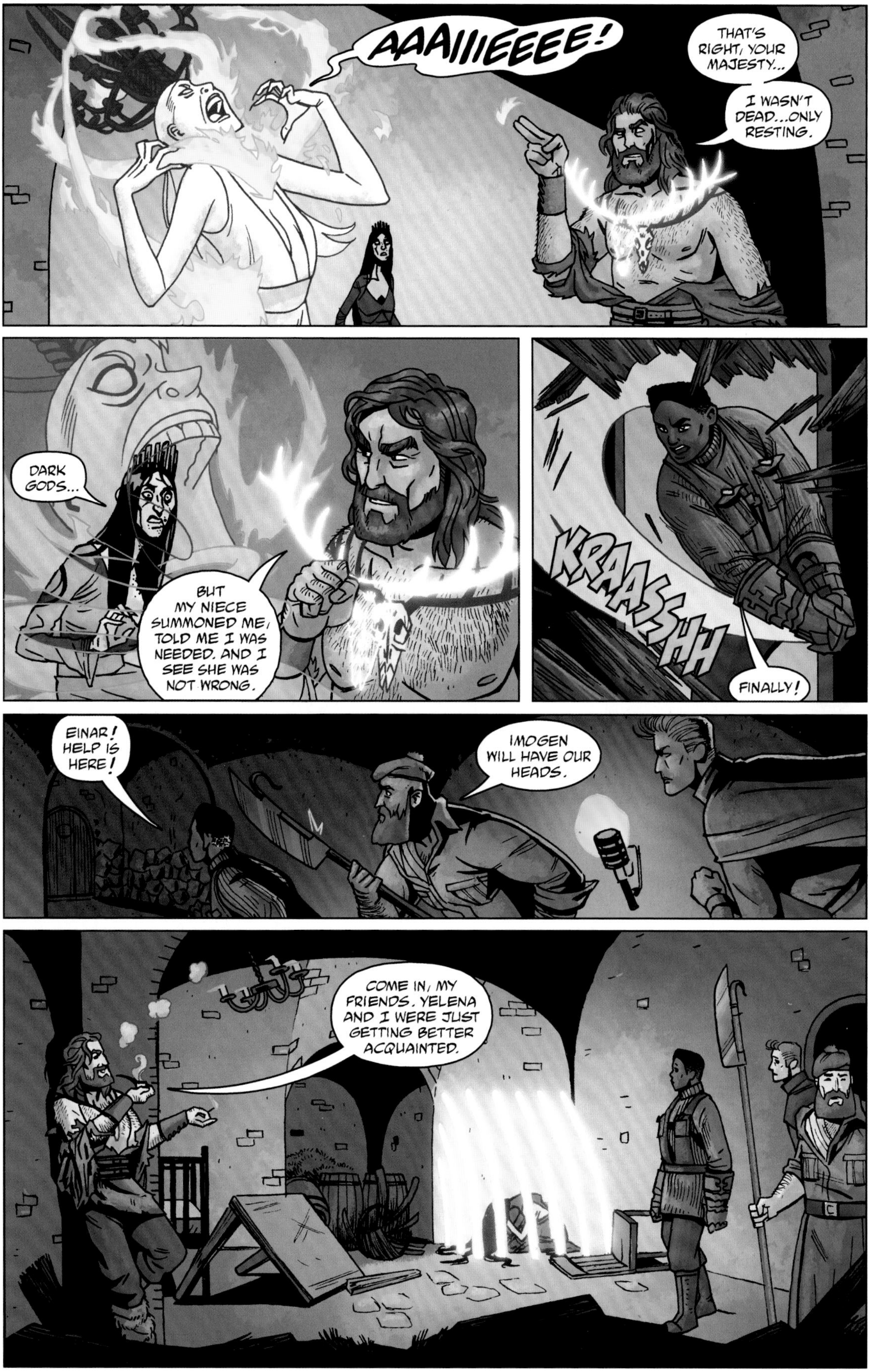
AAAIIIEEEE!
THAT'S RIGHT, YOUR MAJESTY...
I WASN'T DEAD...ONLY RESTING.
DARK GODS...
BUT MY NIECE SUMMONED ME, TOLD ME I WAS NEEDED. AND I SEE SHE WAS NOT WRONG.
KRAASSHH
FINALLY!
EINAR! HELP IS HERE!
IMOGEN WILL HAVE OUR HEADS.
COME IN, MY FRIENDS. YELENA AND I WERE JUST GETTING BETTER ACQUAINTED.

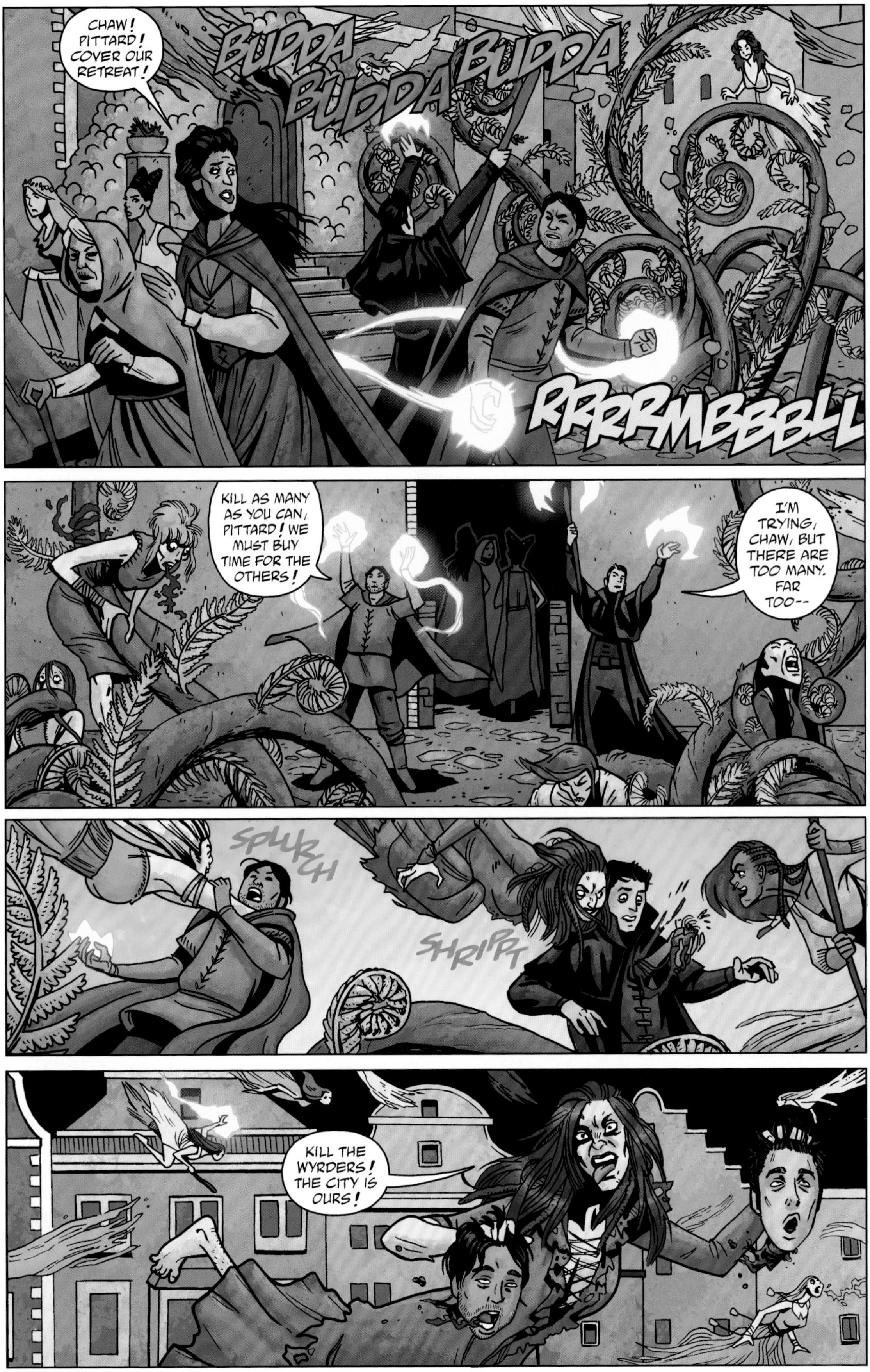
CHAW! PITTARD! COVER OUR RETREAT!
BUDDA BUDDA BUDDA
RRRRMBBBLL
KILL AS MANY AS YOU CAN, PITTARD! WE MUST BUY TIME FOR THE OTHERS!
I'M TRYING, CHAW, BUT THERE ARE TOO MANY. FAR TOO--
SPLURCH
SHRIPPT
KILL THE WYRDERS! THE CITY IS OURS!

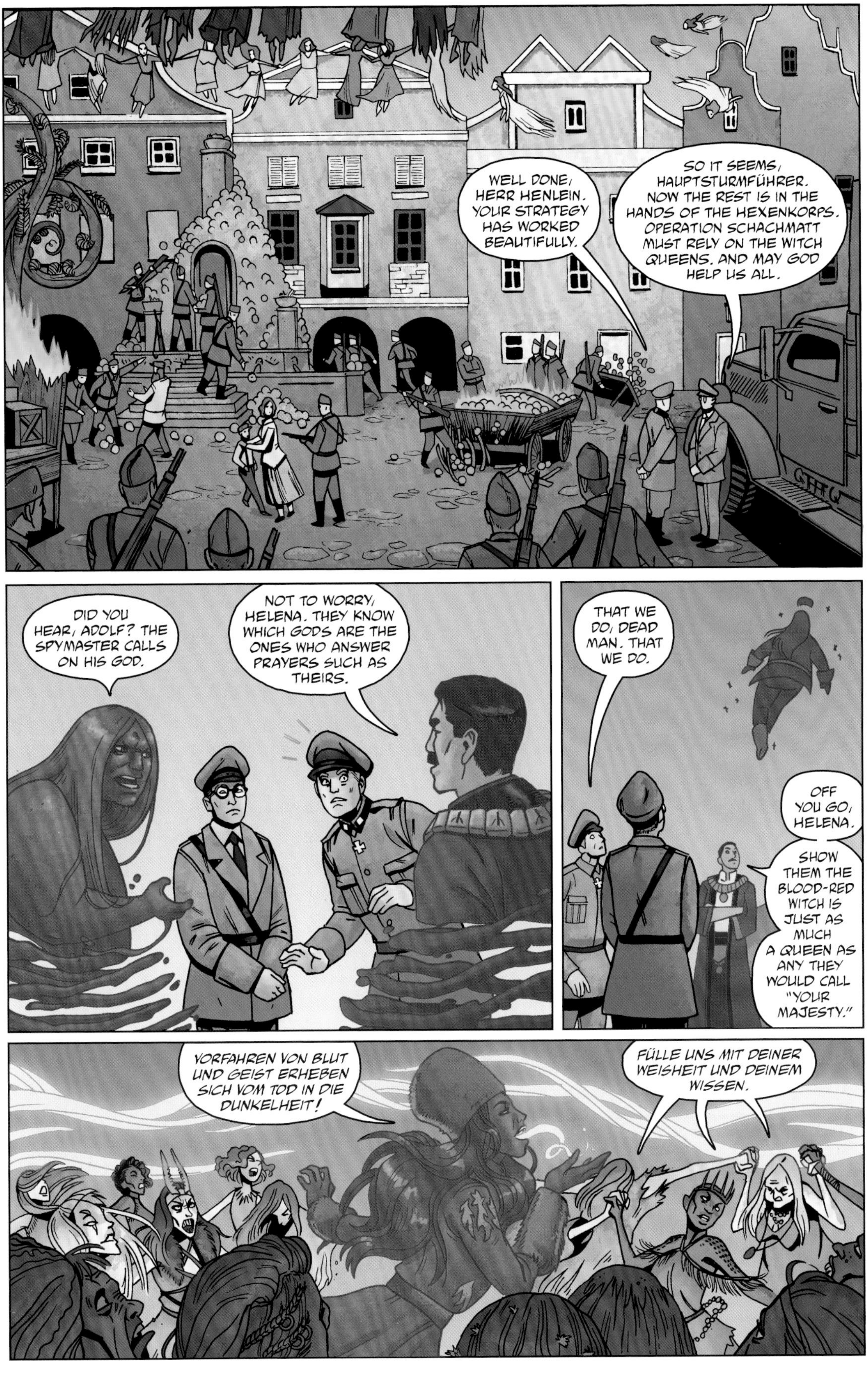
WELL DONE, HERR HENLEIN. YOUR STRATEGY HAS WORKED BEAUTIFULLY.
SO IT SEEMS, HAUPTSTURMFÜHRER. NOW THE REST IS IN THE HANDS OF THE HEXENKORPS. OPERATION SCHACHMATT MUST RELY ON THE WITCH QUEENS. AND MAY GOD HELP US ALL.
DID YOU HEAR, ADOLF? THE SPYMASTER CALLS ON HIS GOD.
NOT TO WORRY, HELENA. THEY KNOW WHICH GODS ARE THE ONES WHO ANSWER PRAYERS SUCH AS THEIRS.
THAT WE DO, DEAD MAN. THAT WE DO.
OFF YOU GO, HELENA.
SHOW THEM THE BLOOD-RED WITCH IS JUST AS MUCH A QUEEN AS ANY THEY WOULD CALL "YOUR MAJESTY."
VORFAHREN VON BLUT UND GEIST ERHEBEN SICH VOM TOD IN DIE DUNKELHEIT!
FÜLLE UNS MIT DEINER WEISHEIT UND DEINEM WISSEN.

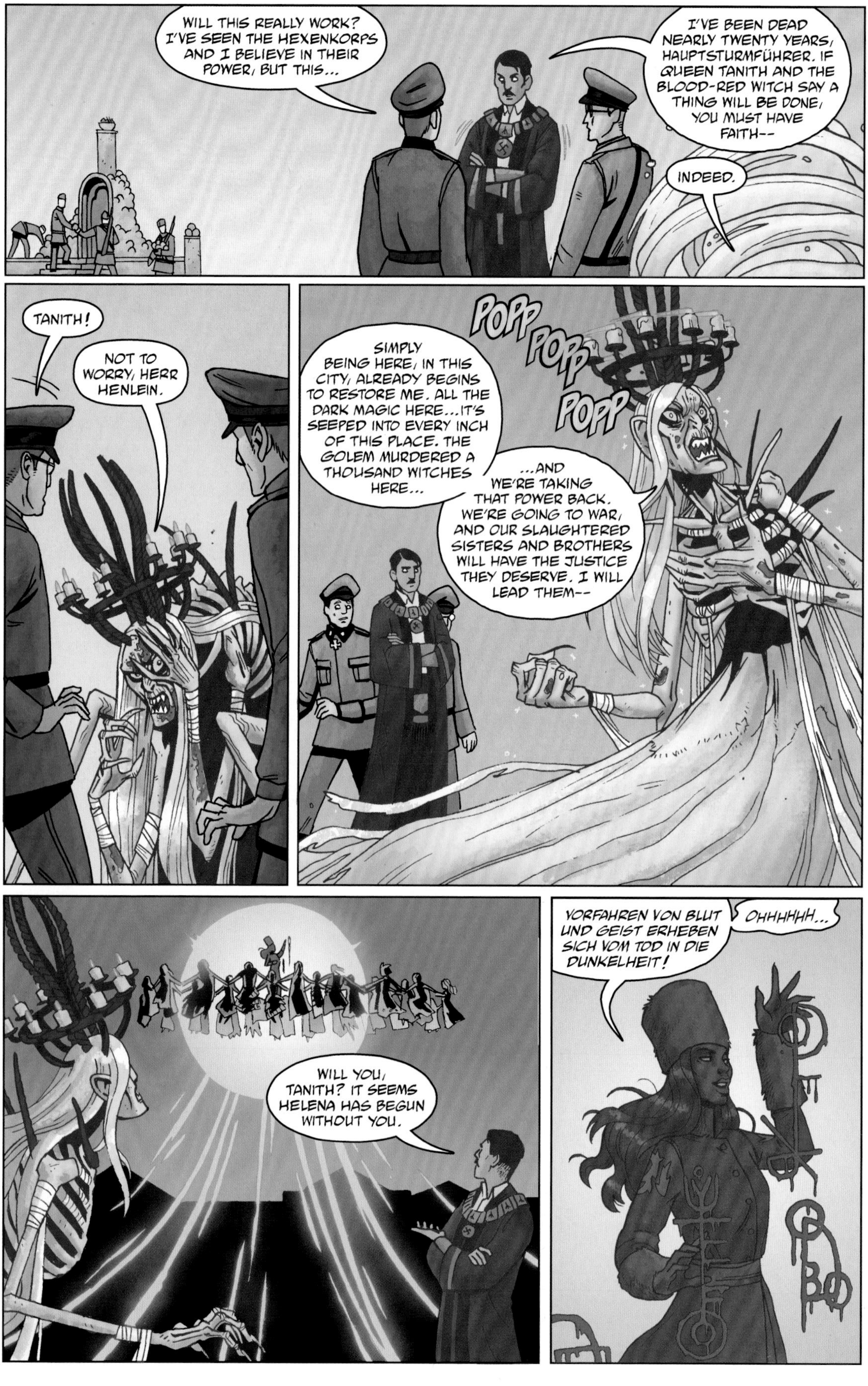
WILL THIS REALLY WORK? I'VE SEEN THE HEXENKORPS AND I BELIEVE IN THEIR POWER, BUT THIS...
I'VE BEEN DEAD NEARLY TWENTY YEARS, HAUPTSTURMFÜHRER. IF QUEEN TANITH AND THE BLOOD-RED WITCH SAY A THING WILL BE DONE, YOU MUST HAVE FAITH--
INDEED.
TANITH!
NOT TO WORRY, HERR HENLEIN.
POPP POPP POPP
SIMPLY BEING HERE, IN THIS CITY, ALREADY BEGINS TO RESTORE ME. ALL THE DARK MAGIC HERE...IT'S SEEPED INTO EVERY INCH OF THIS PLACE. THE GOLEM MURDERED A THOUSAND WITCHES HERE...
...AND WE'RE TAKING THAT POWER BACK. WE'RE GOING TO WAR, AND OUR SLAUGHTERED SISTERS AND BROTHERS WILL HAVE THE JUSTICE THEY DESERVE. I WILL LEAD THEM--
WILL YOU, TANITH? IT SEEMS HELENA HAS BEGUN WITHOUT YOU.
VORFAHREN VON BLUT UND GEIST ERHEBEN SICH VOM TOD IN DIE DUNKELHEIT!
OHHHHHH...

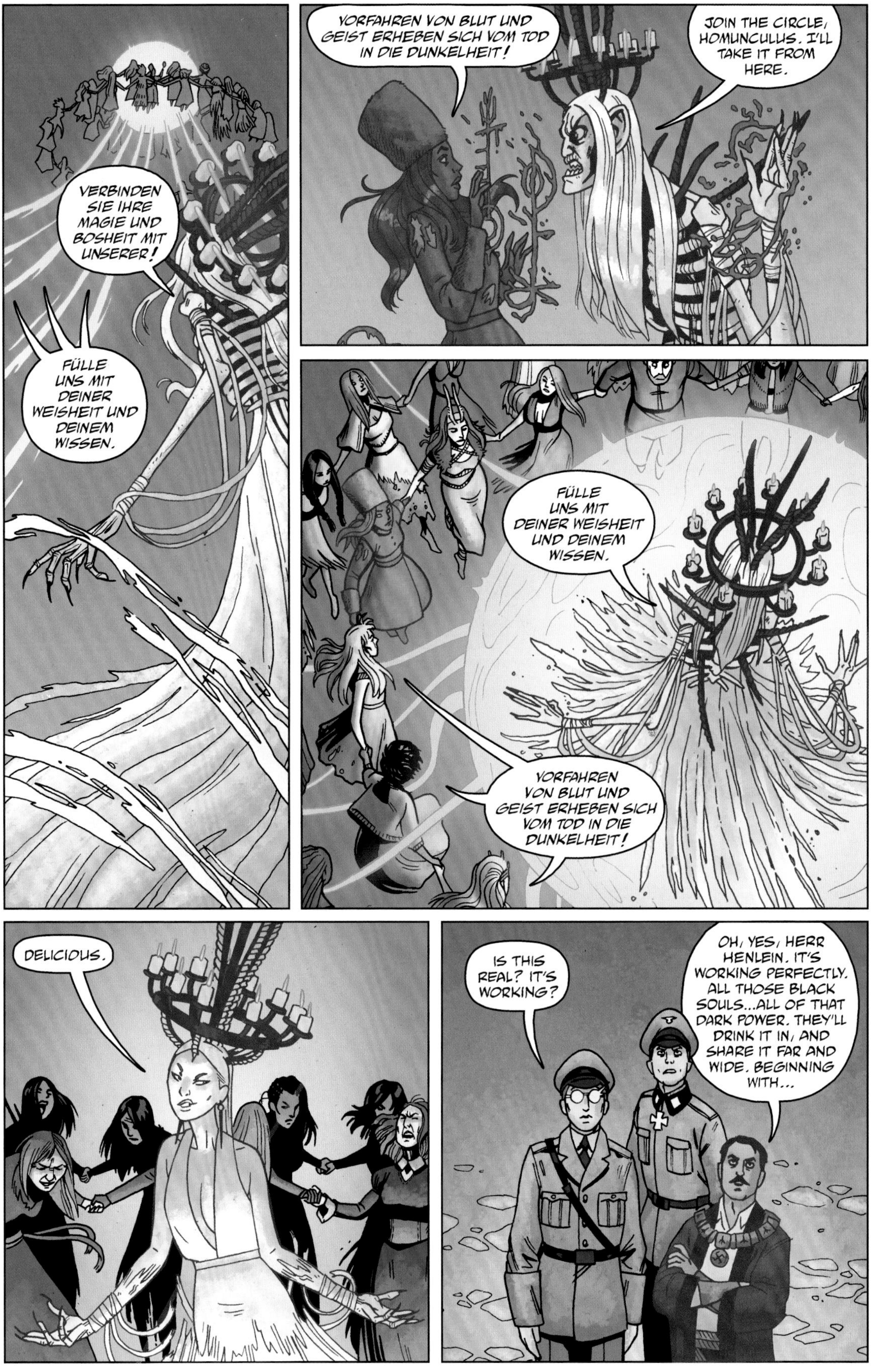
VERBINDEN SIE IHRE MAGIE UND BOSHEIT MIT UNSERER!
FÜLLE UNS MIT DEINER WEISHEIT UND DEINEM WISSEN.
VORFAHREN VON BLUT UND GEIST ERHEBEN SICH VOM TOD IN DIE DUNKELHEIT!
JOIN THE CIRCLE, HOMUNCULUS. I'LL TAKE IT FROM HERE.
FÜLLE UNS MIT DEINER WEISHEIT UND DEINEM WISSEN.
VORFAHREN VON BLUT UND GEIST ERHEBEN SICH VOM TOD IN DIE DUNKELHEIT!
DELICIOUS.
IS THIS REAL? IT'S WORKING?
OH, YES, HERR HENLEIN. IT'S WORKING PERFECTLY. ALL THOSE BLACK SOULS...ALL OF THAT DARK POWER. THEY'LL DRINK IT IN, AND SHARE IT FAR AND WIDE. BEGINNING WITH...

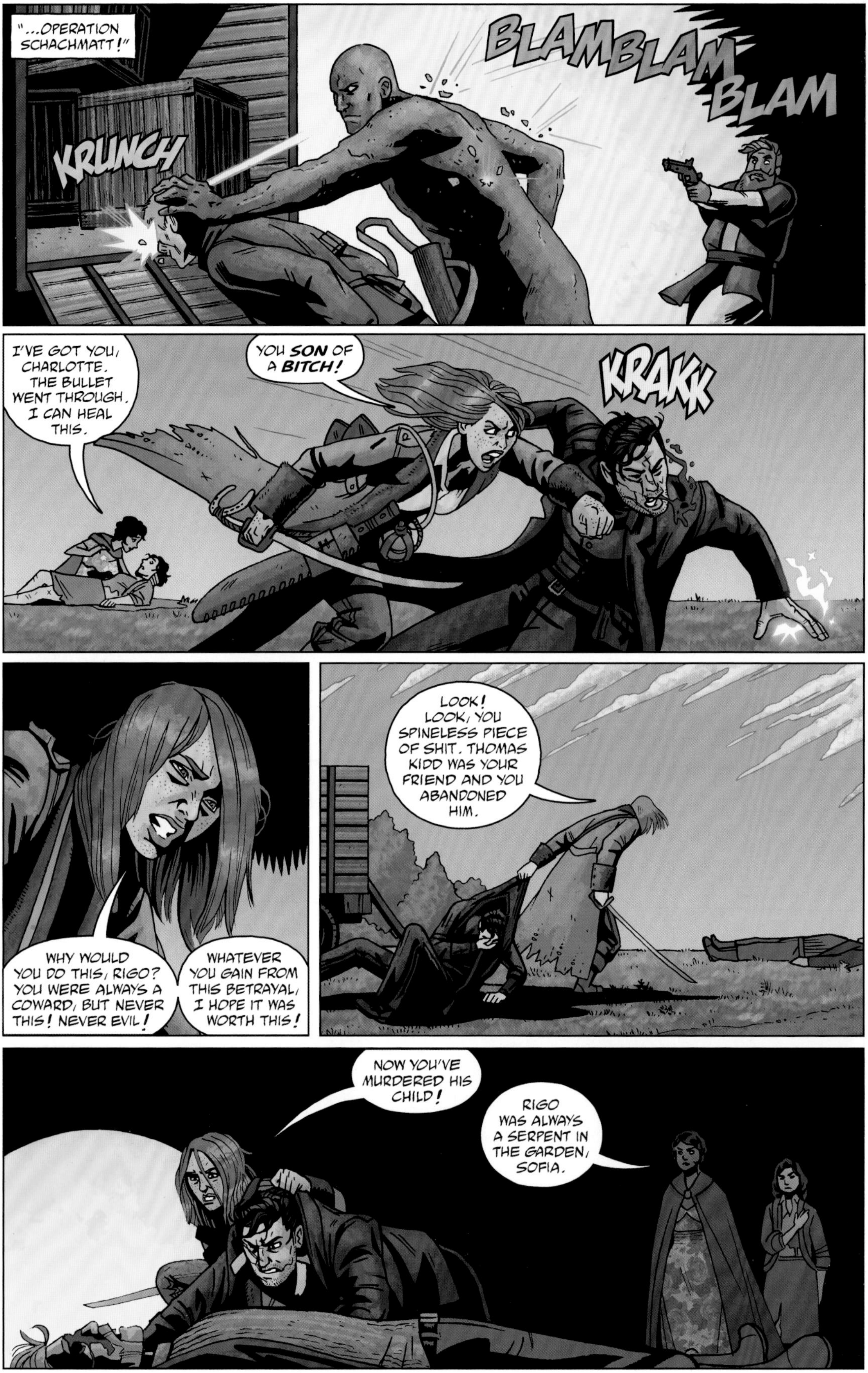
"...OPERATION SCHACHMATT!"
BLAMBLAMBLAM
KRUNCH
BLAM
I'VE GOT YOU, CHARLOTTE. THE BULLET WENT THROUGH. I CAN HEAL THIS.
YOU SON OF A BITCH!
KRAKK
WHY WOULD YOU DO THIS, RIGO? YOU WERE ALWAYS A COWARD, BUT NEVER THIS! NEVER EVIL!
WHATEVER YOU GAIN FROM THIS BETRAYAL, I HOPE IT WAS WORTH THIS!
LOOK! LOOK, YOU SPINELESS PIECE OF SHIT. THOMAS KIDD WAS YOUR FRIEND AND YOU ABANDONED HIM.
NOW YOU'VE MURDERED HIS CHILD!
RIGO WAS ALWAYS A SERPENT IN THE GARDEN, SOFIA.

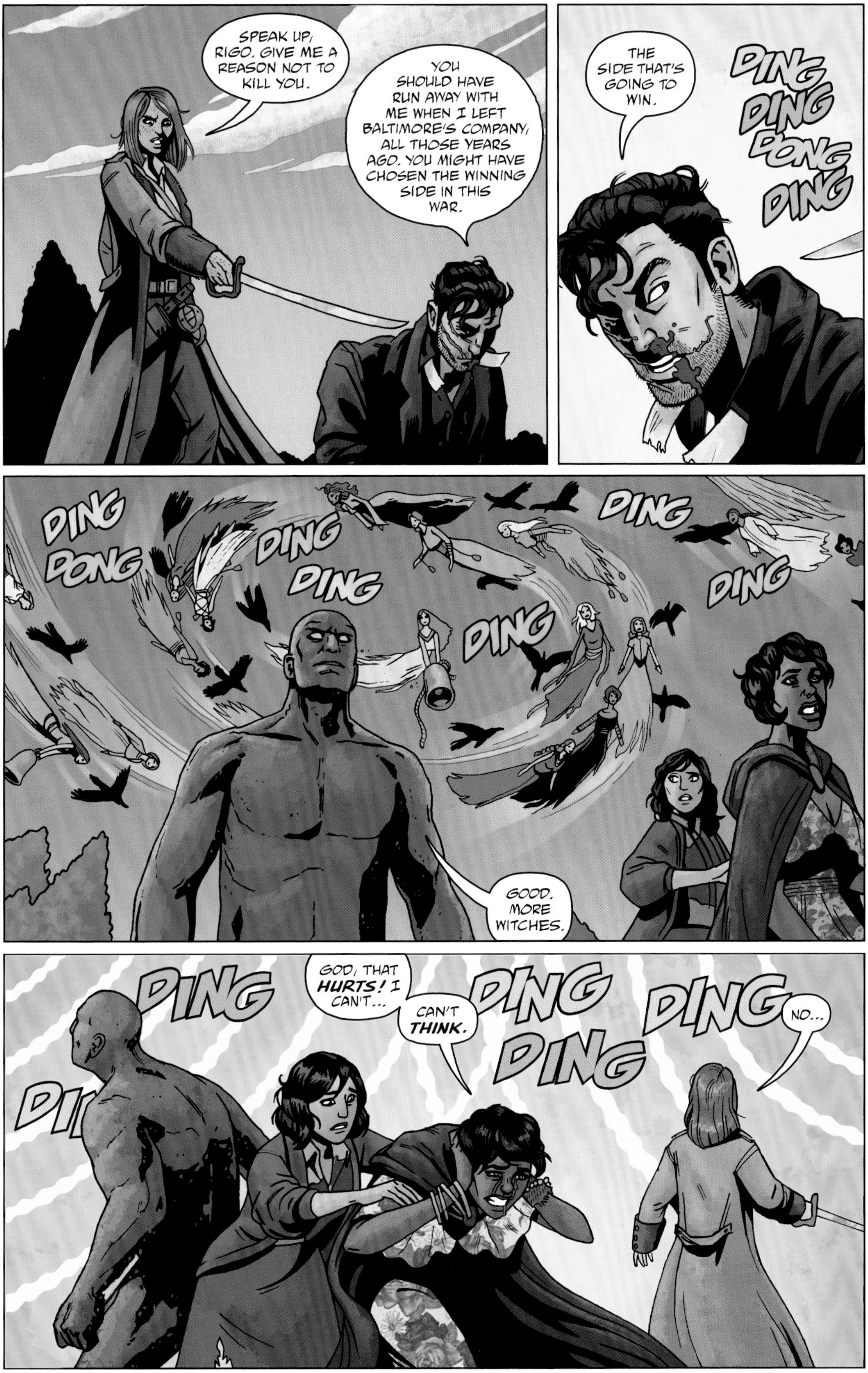
SPEAK UP, RIGO. GIVE ME A REASON NOT TO KILL YOU.
YOU SHOULD HAVE RUN AWAY WITH ME WHEN I LEFT BALTIMORE'S COMPANY, ALL THOSE YEARS AGO. YOU MIGHT HAVE CHOSEN THE WINNING SIDE IN THIS WAR.
THE SIDE THAT'S GOING TO WIN.
DING DING DONG DING
DING DONG
DING DING
DING
DING
DING
GOOD. MORE WITCHES.
DING
GOD, THAT **HURTS!** I CAN'T...
CAN'T **THINK.**
DING DING
DING
NO...

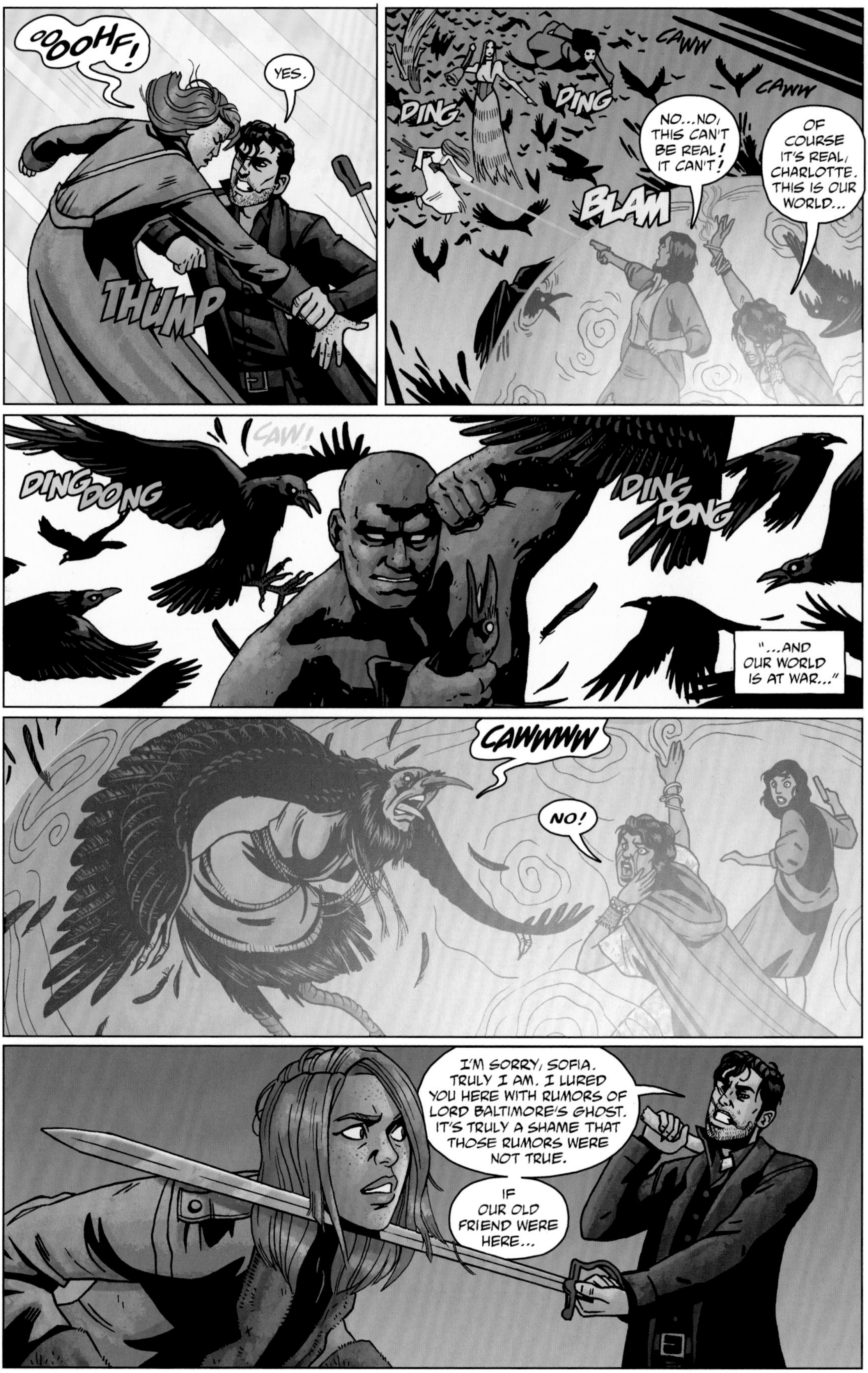
OOOOHF!
YES.
THUMP
CAWW
CAWW
DING
DING
NO...NO, THIS CAN'T BE REAL! IT CAN'T!
OF COURSE IT'S REAL, CHARLOTTE. THIS IS OUR WORLD...
BLAM
CAW!
DING DONG
DING DONG
"...AND OUR WORLD IS AT WAR..."
CAWWWW
NO!
I'M SORRY, SOFIA. TRULY I AM. I LURED YOU HERE WITH RUMORS OF LORD BALTIMORE'S GHOST. IT'S TRULY A SHAME THAT THOSE RUMORS WERE NOT TRUE.
IF OUR OLD FRIEND WERE HERE...

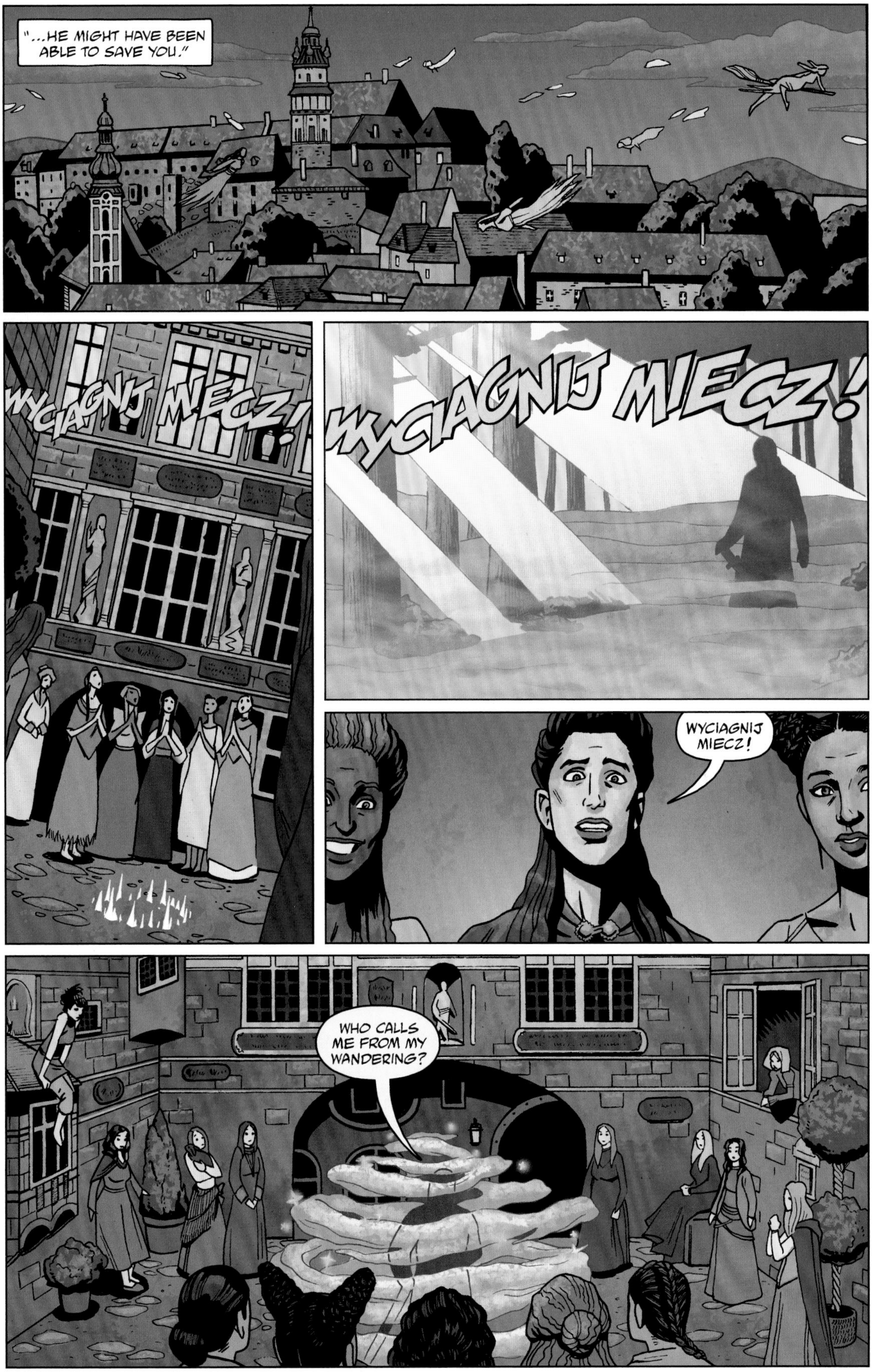
"...HE MIGHT HAVE BEEN ABLE TO SAVE YOU."
WYCIAGNIJ MIECZ!
WYCIAGNIJ MIECZ!
WYCIAGNIJ MIECZ!
WHO CALLS ME FROM MY WANDERING?

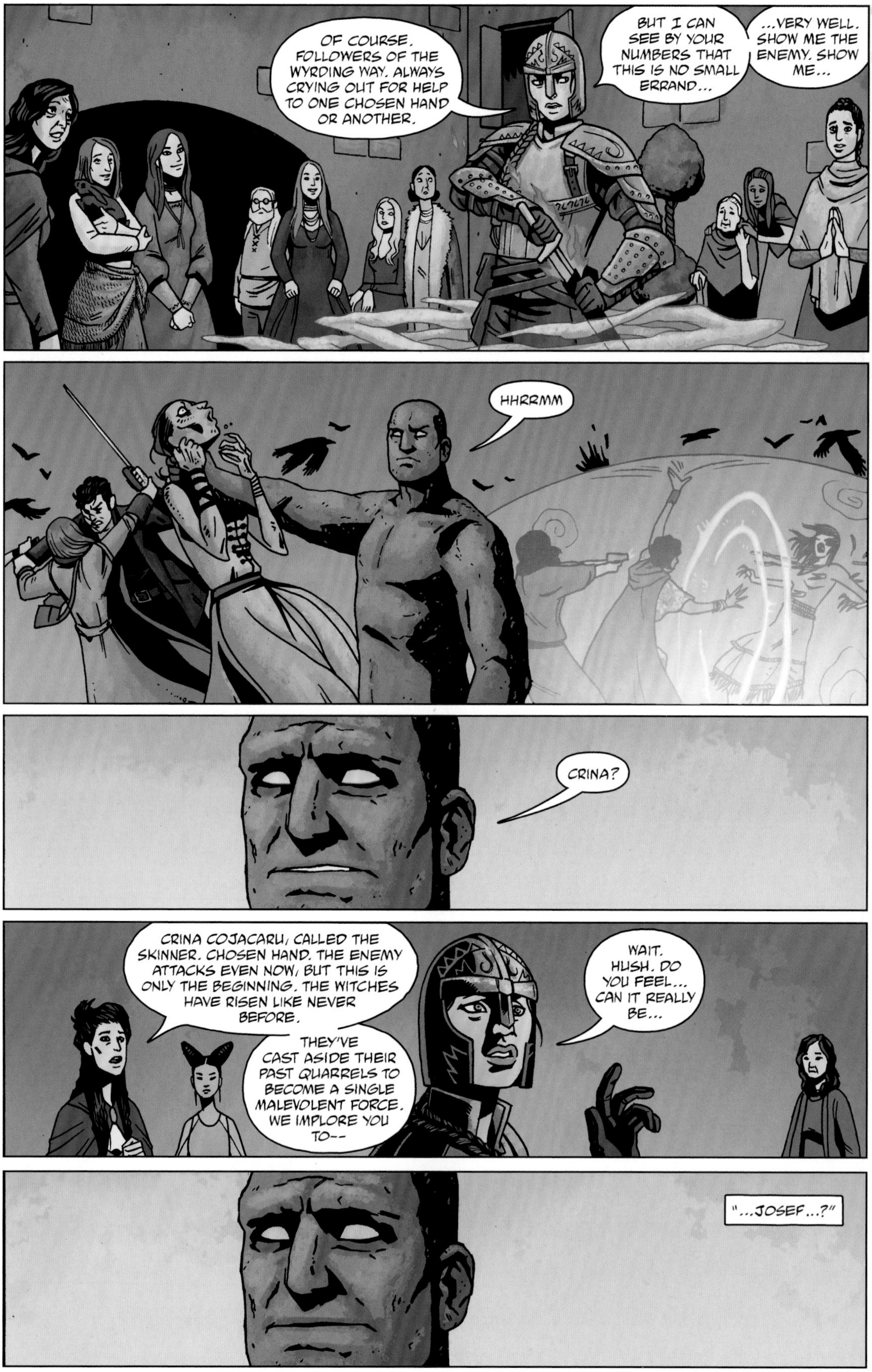
OF COURSE. FOLLOWERS OF THE WYRDING WAY. ALWAYS CRYING OUT FOR HELP TO ONE CHOSEN HAND OR ANOTHER.
BUT I CAN SEE BY YOUR NUMBERS THAT THIS IS NO SMALL ERRAND...
...VERY WELL. SHOW ME THE ENEMY. SHOW ME...
HHRRMM
CRINA?
CRINA COJACARU, CALLED THE SKINNER. CHOSEN HAND. THE ENEMY ATTACKS EVEN NOW, BUT THIS IS ONLY THE BEGINNING. THE WITCHES HAVE RISEN LIKE NEVER BEFORE.
THEY'VE CAST ASIDE THEIR PAST QUARRELS TO BECOME A SINGLE MALEVOLENT FORCE. WE IMPLORE YOU TO--
WAIT. HUSH. DO YOU FEEL... CAN IT REALLY BE...
"...JOSEF...?"

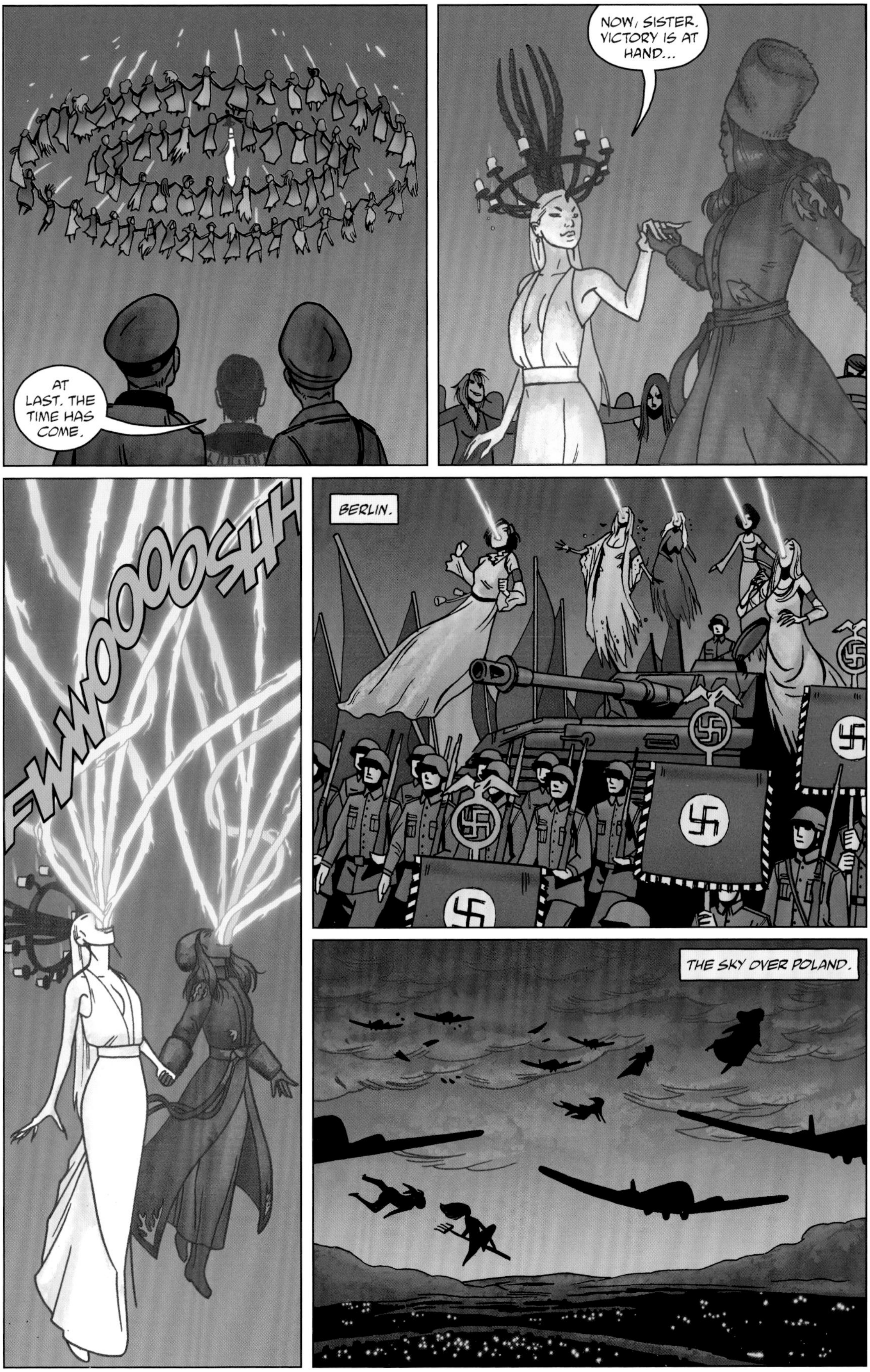
AT LAST. THE TIME HAS COME.
NOW, SISTER. VICTORY IS AT HAND...
FWOOOOSHH
BERLIN.
THE SKY OVER POLAND.

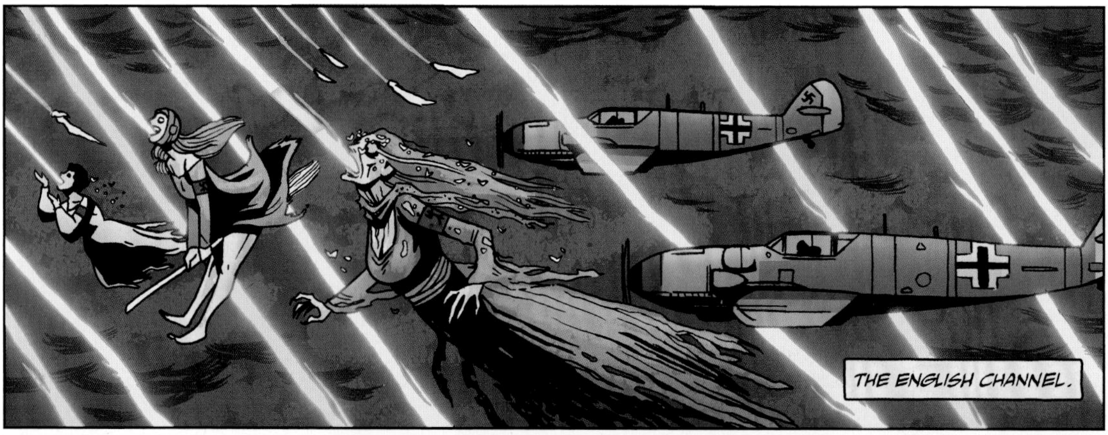
THE ENGLISH CHANNEL.

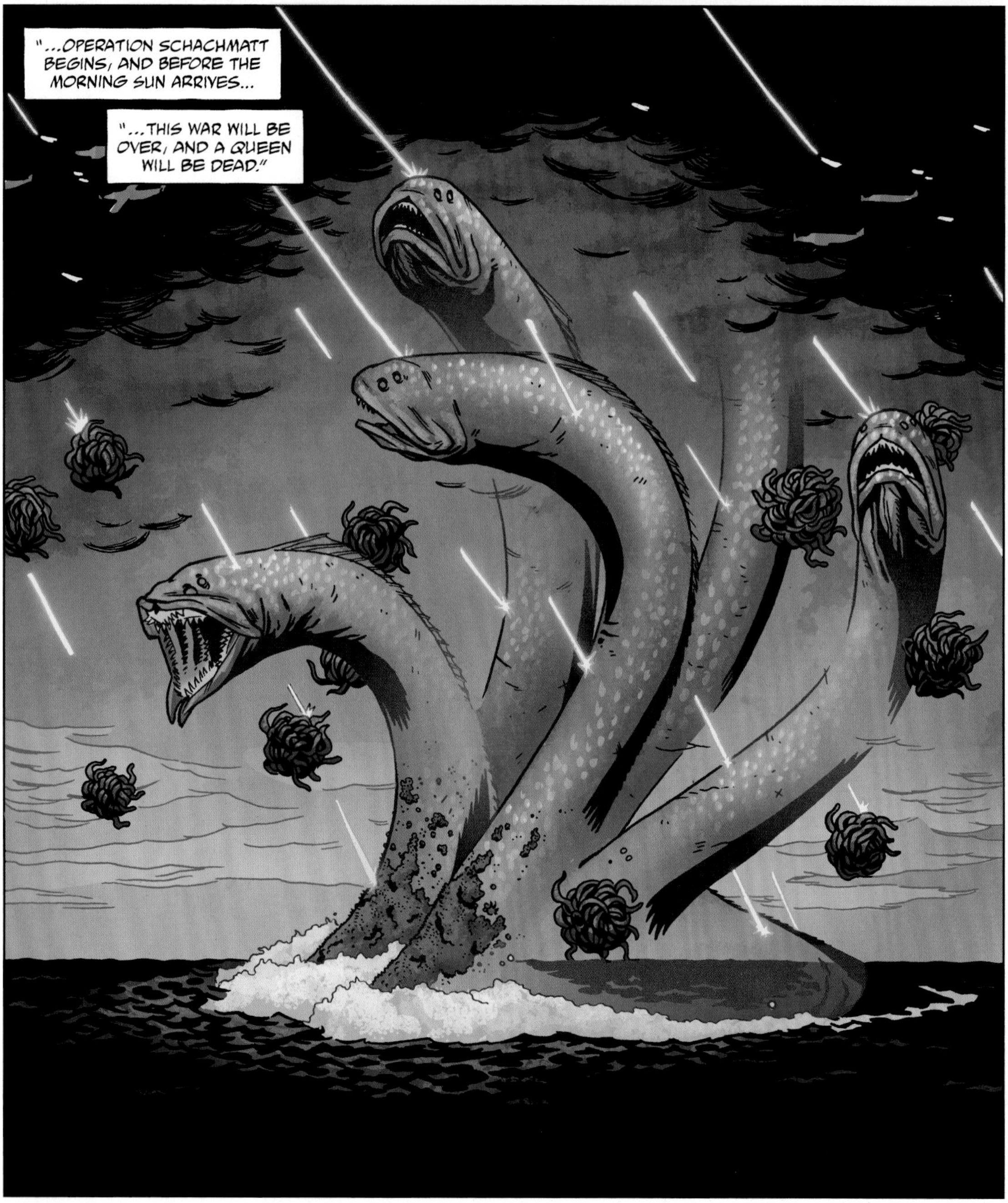
"...OPERATION SCHACHMATT BEGINS, AND BEFORE THE MORNING SUN ARRIVES...
"...THIS WAR WILL BE OVER, AND A QUEEN WILL BE DEAD."

CHAPTER FIVE

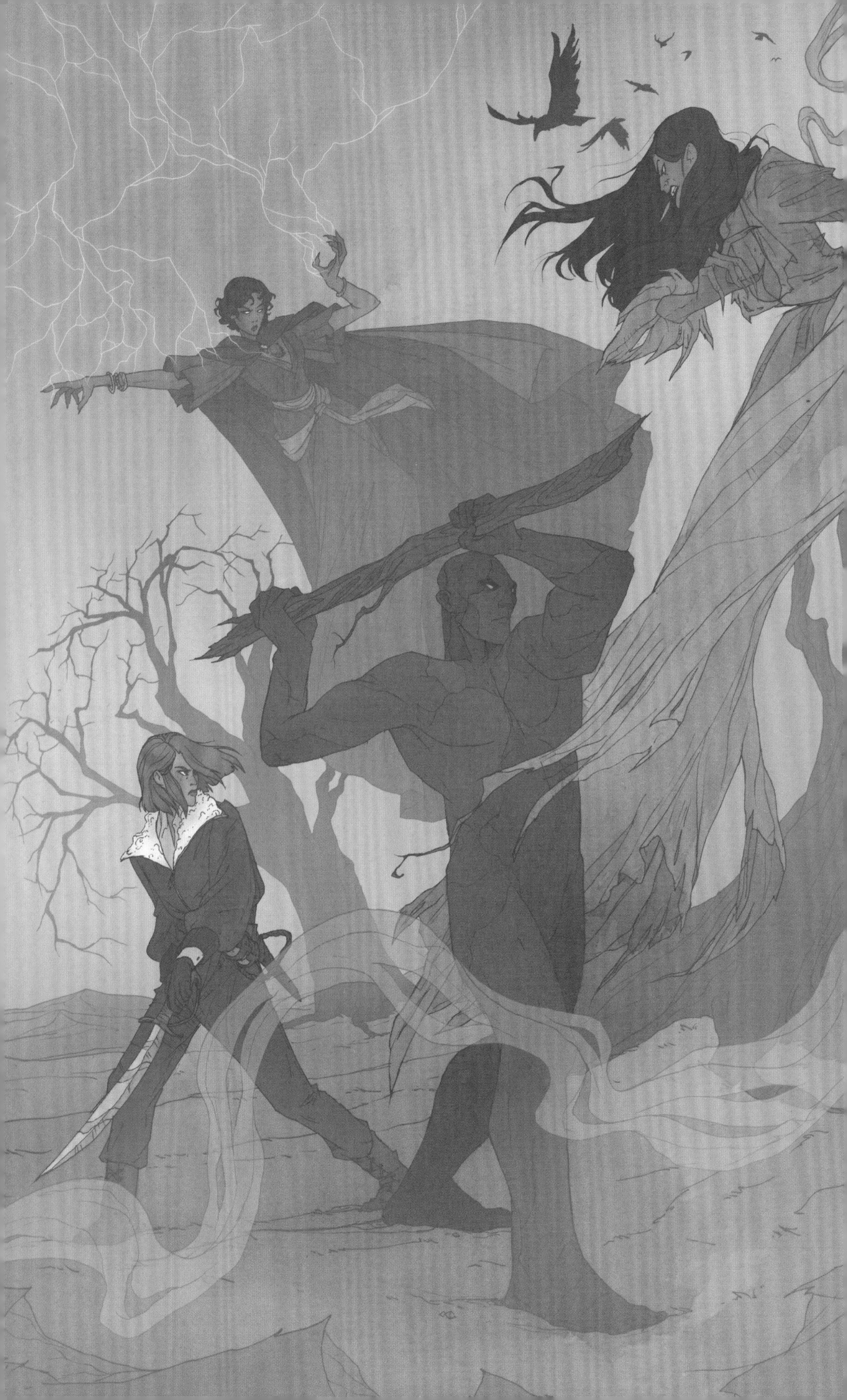

"OH, SOFIA... *LADY* BALTIMORE..."

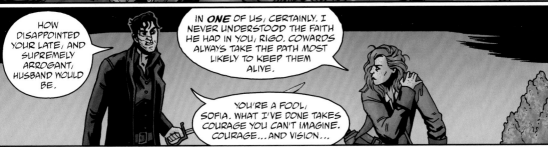

HOW DISAPPOINTED YOUR LATE, AND SUPREMELY ARROGANT, HUSBAND WOULD BE.

IN *ONE* OF US, CERTAINLY. I NEVER UNDERSTOOD THE FAITH HE HAD IN YOU, RIGO. COWARDS ALWAYS TAKE THE PATH MOST LIKELY TO KEEP THEM ALIVE.

YOU'RE A FOOL, SOFIA. WHAT I'VE DONE TAKES COURAGE YOU CAN'T IMAGINE. COURAGE...AND VISION...

"THE RED KING MIGHT HAVE DESTROYED HUMANITY. I'M GRATEFUL BALTIMORE DESTROYED HIM. BUT THE NAZIS AND THE HEXENKORPS MERELY WANT TO CONQUER--"

"YES, AND 'PURIFY,' RIGO--DON'T FORGET THAT. THEY WANT TO ERADICATE THOSE WHO ARE DIFFERENT, OR WHO DISAGREE. THEY'RE MONSTROUS!"

YES, THEY ARE! AND YOU'VE FAILED TO LEARN THE LESSON.

WHEN THE MONSTERS COME FOR THOSE WHO DISAGREE, THE ONLY WAY TO SURVIVE IS TO BECOME ONE OF THEM! THE PATH TO POWER IS ALWAYS OVER THE BONES OF THOSE WHO ARE *DIFFERENT*.

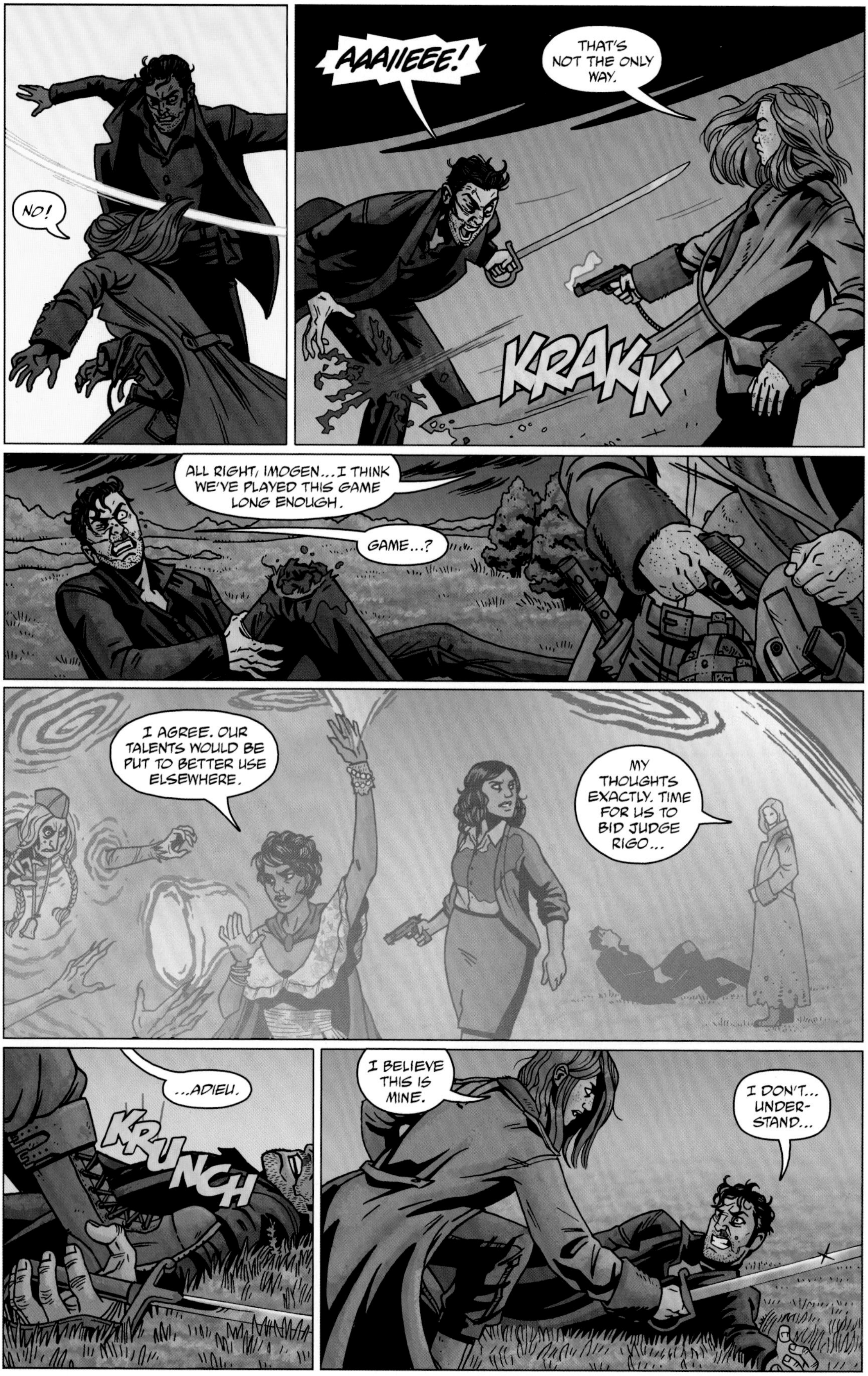
NO!
AAAIIEEE!
THAT'S NOT THE ONLY WAY.
KRAKK
ALL RIGHT, IMOGEN... I THINK WE'VE PLAYED THIS GAME LONG ENOUGH.
GAME...?
I AGREE. OUR TALENTS WOULD BE PUT TO BETTER USE ELSEWHERE.
MY THOUGHTS EXACTLY. TIME FOR US TO BID JUDGE RIGO...
...ADIEU.
KRUNCH
I BELIEVE THIS IS MINE.
I DON'T... UNDER-STAND...

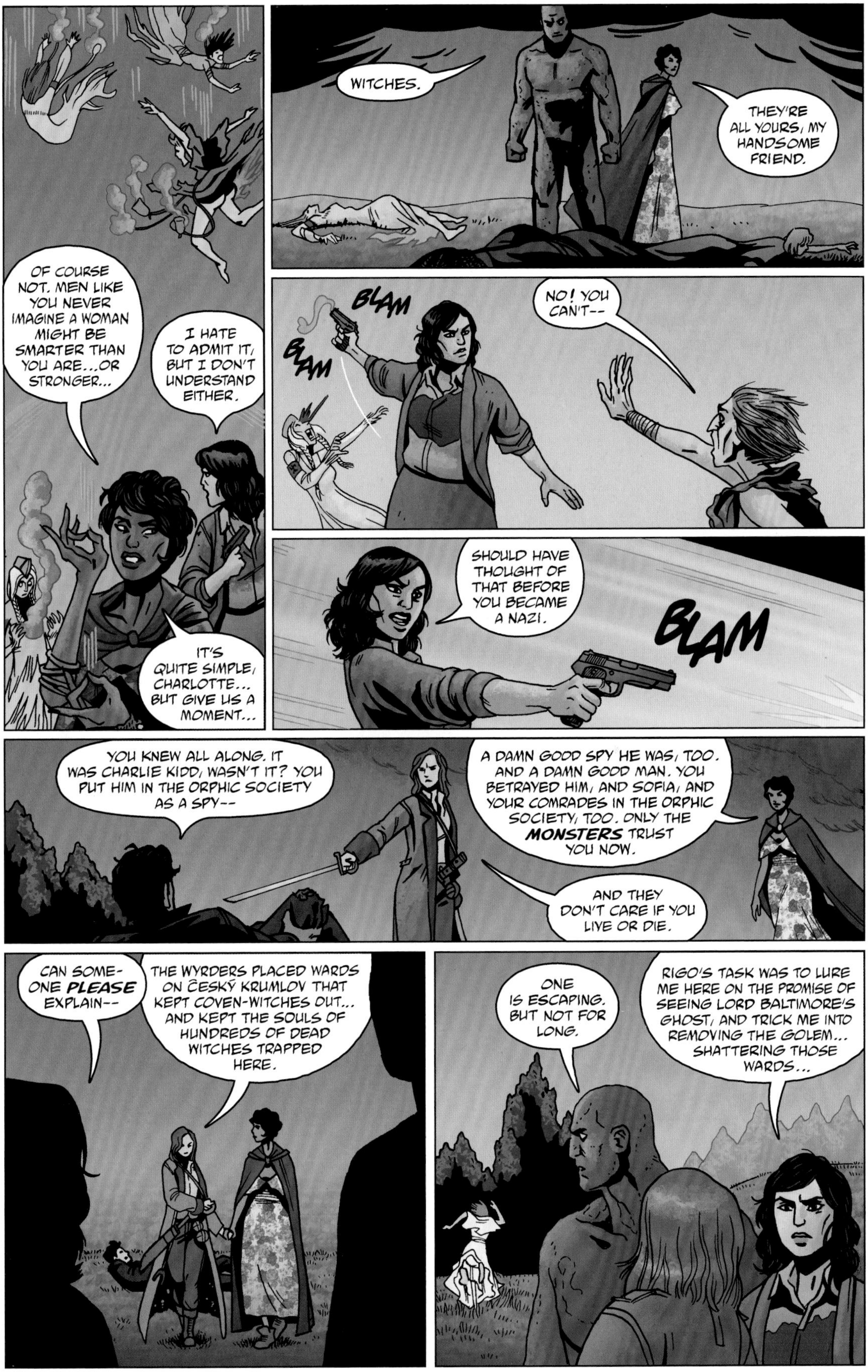
WITCHES.
THEY'RE ALL YOURS, MY HANDSOME FRIEND.
OF COURSE NOT. MEN LIKE YOU NEVER IMAGINE A WOMAN MIGHT BE SMARTER THAN YOU ARE...OR STRONGER...
I HATE TO ADMIT IT, BUT I DON'T UNDERSTAND EITHER.
IT'S QUITE SIMPLE, CHARLOTTE... BUT GIVE US A MOMENT...
BLAM
BLAM
NO! YOU CAN'T--
SHOULD HAVE THOUGHT OF THAT BEFORE YOU BECAME A NAZI.
BLAM
YOU KNEW ALL ALONG. IT WAS CHARLIE KIDD, WASN'T IT? YOU PUT HIM IN THE ORPHIC SOCIETY AS A SPY--
A DAMN GOOD SPY HE WAS, TOO. AND A DAMN GOOD MAN. YOU BETRAYED HIM, AND SOFIA, AND YOUR COMRADES IN THE ORPHIC SOCIETY, TOO. ONLY THE MONSTERS TRUST YOU NOW.
AND THEY DON'T CARE IF YOU LIVE OR DIE.
CAN SOMEONE PLEASE EXPLAIN--
THE WYRDERS PLACED WARDS ON ČESKÝ KRUMLOV THAT KEPT COVEN-WITCHES OUT... AND KEPT THE SOULS OF HUNDREDS OF DEAD WITCHES TRAPPED HERE.
ONE IS ESCAPING. BUT NOT FOR LONG.
RIGO'S TASK WAS TO LURE ME HERE ON THE PROMISE OF SEEING LORD BALTIMORE'S GHOST, AND TRICK ME INTO REMOVING THE GOLEM... SHATTERING THOSE WARDS...

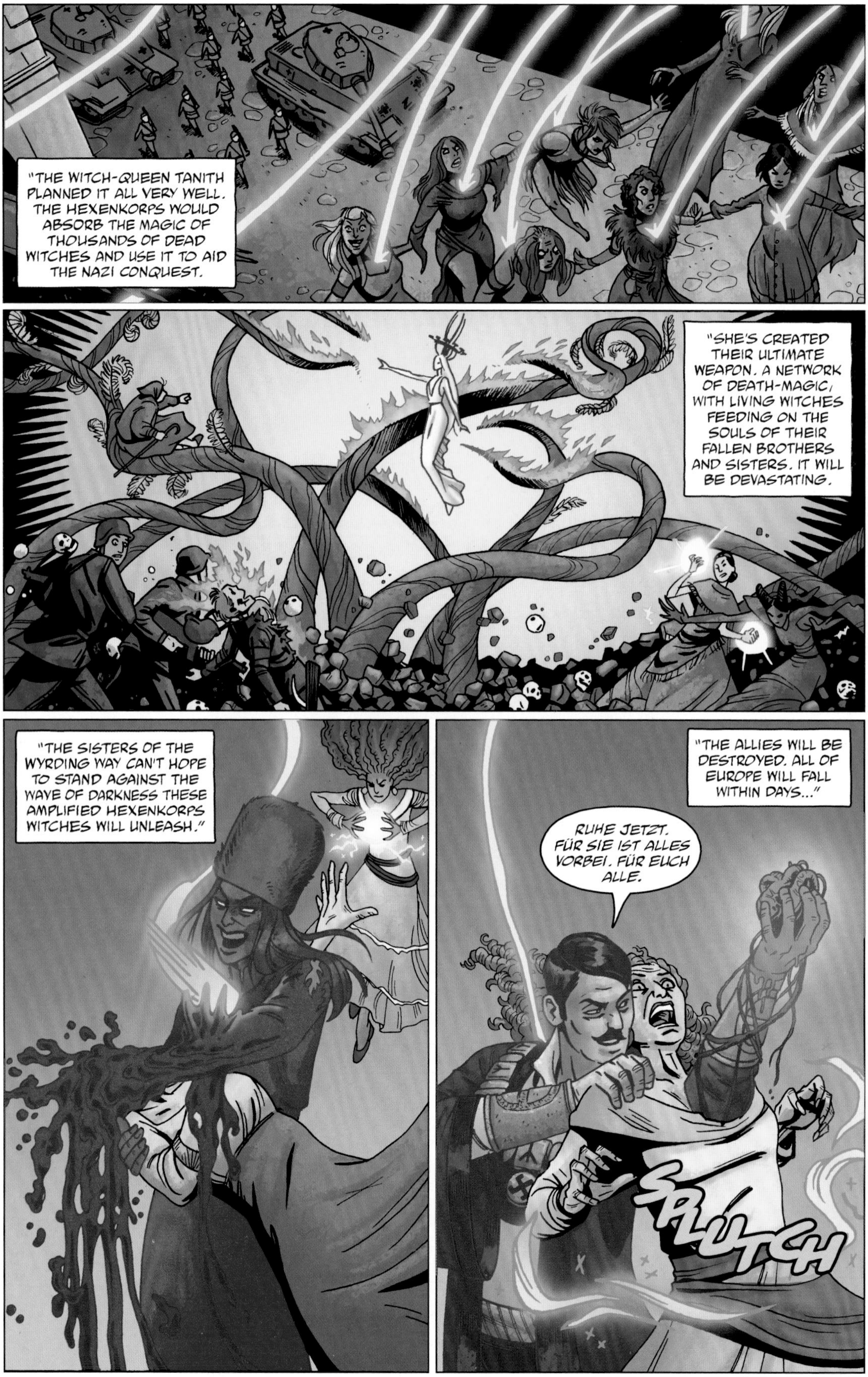
"THE WITCH-QUEEN TANITH PLANNED IT ALL VERY WELL. THE HEXENKORPS WOULD ABSORB THE MAGIC OF THOUSANDS OF DEAD WITCHES AND USE IT TO AID THE NAZI CONQUEST.
"SHE'S CREATED THEIR ULTIMATE WEAPON. A NETWORK OF DEATH-MAGIC, WITH LIVING WITCHES FEEDING ON THE SOULS OF THEIR FALLEN BROTHERS AND SISTERS. IT WILL BE DEVASTATING.
"THE SISTERS OF THE WYRDING WAY CAN'T HOPE TO STAND AGAINST THE WAVE OF DARKNESS THESE AMPLIFIED HEXENKORPS WITCHES WILL UNLEASH."
"THE ALLIES WILL BE DESTROYED. ALL OF EUROPE WILL FALL WITHIN DAYS..."
RUHE JETZT. FÜR SIE IST ALLES VORBEI. FÜR EUCH ALLE.
SPLUTCH

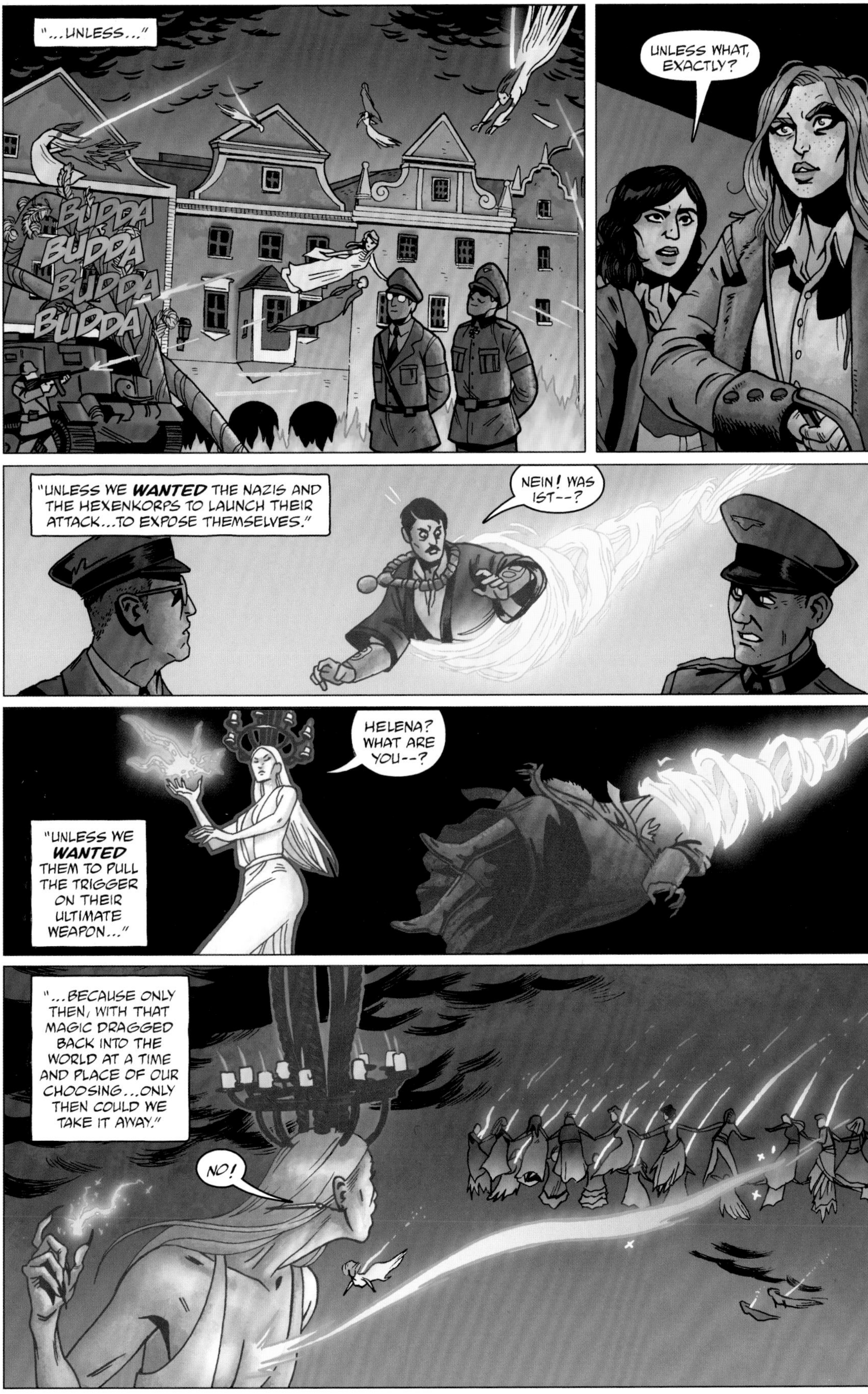
"...UNLESS..."
BUDDA BUDDA BUDDA BUDDA
UNLESS WHAT, EXACTLY?
"UNLESS WE **WANTED** THE NAZIS AND THE HEXENKORPS TO LAUNCH THEIR ATTACK...TO EXPOSE THEMSELVES."
NEIN! WAS IST--?
HELENA? WHAT ARE YOU--?
"UNLESS WE **WANTED** THEM TO PULL THE TRIGGER ON THEIR ULTIMATE WEAPON..."
"...BECAUSE ONLY THEN, WITH THAT MAGIC DRAGGED BACK INTO THE WORLD AT A TIME AND PLACE OF OUR CHOOSING...ONLY THEN COULD WE TAKE IT AWAY."
NO!

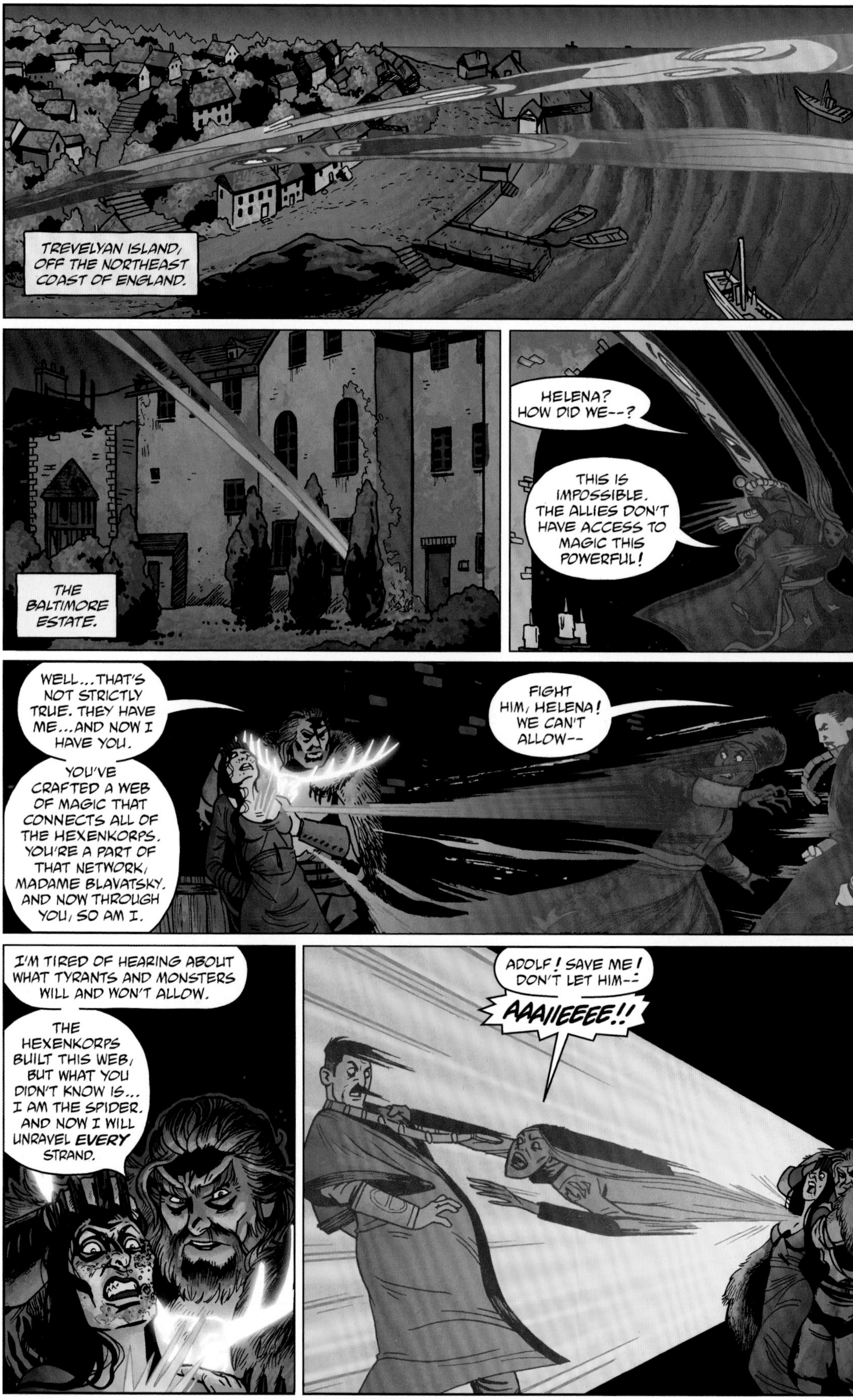
TREVELYAN ISLAND, OFF THE NORTHEAST COAST OF ENGLAND.
THE BALTIMORE ESTATE.
HELENA? HOW DID WE--?
THIS IS IMPOSSIBLE. THE ALLIES DON'T HAVE ACCESS TO MAGIC THIS POWERFUL!
WELL...THAT'S NOT STRICTLY TRUE. THEY HAVE ME...AND NOW I HAVE YOU.
YOU'VE CRAFTED A WEB OF MAGIC THAT CONNECTS ALL OF THE HEXENKORPS. YOU'RE A PART OF THAT NETWORK, MADAME BLAVATSKY. AND NOW THROUGH YOU, SO AM I.
FIGHT HIM, HELENA! WE CAN'T ALLOW--
I'M TIRED OF HEARING ABOUT WHAT TYRANTS AND MONSTERS WILL AND WON'T ALLOW.
THE HEXENKORPS BUILT THIS WEB, BUT WHAT YOU DIDN'T KNOW IS... I AM THE SPIDER. AND NOW I WILL UNRAVEL *EVERY* STRAND.
ADOLF! SAVE ME! DON'T LET HIM--
AAAIIEEEE!!

IT CANNOT END THIS WAY.

MY GOD.

KARTHYS UND DARMAG, HERREN DER DUNKELWELT, TRAGT MICH HINFORT!

DAMN IT!

YOU SNEAKY LITTLE BASTARD!

WHAT DO WE REALLY KNOW ABOUT EINAR? I TRUST IMOGEN, BUT WE'VE ONLY JUST MET HIM AND SUDDENLY HE HAS THE RUN OF THE PLACE.

HAPPY TO GIVE HIM THE RUN OF MY PLACE. I LIKE THEM BIG AND FUZZY LIKE THAT.

CAREFUL, HEN. YOU'LL GIVE AN OLD MAN IDEAS. BESIDES...

"...SEEMS TO ME OUR NEW FRIEND'S GOT ENOUGH ON HIS PLATE ALREADY."

THAT'S THE THING ABOUT TAPPING INTO ANCIENT, DANGEROUS MAGICKS...

THERE'S ALWAYS SOMETHING EVEN OLDER...AND MORE DANGEROUS. I'VE SENT A LITTLE SPELL OF MY OWN INTO YOUR WEB, TO DISPERSE ALL THE OLD, DEAD MAGIC YOU HARVESTED.

THE SIDES IN THIS WAR ARE A LITTLE MORE EVEN NOW. REST WELL, YELENA. I HAVE NO DOUBT WE WILL MEET AGAIN.

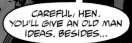

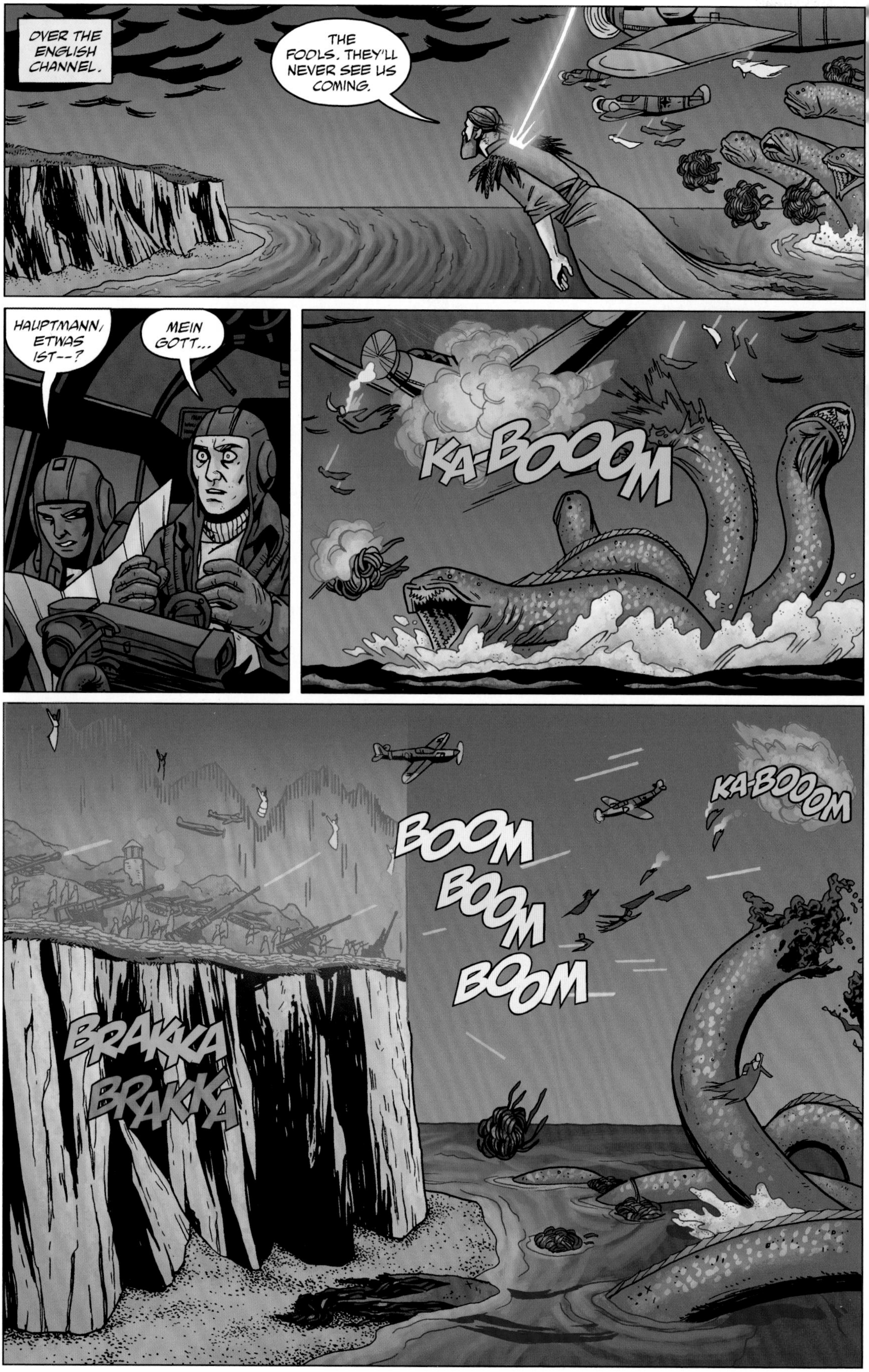
OVER THE ENGLISH CHANNEL.
THE FOOLS. THEY'LL NEVER SEE US COMING.
HAUPTMANN, ETWAS IST--?
MEIN GOTT...
KA-BOOOM
KA-BOOOM
BOOM
BOOM
BOOM
BRAKKA
BRAKKA

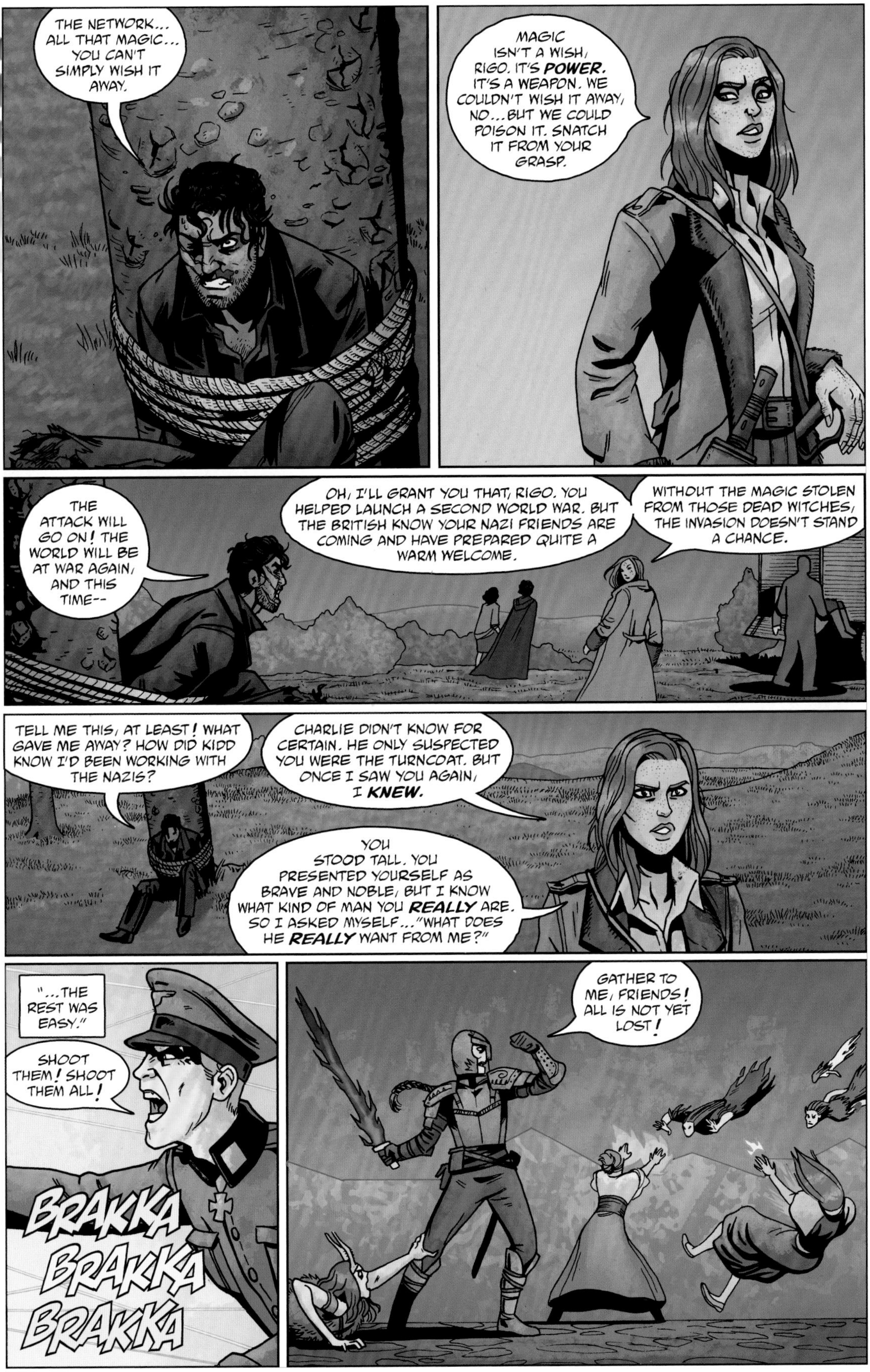
THE NETWORK... ALL THAT MAGIC... YOU CAN'T SIMPLY WISH IT AWAY.
MAGIC ISN'T A WISH, RIGO. IT'S POWER. IT'S A WEAPON. WE COULDN'T WISH IT AWAY, NO...BUT WE COULD POISON IT. SNATCH IT FROM YOUR GRASP.
THE ATTACK WILL GO ON! THE WORLD WILL BE AT WAR AGAIN, AND THIS TIME--
OH, I'LL GRANT YOU THAT, RIGO. YOU HELPED LAUNCH A SECOND WORLD WAR. BUT THE BRITISH KNOW YOUR NAZI FRIENDS ARE COMING AND HAVE PREPARED QUITE A WARM WELCOME.
WITHOUT THE MAGIC STOLEN FROM THOSE DEAD WITCHES, THE INVASION DOESN'T STAND A CHANCE.
TELL ME THIS, AT LEAST! WHAT GAVE ME AWAY? HOW DID KIDD KNOW I'D BEEN WORKING WITH THE NAZIS?
CHARLIE DIDN'T KNOW FOR CERTAIN. HE ONLY SUSPECTED YOU WERE THE TURNCOAT. BUT ONCE I SAW YOU AGAIN, I KNEW.
YOU STOOD TALL. YOU PRESENTED YOURSELF AS BRAVE AND NOBLE, BUT I KNOW WHAT KIND OF MAN YOU REALLY ARE. SO I ASKED MYSELF..."WHAT DOES HE REALLY WANT FROM ME?"
"...THE REST WAS EASY."
SHOOT THEM! SHOOT THEM ALL!
BRAKKA
BRAKKA
BRAKKA
GATHER TO ME, FRIENDS! ALL IS NOT YET LOST!

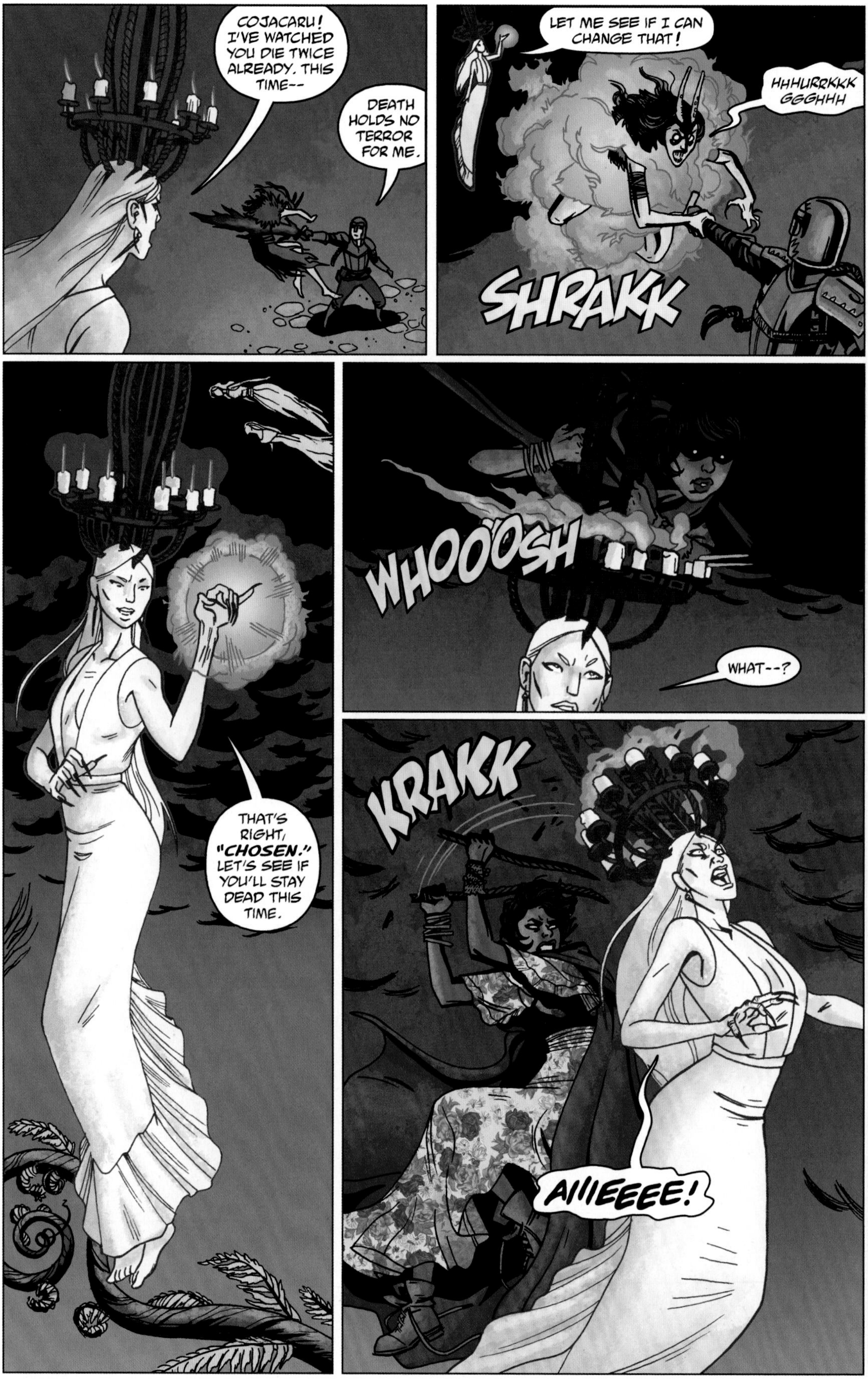
COJACARU! I'VE WATCHED YOU DIE TWICE ALREADY. THIS TIME--
DEATH HOLDS NO TERROR FOR ME.
LET ME SEE IF I CAN CHANGE THAT!
HHHURRKKK GGGHHH
SHRAKK
THAT'S RIGHT, "CHOSEN." LET'S SEE IF YOU'LL STAY DEAD THIS TIME.
WHOOOSH
WHAT--?
KRAKK
AIIIEEEE!

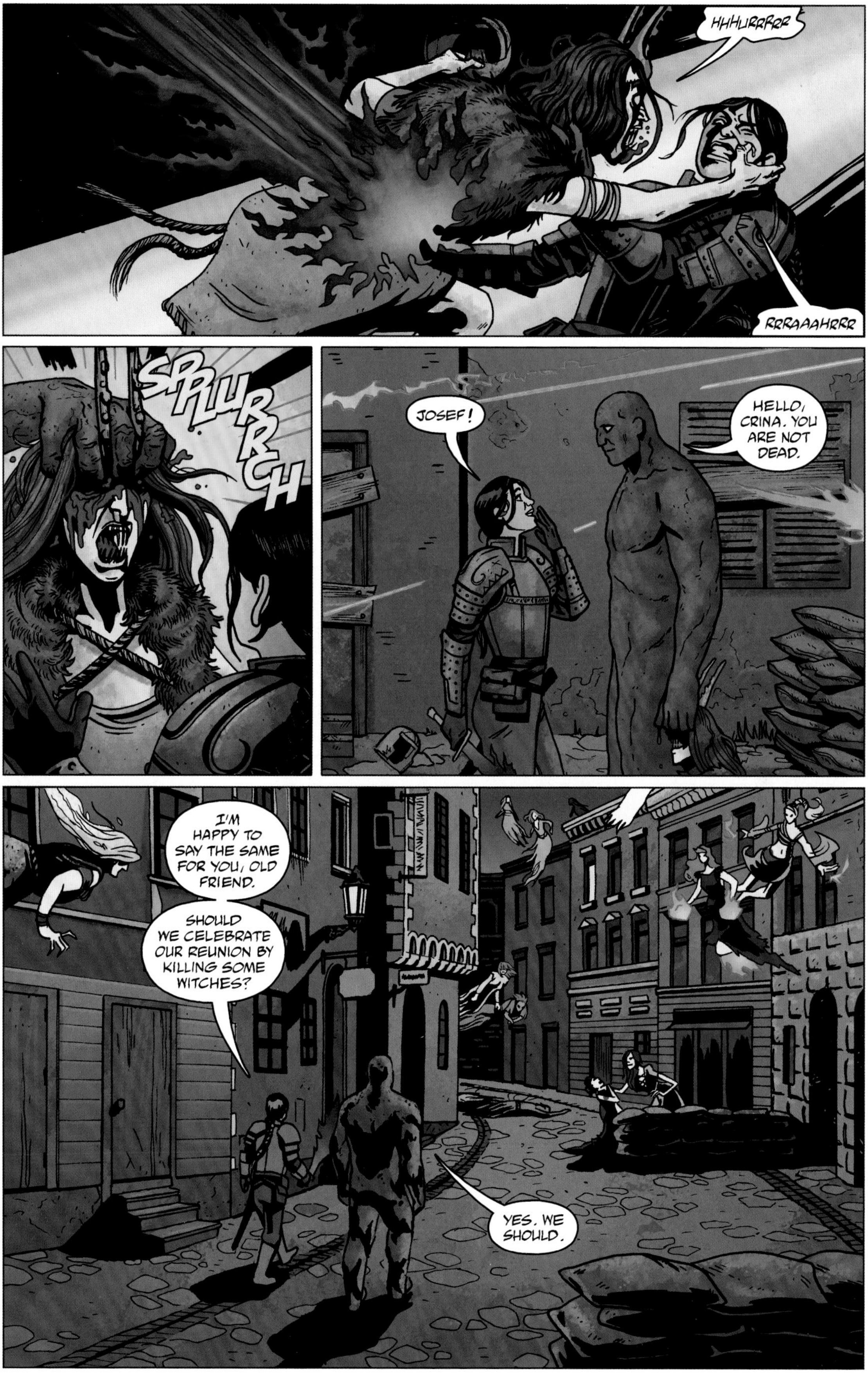
HHHURRRRR
RRRAAAHRRR
SPRLURRCH
JOSEF!
HELLO, CRINA. YOU ARE NOT DEAD.
I'M HAPPY TO SAY THE SAME FOR YOU, OLD FRIEND.
SHOULD WE CELEBRATE OUR REUNION BY KILLING SOME WITCHES?
YES. WE SHOULD.

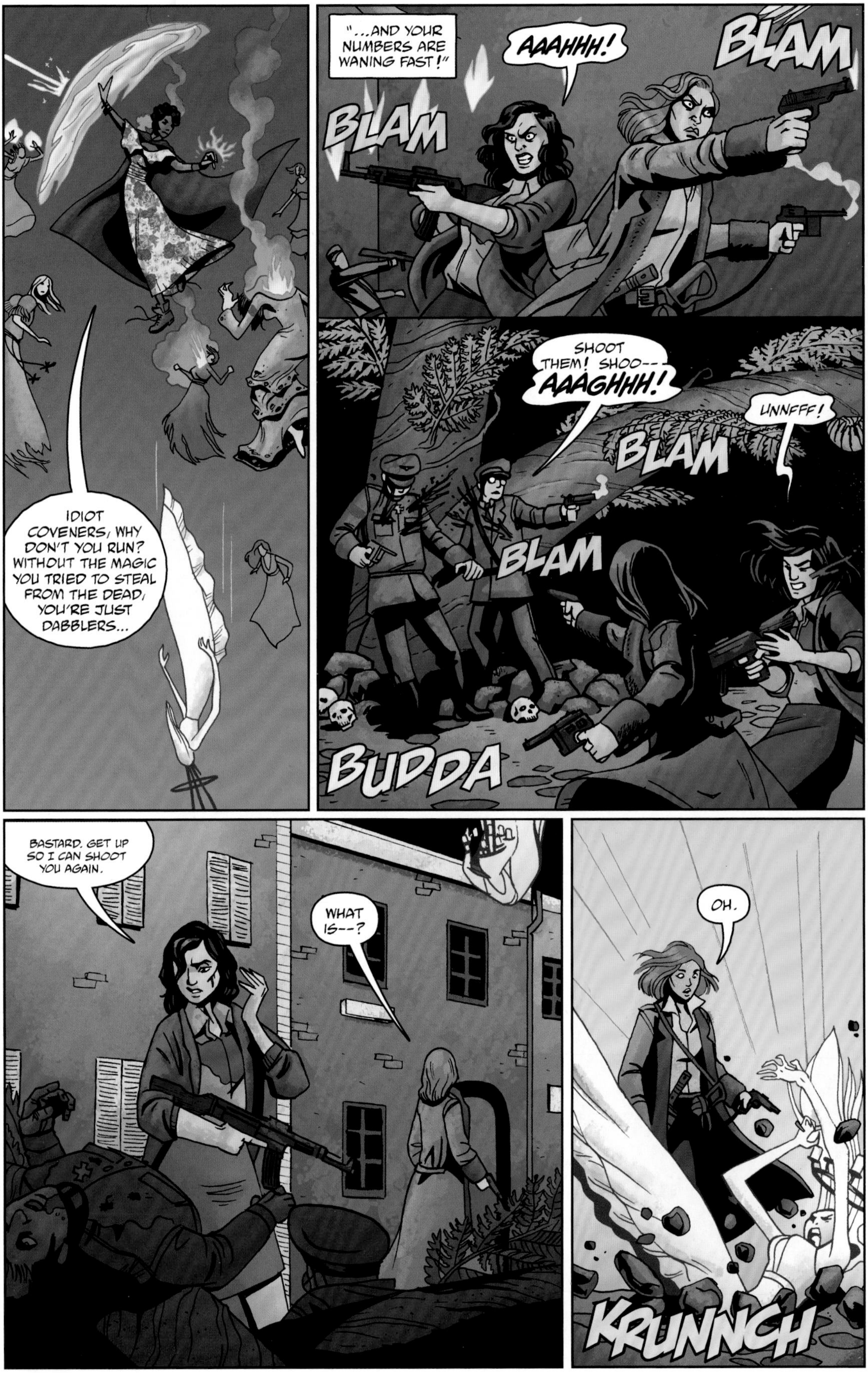
IDIOT COVENERS, WHY DON'T YOU RUN? WITHOUT THE MAGIC YOU TRIED TO STEAL FROM THE DEAD, YOU'RE JUST DABBLERS...
"...AND YOUR NUMBERS ARE WANING FAST!"
AAAHHH!
BLAM
BLAM
SHOOT THEM! SHOO-- AAAGHHH!
UNNFFF!
BLAM
BLAM
BUDDA
BASTARD. GET UP SO I CAN SHOOT YOU AGAIN.
WHAT IS--?
OH.
KRUNNCH

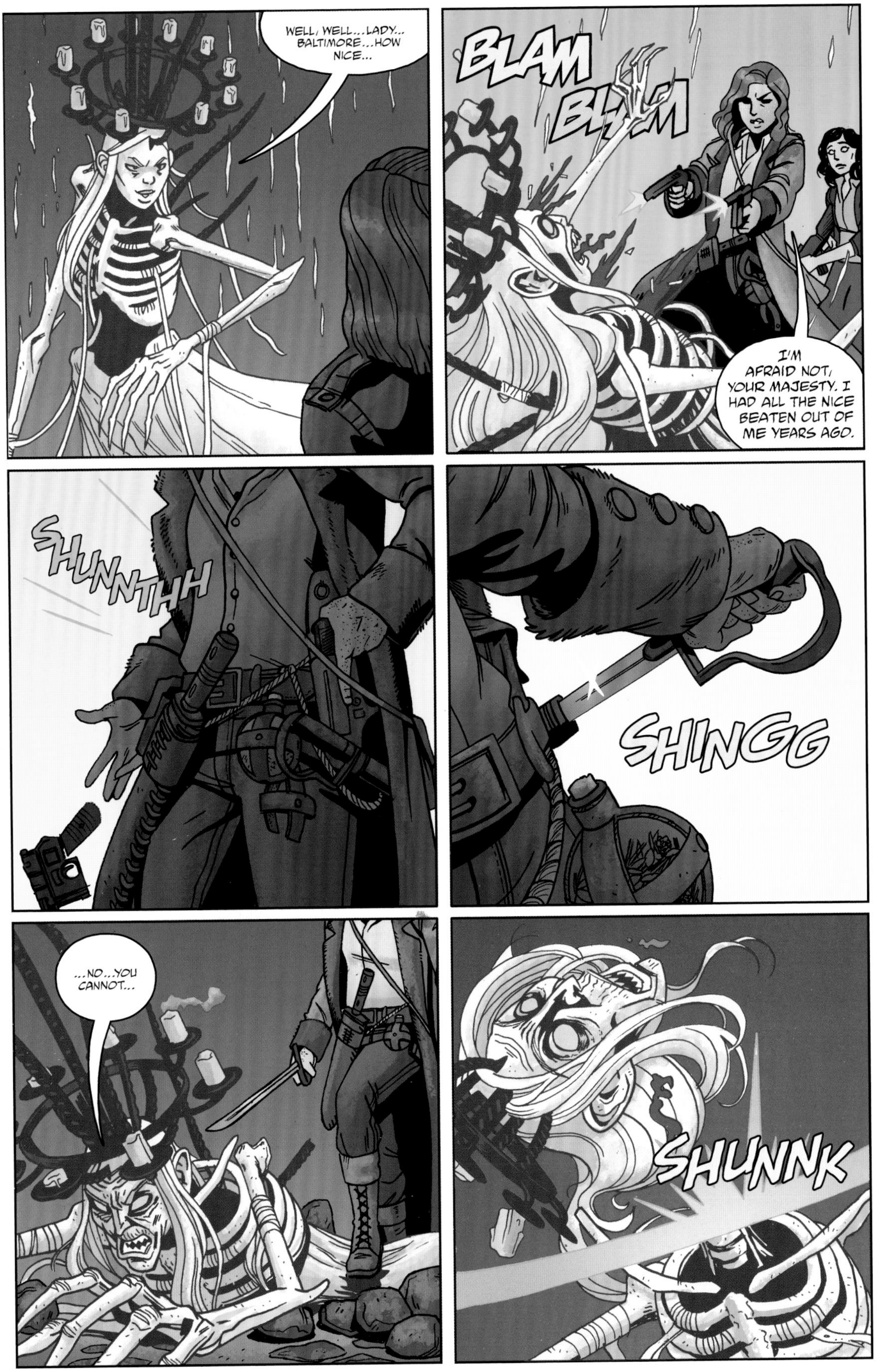
WELL, WELL...LADY... BALTIMORE...HOW NICE...
BLAM
BLAM
I'M AFRAID NOT, YOUR MAJESTY. I HAD ALL THE NICE BEATEN OUT OF ME YEARS AGO.
SHUNNTHH
SHINGG
...NO...YOU CANNOT...
SHUNNK

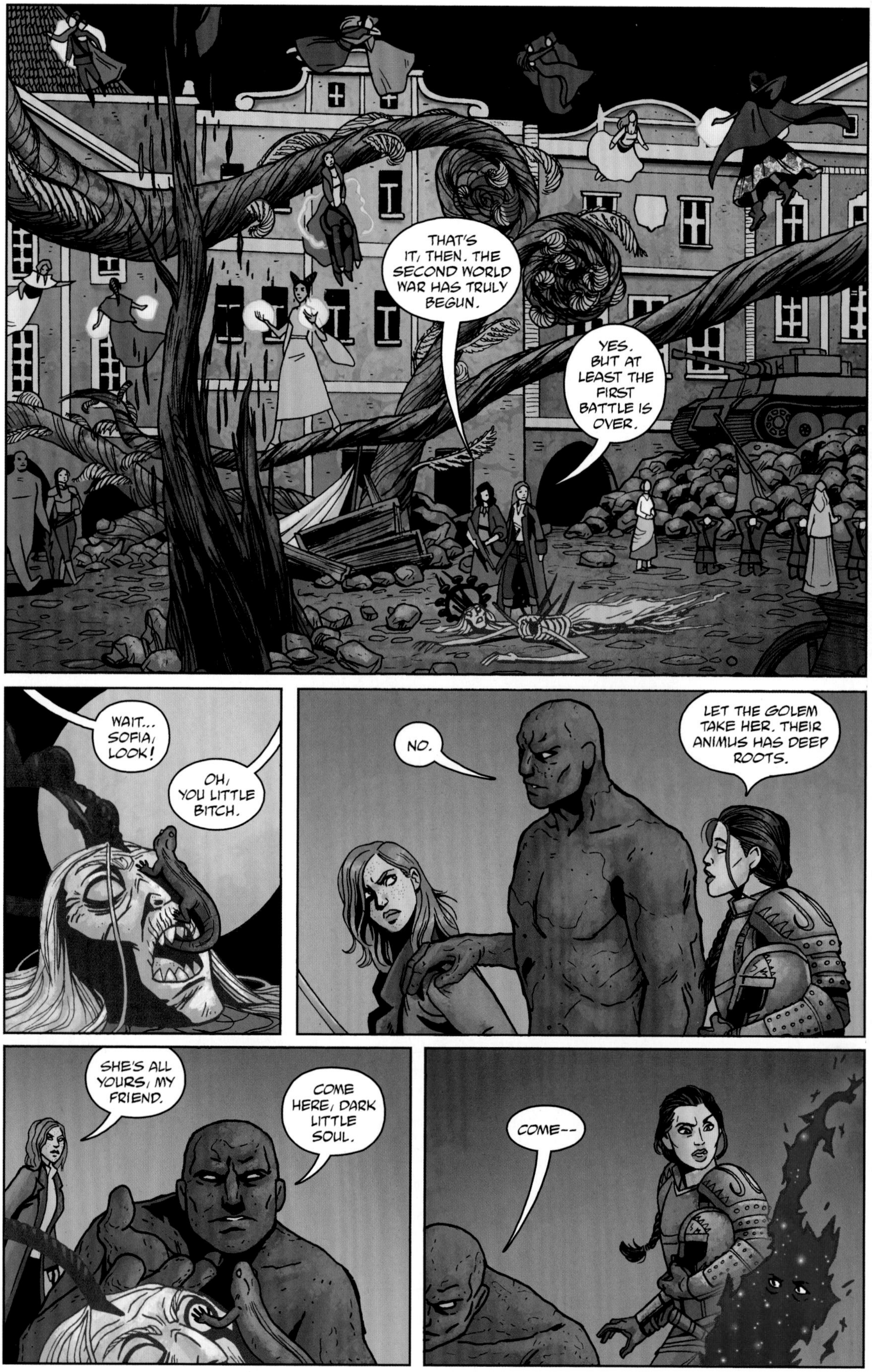
THAT'S IT, THEN. THE SECOND WORLD WAR HAS TRULY BEGUN.
YES. BUT AT LEAST THE FIRST BATTLE IS OVER.
WAIT... SOFIA, LOOK!
OH, YOU LITTLE BITCH.
NO.
LET THE GOLEM TAKE HER. THEIR ANIMUS HAS DEEP ROOTS.
SHE'S ALL YOURS, MY FRIEND.
COME HERE, DARK LITTLE SOUL.
COME--

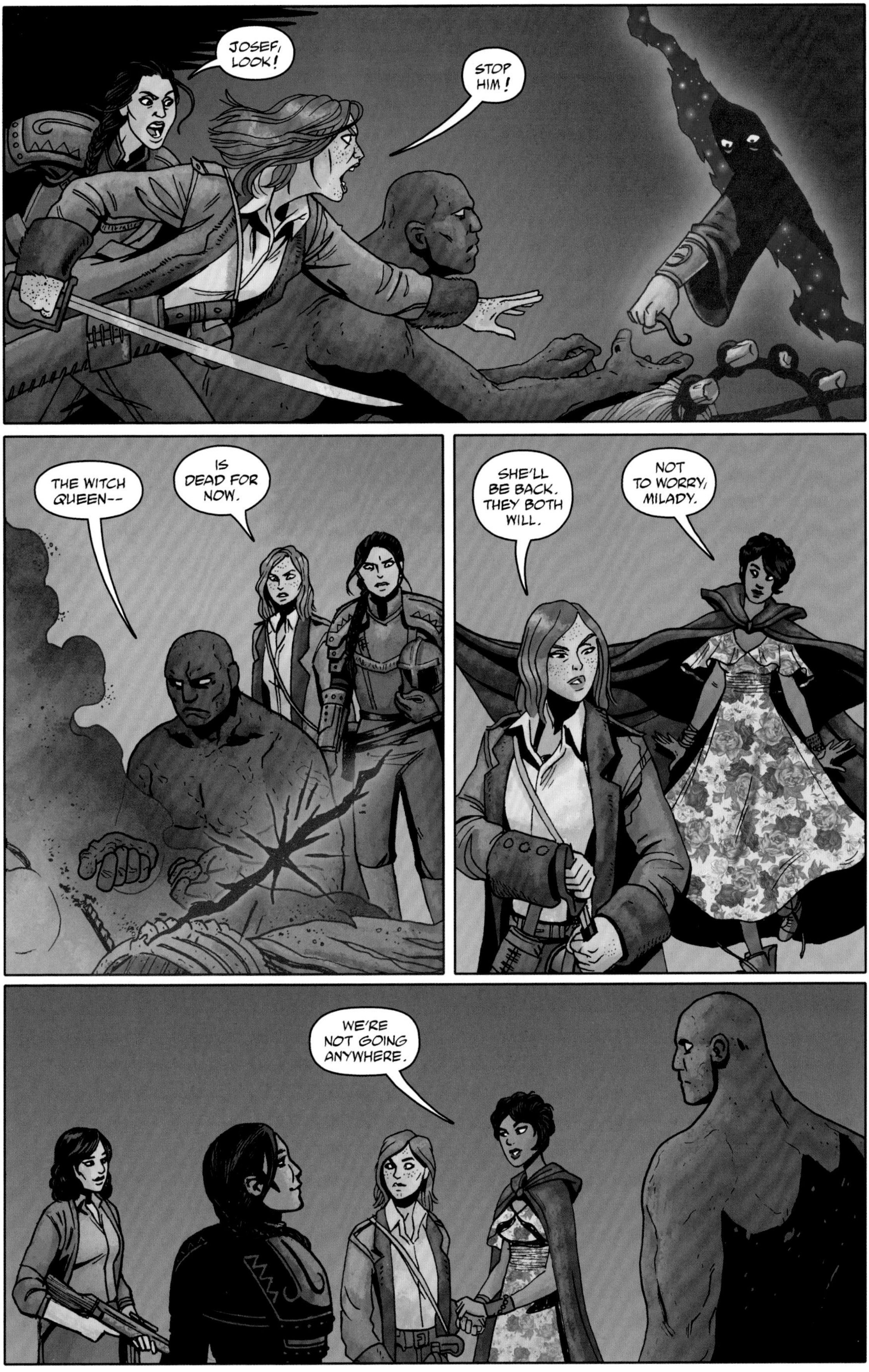
JOSEF, LOOK!
STOP HIM!
THE WITCH QUEEN--
IS DEAD FOR NOW.
SHE'LL BE BACK. THEY BOTH WILL.
NOT TO WORRY, MILADY.
WE'RE NOT GOING ANYWHERE.

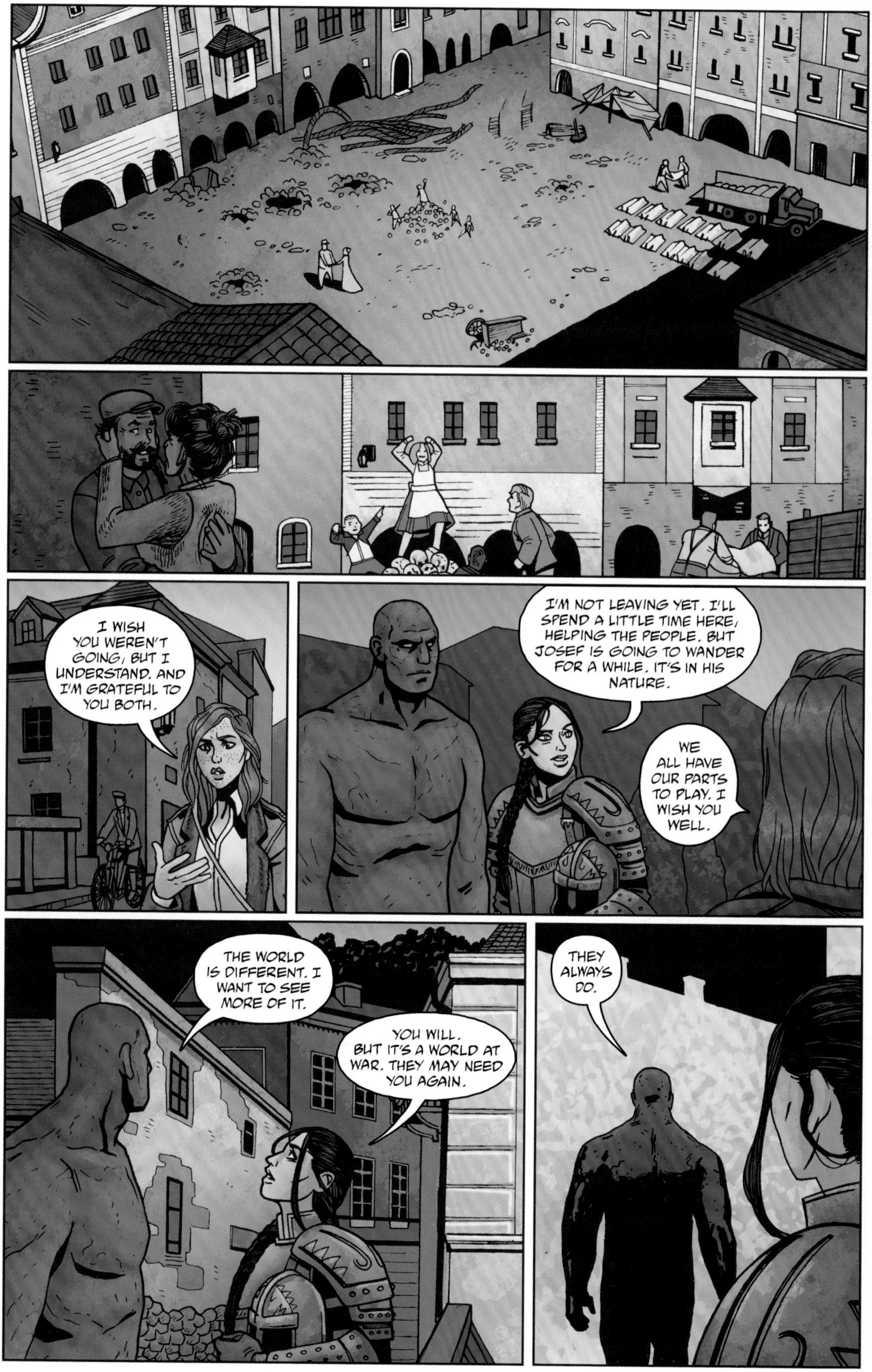
I WISH YOU WEREN'T GOING, BUT I UNDERSTAND. AND I'M GRATEFUL TO YOU BOTH.
I'M NOT LEAVING YET. I'LL SPEND A LITTLE TIME HERE, HELPING THE PEOPLE. BUT JOSEF IS GOING TO WANDER FOR A WHILE. IT'S IN HIS NATURE.
WE ALL HAVE OUR PARTS TO PLAY. I WISH YOU WELL.
THE WORLD IS DIFFERENT. I WANT TO SEE MORE OF IT.
YOU WILL. BUT IT'S A WORLD AT WAR. THEY MAY NEED YOU AGAIN.
THEY ALWAYS DO.

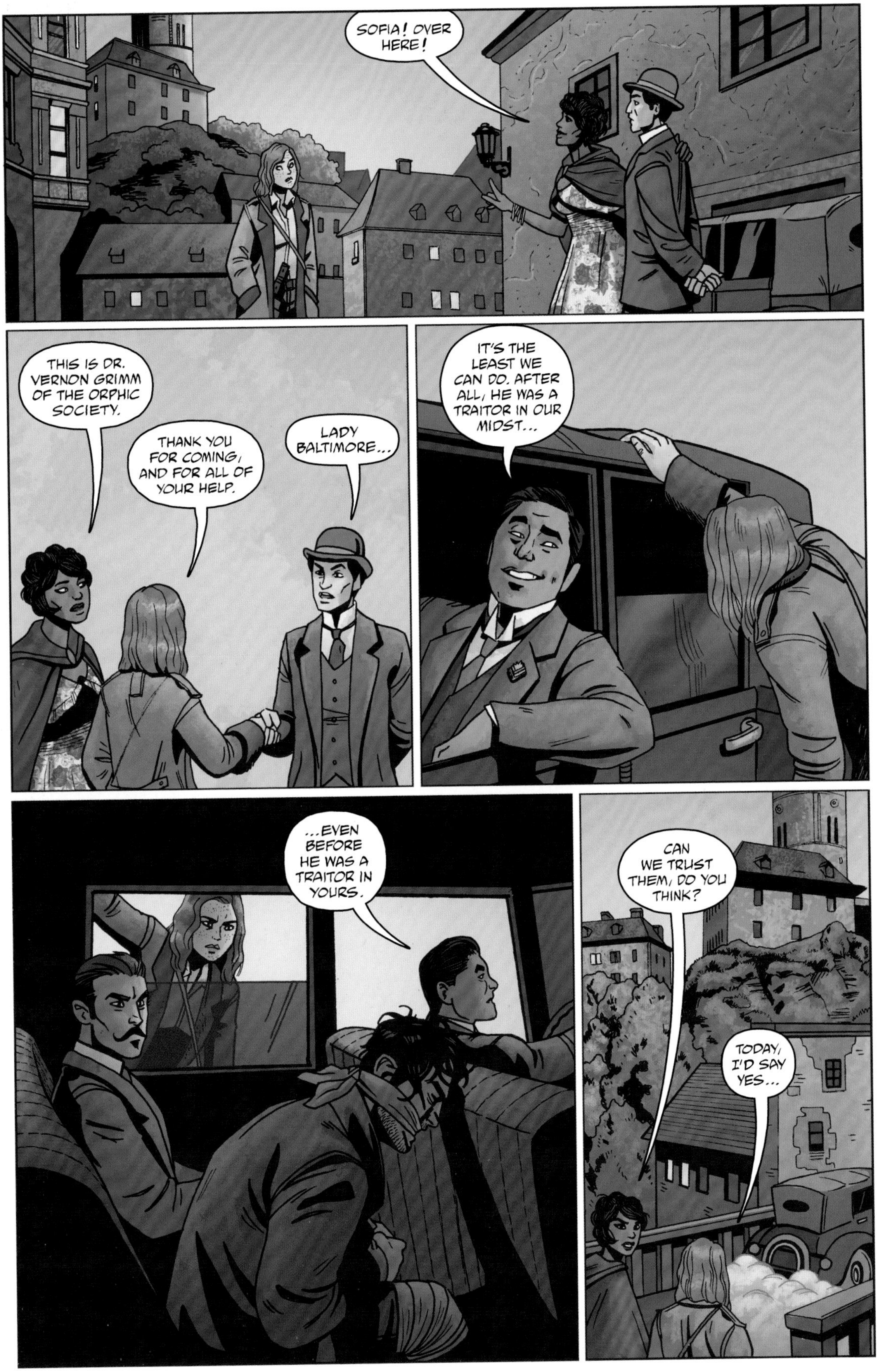
SOFIA! OVER HERE!
THIS IS DR. VERNON GRIMM OF THE ORPHIC SOCIETY.
THANK YOU FOR COMING, AND FOR ALL OF YOUR HELP.
LADY BALTIMORE...
IT'S THE LEAST WE CAN DO. AFTER ALL, HE WAS A TRAITOR IN OUR MIDST...
...EVEN BEFORE HE WAS A TRAITOR IN YOURS.
CAN WE TRUST THEM, DO YOU THINK?
TODAY, I'D SAY YES...

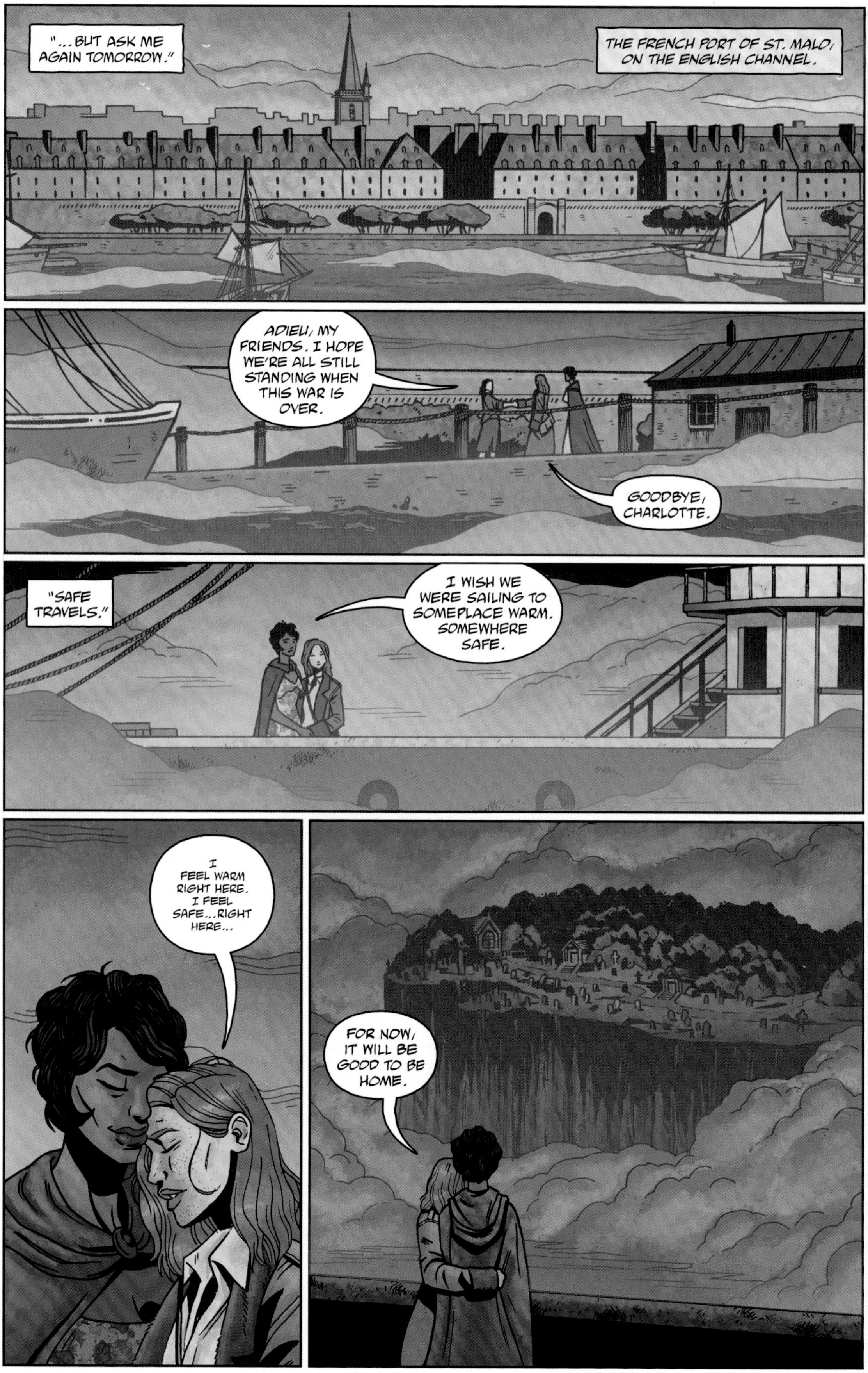
"...BUT ASK ME AGAIN TOMORROW."
THE FRENCH PORT OF ST. MALO, ON THE ENGLISH CHANNEL.
ADIEU, MY FRIENDS. I HOPE WE'RE ALL STILL STANDING WHEN THIS WAR IS OVER.
GOODBYE, CHARLOTTE.
"SAFE TRAVELS."
I WISH WE WERE SAILING TO SOMEPLACE WARM. SOMEWHERE SAFE.
I FEEL WARM RIGHT HERE. I FEEL SAFE...RIGHT HERE...
FOR NOW, IT WILL BE GOOD TO BE HOME.

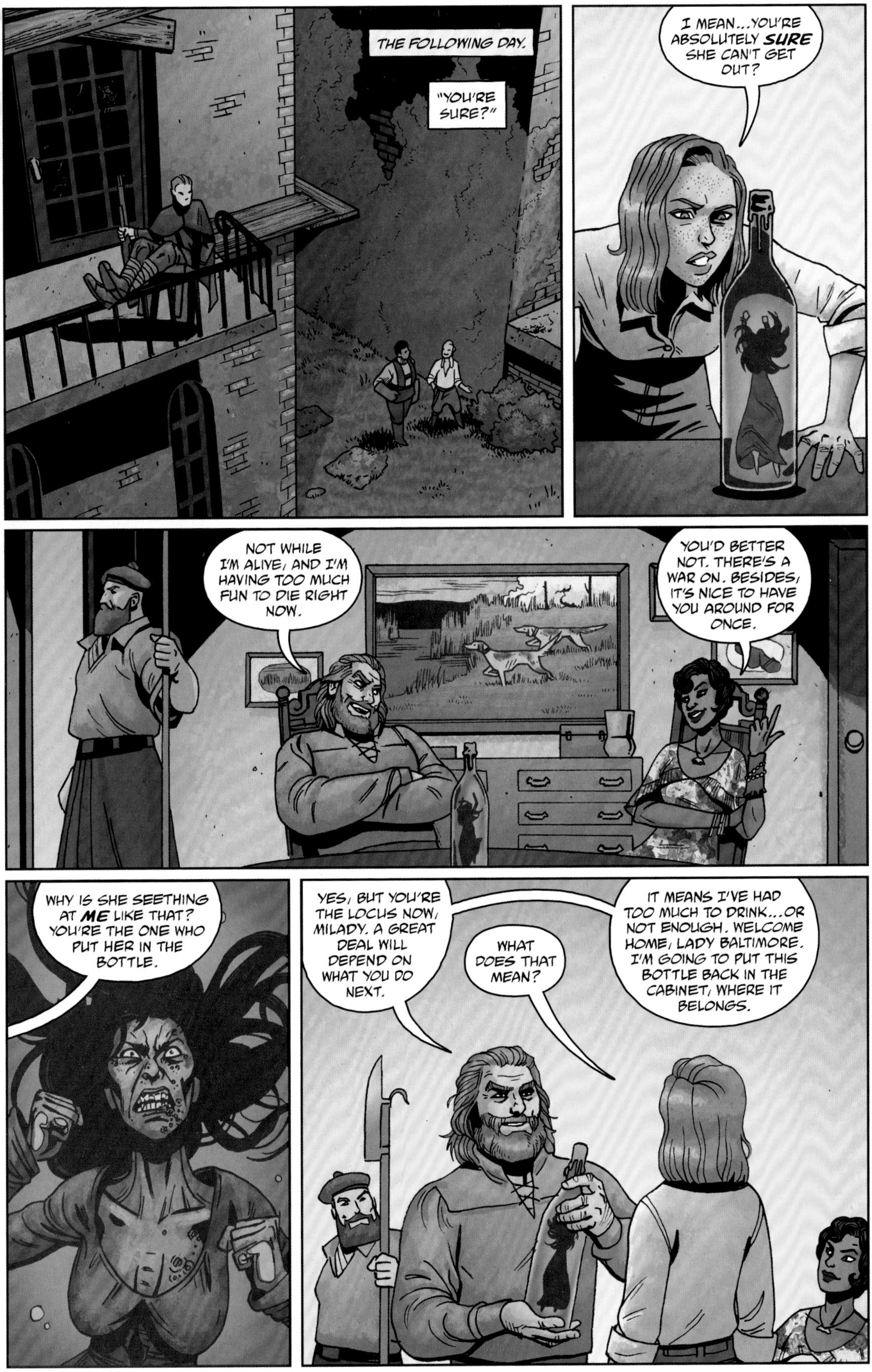
THE FOLLOWING DAY.
"YOU'RE SURE?"
I MEAN...YOU'RE ABSOLUTELY SURE SHE CAN'T GET OUT?
NOT WHILE I'M ALIVE, AND I'M HAVING TOO MUCH FUN TO DIE RIGHT NOW.
YOU'D BETTER NOT. THERE'S A WAR ON. BESIDES, IT'S NICE TO HAVE YOU AROUND FOR ONCE.
WHY IS SHE SEETHING AT ME LIKE THAT? YOU'RE THE ONE WHO PUT HER IN THE BOTTLE.
YES, BUT YOU'RE THE LOCUS NOW, MILADY. A GREAT DEAL WILL DEPEND ON WHAT YOU DO NEXT.
WHAT DOES THAT MEAN?
IT MEANS I'VE HAD TOO MUCH TO DRINK...OR NOT ENOUGH. WELCOME HOME, LADY BALTIMORE. I'M GOING TO PUT THIS BOTTLE BACK IN THE CABINET, WHERE IT BELONGS.

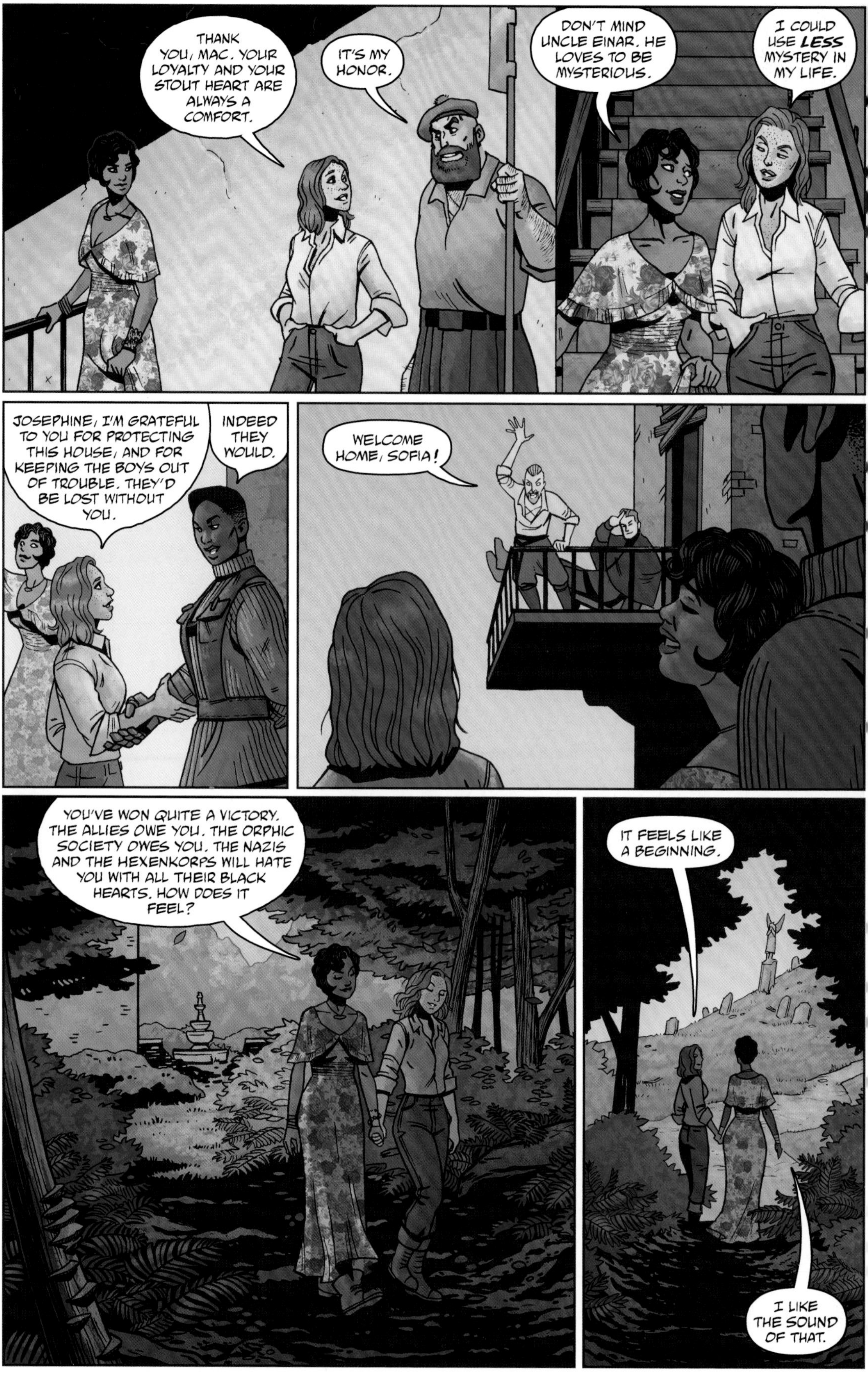
THANK YOU, MAC. YOUR LOYALTY AND YOUR STOUT HEART ARE ALWAYS A COMFORT.
IT'S MY HONOR.
DON'T MIND UNCLE EINAR. HE LOVES TO BE MYSTERIOUS.
I COULD USE LESS MYSTERY IN MY LIFE.
JOSEPHINE, I'M GRATEFUL TO YOU FOR PROTECTING THIS HOUSE, AND FOR KEEPING THE BOYS OUT OF TROUBLE. THEY'D BE LOST WITHOUT YOU.
INDEED THEY WOULD.
WELCOME HOME, SOFIA!
YOU'VE WON QUITE A VICTORY. THE ALLIES OWE YOU. THE ORPHIC SOCIETY OWES YOU. THE NAZIS AND THE HEXENKORPS WILL HATE YOU WITH ALL THEIR BLACK HEARTS. HOW DOES IT FEEL?
IT FEELS LIKE A BEGINNING.
I LIKE THE SOUND OF THAT.

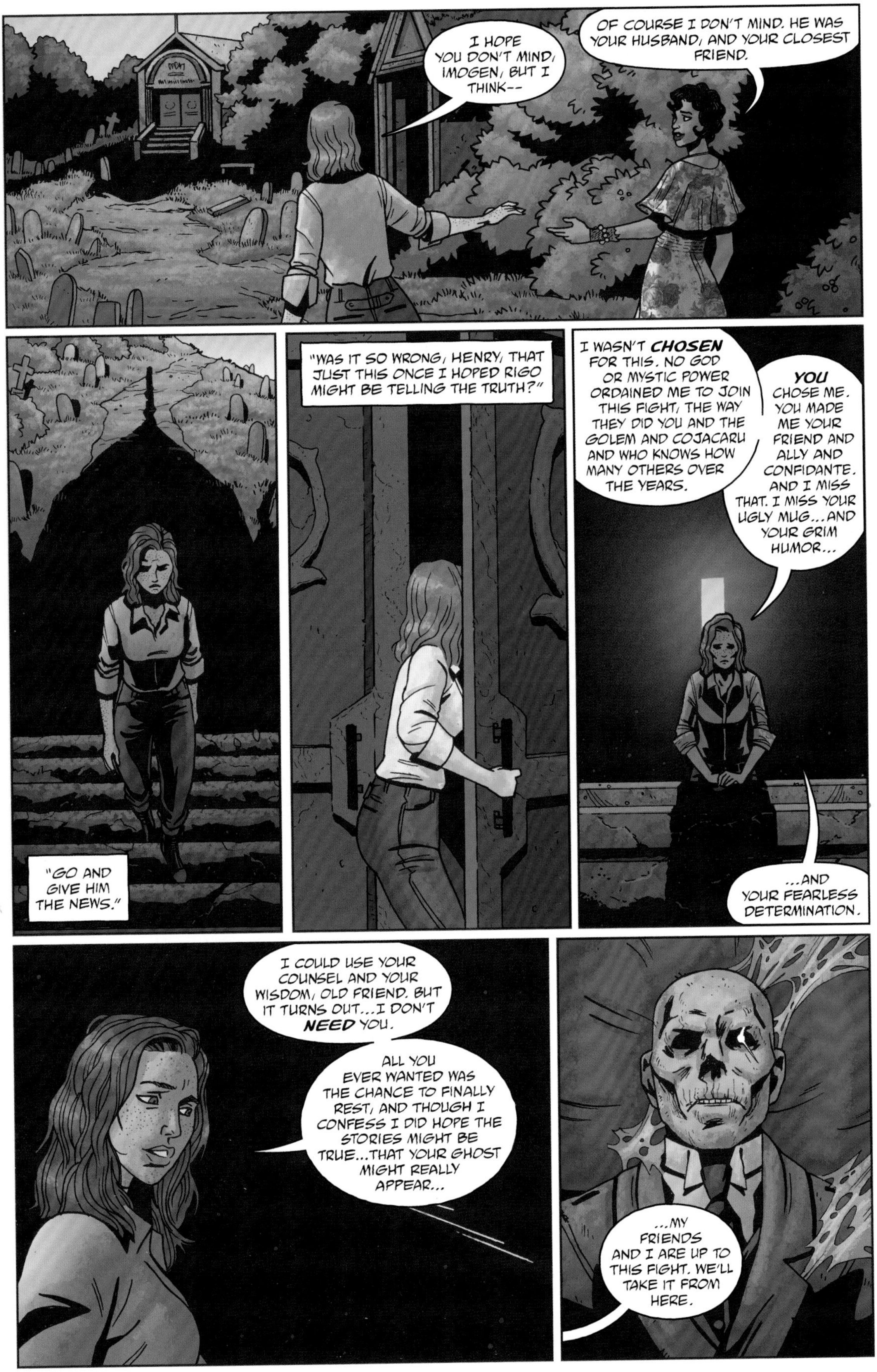
I HOPE YOU DON'T MIND, IMOGEN, BUT I THINK--
OF COURSE I DON'T MIND. HE WAS YOUR HUSBAND, AND YOUR CLOSEST FRIEND.
"GO AND GIVE HIM THE NEWS."
"WAS IT SO WRONG, HENRY, THAT JUST THIS ONCE I HOPED RIGO MIGHT BE TELLING THE TRUTH?"
I WASN'T **CHOSEN** FOR THIS. NO GOD OR MYSTIC POWER ORDAINED ME TO JOIN THIS FIGHT, THE WAY THEY DID YOU AND THE GOLEM AND COJACARU AND WHO KNOWS HOW MANY OTHERS OVER THE YEARS.
YOU CHOSE ME. YOU MADE ME YOUR FRIEND AND ALLY AND CONFIDANTE. AND I MISS THAT. I MISS YOUR UGLY MUG...AND YOUR GRIM HUMOR...
...AND YOUR FEARLESS DETERMINATION.
I COULD USE YOUR COUNSEL AND YOUR WISDOM, OLD FRIEND. BUT IT TURNS OUT...I DON'T **NEED** YOU.
ALL YOU EVER WANTED WAS THE CHANCE TO FINALLY REST, AND THOUGH I CONFESS I DID HOPE THE STORIES MIGHT BE TRUE...THAT YOUR GHOST MIGHT REALLY APPEAR...
...MY FRIENDS AND I ARE UP TO THIS FIGHT. WE'LL TAKE IT FROM HERE.

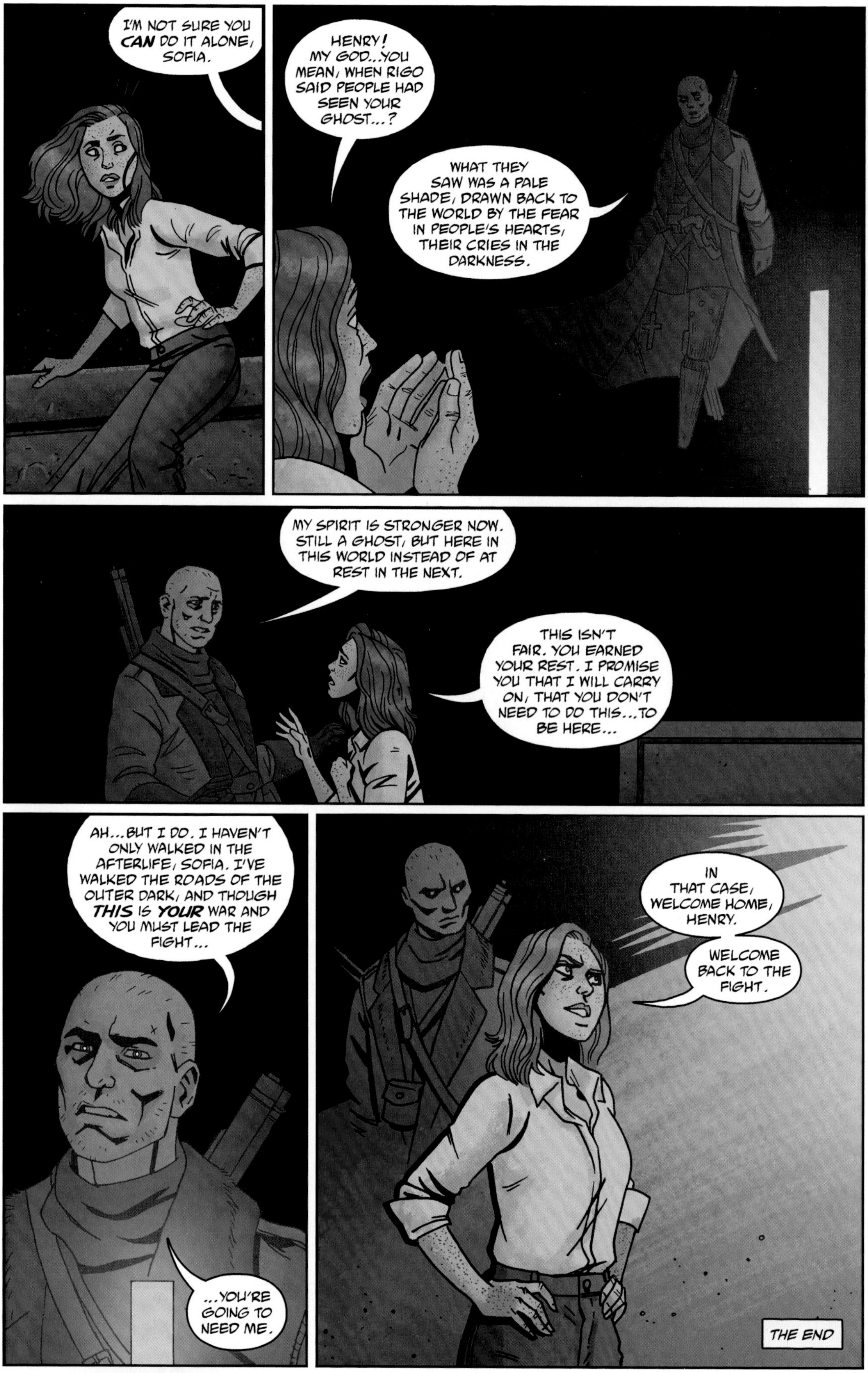
I'M NOT SURE YOU CAN DO IT ALONE, SOFIA.
HENRY! MY GOD...YOU MEAN, WHEN RIGO SAID PEOPLE HAD SEEN YOUR GHOST...?
WHAT THEY SAW WAS A PALE SHADE, DRAWN BACK TO THE WORLD BY THE FEAR IN PEOPLE'S HEARTS, THEIR CRIES IN THE DARKNESS.
MY SPIRIT IS STRONGER NOW. STILL A GHOST, BUT HERE IN THIS WORLD INSTEAD OF AT REST IN THE NEXT.
THIS ISN'T FAIR. YOU EARNED YOUR REST. I PROMISE YOU THAT I WILL CARRY ON, THAT YOU DON'T NEED TO DO THIS...TO BE HERE...
AH...BUT I DO. I HAVEN'T ONLY WALKED IN THE AFTERLIFE, SOFIA. I'VE WALKED THE ROADS OF THE OUTER DARK, AND THOUGH THIS IS YOUR WAR AND YOU MUST LEAD THE FIGHT...
...YOU'RE GOING TO NEED ME.
IN THAT CASE, WELCOME HOME, HENRY.
WELCOME BACK TO THE FIGHT.
THE END

LADY BALTIMORE
THE WITCH QUEENS

SKETCHBOOK

Notes by the editor

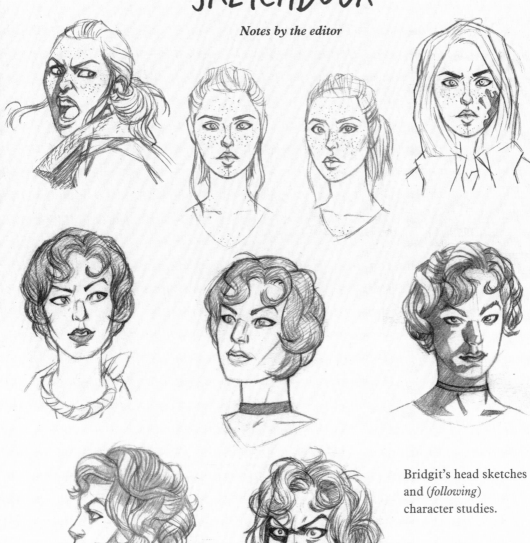

Bridgit's head sketches
and (*following*)
character studies.

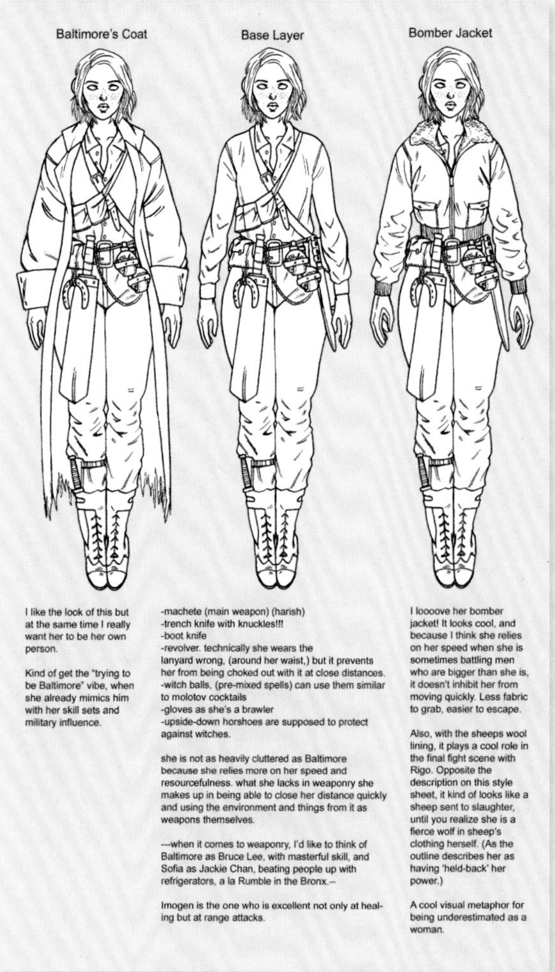

Baltimore's Coat
Base Layer
Bomber Jacket
I like the look of this but at the same time I really want her to be her own person.
Kind of get the "trying to be Baltimore" vibe, when she already mimics him with her skill sets and military influence.
-machete (main weapon) (harish)
-trench knife with knuckles!!!
-boot knife
-revolver. technically she wears the lanyard wrong, (around her waist,) but it prevents her from being choked out with it at close distances.
-witch balls, (pre-mixed spells) can use them similar to molotov cocktails
-gloves as she's a brawler
-upside-down horshoes are supposed to protect against witches.
she is not as heavily cluttered as Baltimore because she relies more on her speed and resourcefulness. what she lacks in weaponry she makes up in being able to close her distance quickly and using the environment and things from it as weapons themselves.
---when it comes to weaponry, I'd like to think of Baltimore as Bruce Lee, with masterful skill, and Sofia as Jackie Chan, beating people up with refrigerators, a la Rumble in the Bronx.--
Imogen is the one who is excellent not only at healing but at range attacks.
I loooove her bomber jacket! It looks cool, and because I think she relies on her speed when she is sometimes battling men who are bigger than she is, it doesn't inhibit her from moving quickly. Less fabric to grab, easier to escape.
Also, with the sheeps wool lining, it plays a cool role in the final fight scene with Rigo. Opposite the description on this style sheet, it kind of looks like a sheep sent to slaughter, until you realize she is a fierce wolf in sheep's clothing herself. (As the outline describes her as having 'held-back' her power.)
A cool visual metaphor for being underestimated as a woman.

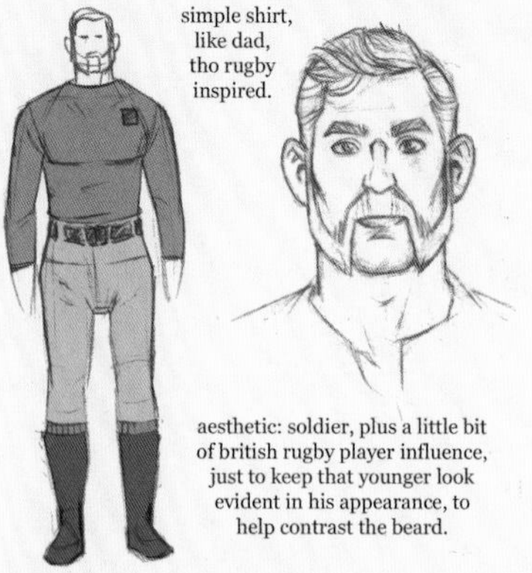

simple shirt, like dad, tho rugby inspired.
aesthetic: soldier, plus a little bit of british rugby player influence, just to keep that younger look evident in his appearance, to help contrast the beard.

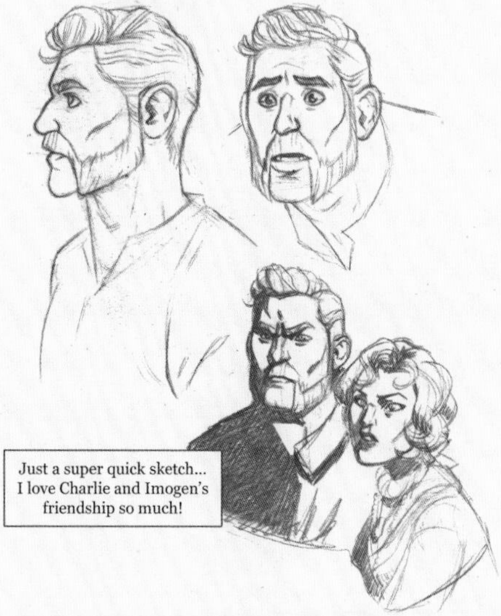

Just a super quick sketch... I love Charlie and Imogen's friendship so much!

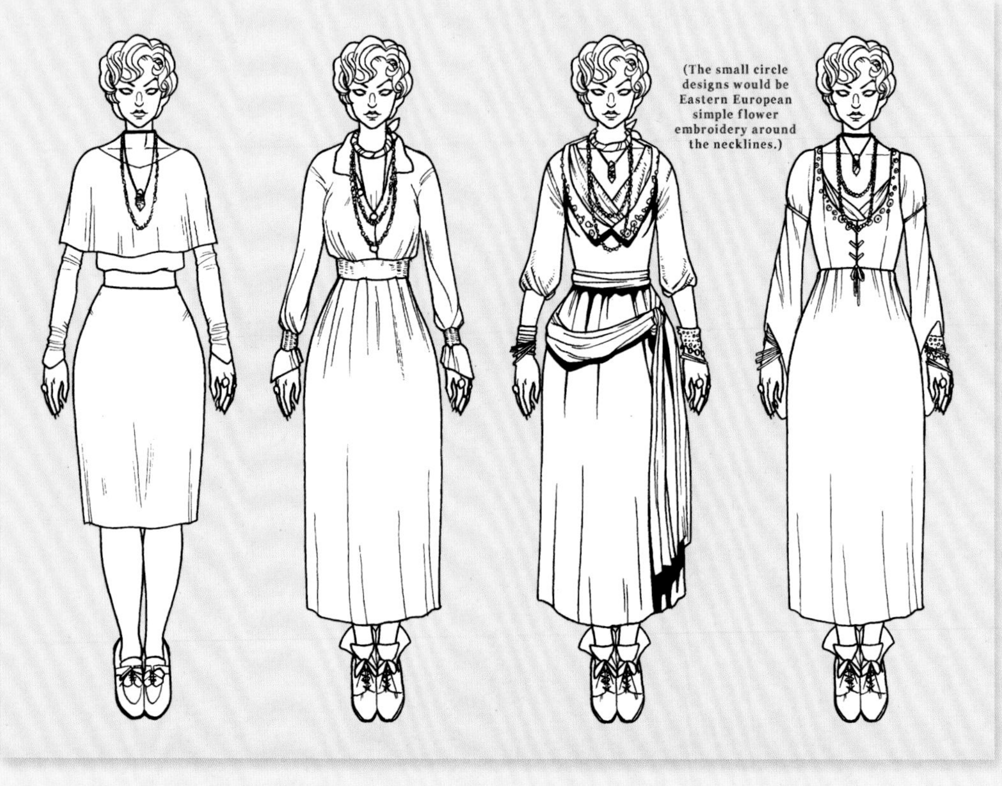

(The small circle designs would be Eastern European simple flower embroidery around the necklines.)

EINAR

-torc necklace
-giant bear hide cloak
-long hair with hidden
 dreads and braids
-two braids in beard
-rune for "life" under
 right eye.
-stag skull across entire
 chest
-hides and furs.
-will have a bit of a larger
 build than seen here.
-will have the longer hair
 from bottom right sketch.

JOSEPHINE

-cynthia erivo + grace jones
-around 6'0"
-built like Gina Carano.
-probably dressed in warmer
clothes since england would
be considerably colder for her.
-planning on doing winter
scene for czechy krumlov so it
would definitely be at least
nearing fall/winter

military sweater with
bren assault vest

african military coat
(can use this later as
well if there is a bit
more of a military
war/battle scene as
opposed to an ambush)

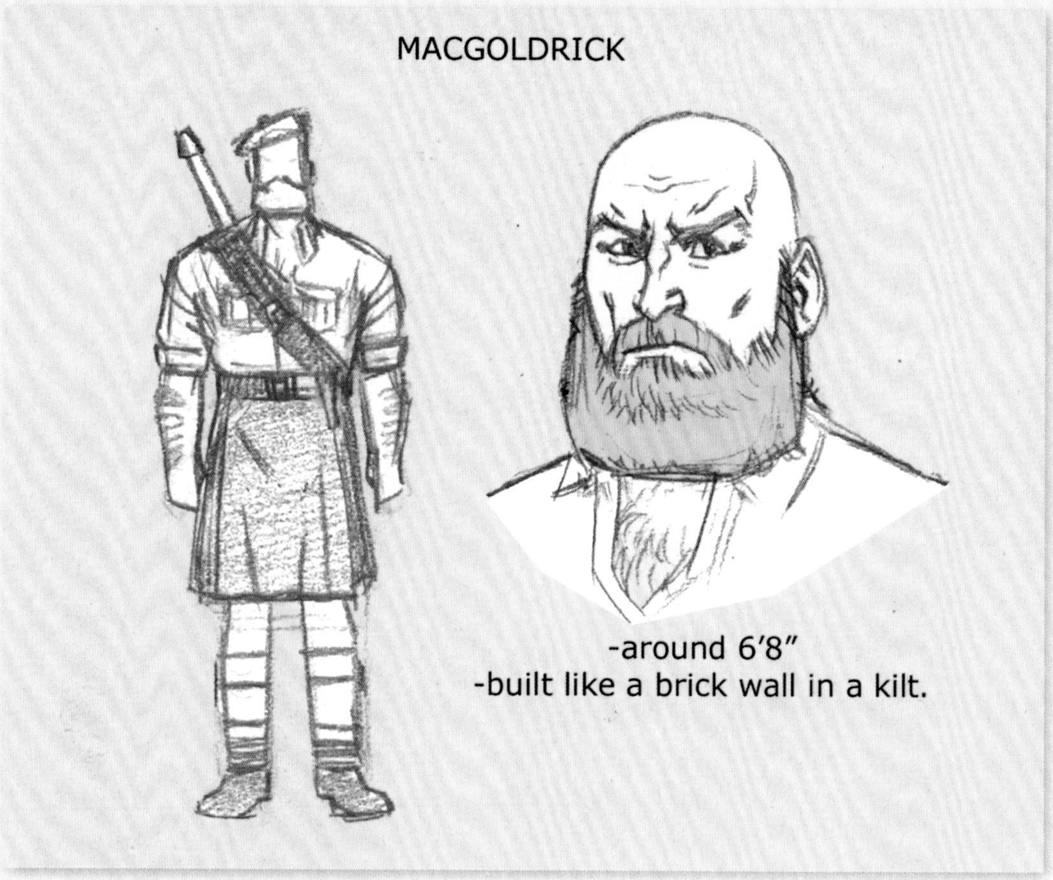
MACGOLDRICK
-around 6'8"
-built like a brick wall in a kilt.

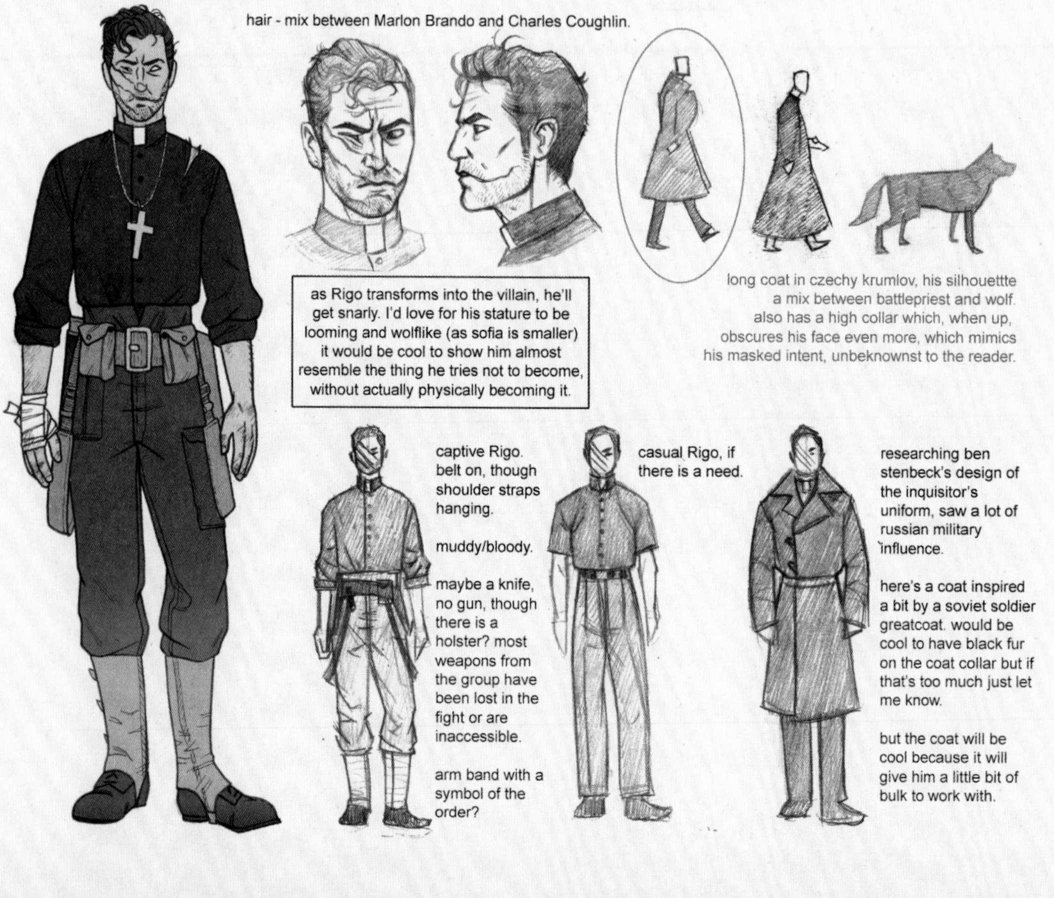
hair - mix between Marlon Brando and Charles Coughlin.
as Rigo transforms into the villain, he'll get snarly. I'd love for his stature to be looming and wolflike (as sofia is smaller) it would be cool to show him almost resemble the thing he tries not to become, without actually physically becoming it.
long coat in czechy krumlov, his silhouettte a mix between battlepriest and wolf. also has a high collar which, when up, obscures his face even more, which mimics his masked intent, unbeknownst to the reader.
captive Rigo. belt on, though shoulder straps hanging.
muddy/bloody.
maybe a knife, no gun, though there is a holster? most weapons from the group have been lost in the fight or are inaccessible.
arm band with a symbol of the order?
casual Rigo, if there is a need.
researching ben stenbeck's design of the inquisitor's uniform, saw a lot of russian military influence.
here's a coat inspired a bit by a soviet soldier greatcoat. would be cool to have black fur on the coat collar but if that's too much just let me know.
but the coat will be cool because it will give him a little bit of bulk to work with.

NJAL

-around 5'10"
-military shirt undone a bit -
he's scandinavian so a little more used
to cold weather (plus we gotta show off
those cool tattoos!)
-viking belt and style pants, though they
blend well with the style of military pants
during WW2, just a little baggier, which
would help his quick fighting style.
-hair is viking-esque but I think it also
blends in well with the styles of that time.
-tattoos will creep up side of his neck and
onto his shaved head.

RUTGER

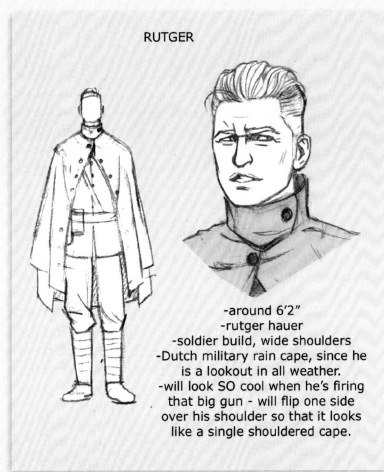

-around 6'2"
-rutger hauer
-soldier build, wide shoulders
-Dutch military rain cape, since he
is a lookout in all weather.
-will look SO cool when he's firing
that big gun - will flip one side
over his shoulder so that it looks
like a single shouldered cape.

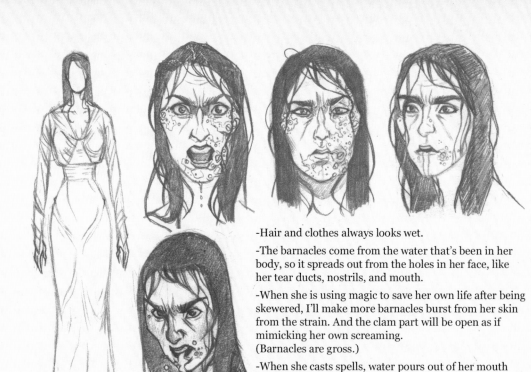

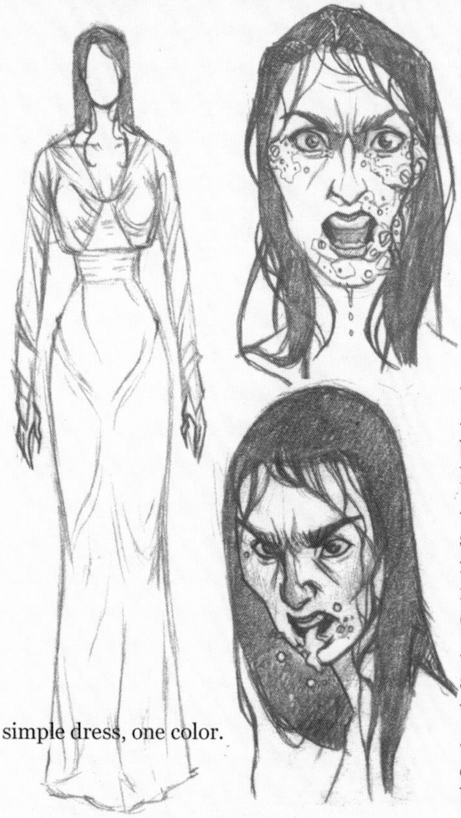
simple dress, one color.

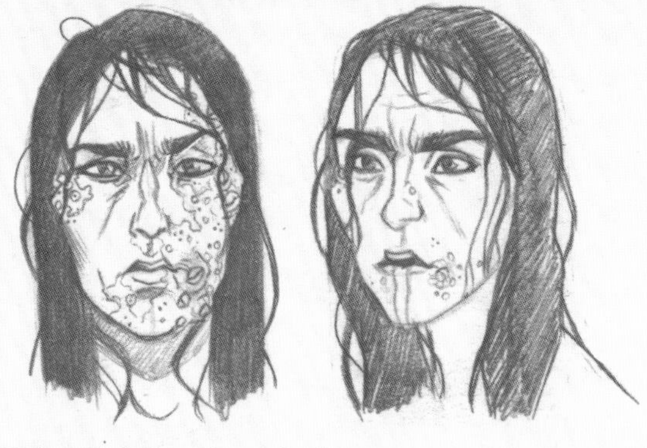

-Hair and clothes always looks wet.

-The barnacles come from the water that's been in her body, so it spreads out from the holes in her face, like her tear ducts, nostrils, and mouth.

-When she is using magic to save her own life after being skewered, I'll make more barnacles burst from her skin from the strain. And the clam part will be open as if mimicking her own screaming.
(Barnacles are gross.)

-When she casts spells, water pours out of her mouth and she might always be a little drooly, but especially when she's angry.

-Would love to keep her dress white, or at least a light color so I can show the wet drapery effect. It also might be cool for Michelle to the wet cloth/skin.

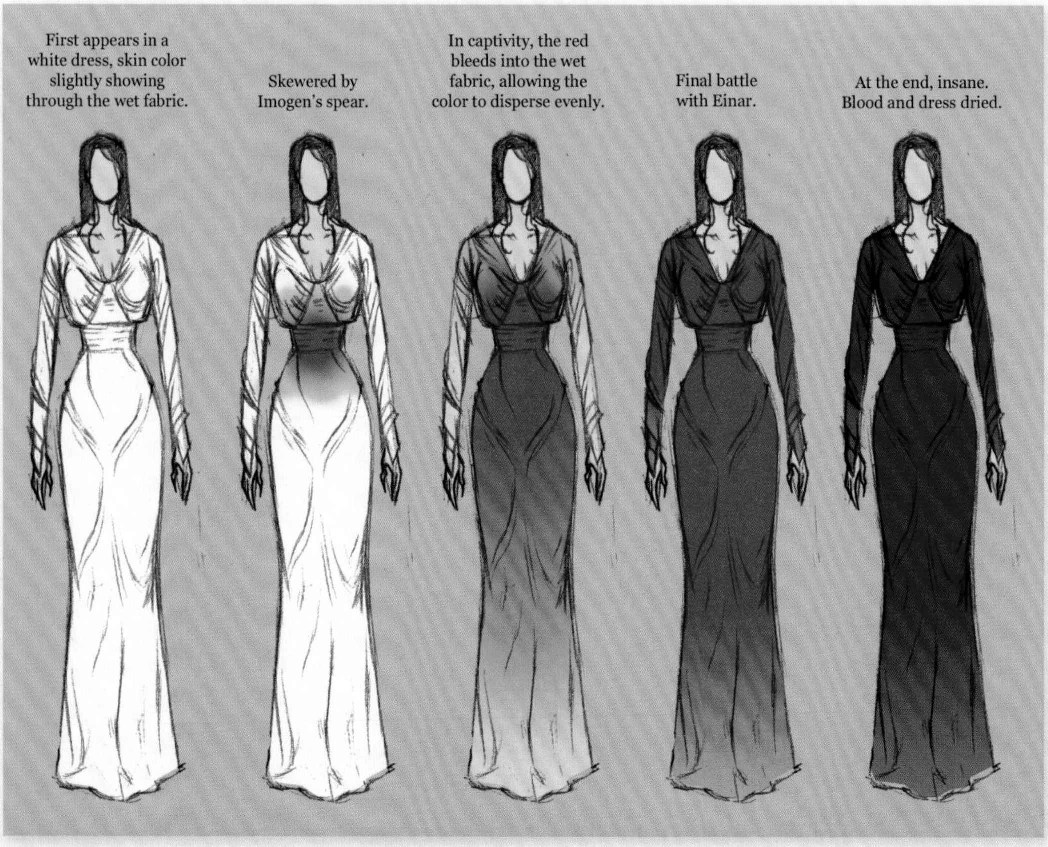
First appears in a white dress, skin color slightly showing through the wet fabric.
Skewered by Imogen's spear.
In captivity, the red bleeds into the wet fabric, allowing the color to disperse evenly.
Final battle with Einar.
At the end, insane. Blood and dress dried.

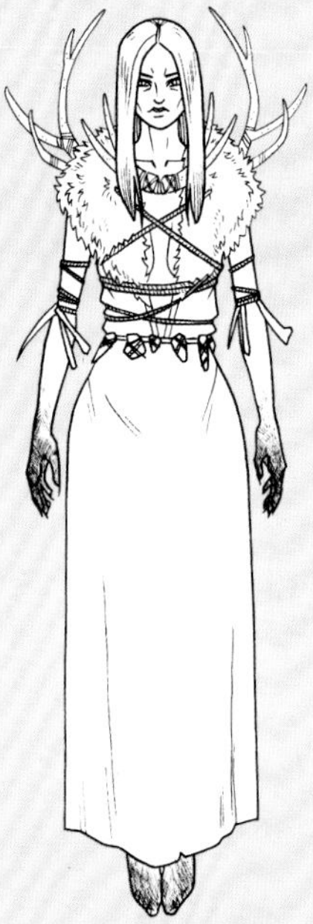

BONE WITCH

aesthetic: animal skins/furs, bones. hair is caked with dirt, hands and feet always brown/black with dirt.
rite of passage: chanting, dancing.
elderly witches: their skeleton overtakes them as they defy mortal death, their bones protrude through their skin more and more as they age.
(several w/skull masks)

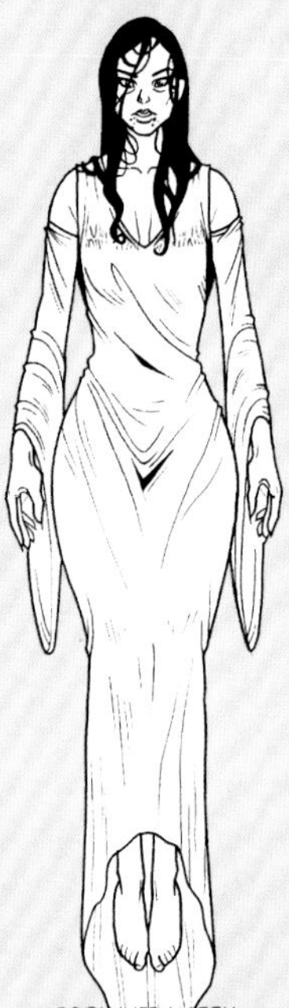

DROWNED WITCH

aesthetic: hair and skin always looks moist. wet drapery effect on their clothes. water pours from their mouths when they speak.
rite of passage: a cursed baptism- through being drawned or almost drowned.
elderly witches: develop barnacle type lesions all over their body. or just plain barnacles. maybe the eldest has a tentacle or two.

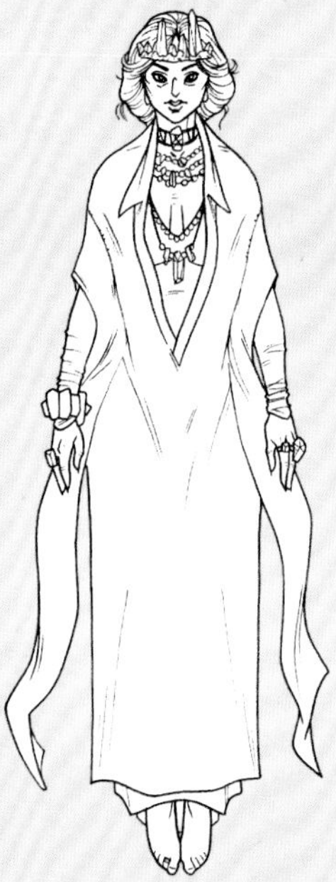

ROCK WITCH

aesthetic: beautiful, covered in stone and gem jewelry and adornments.
rite of passage: crystal arrangement ceremony
elderly witches: the posture of their true form becomes misshapen, as if they are being crushed beneath the weight of an unseen mountain. Use glamour frequently.

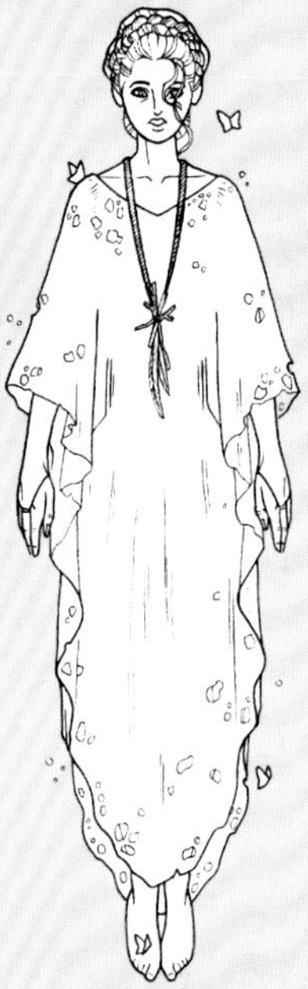

FIRELIGHT WITCH

aesthetic: warm colors? a few moths have a tendancy to be flying around them, or creeping from their orafices.
rite of passage: prove the can physically hold fire? walk through fire?
elderly witches: burns creep along their body as they age. eyes glow and moths are always near face. eldest are crispy.
(moth holes in clothes)
(wicker/kindlewood adornments)
(sleeves attached to dress so as not to burn)

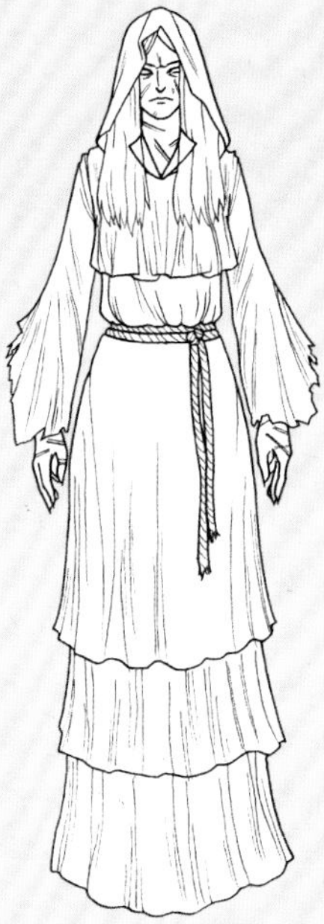

BLOOD WITCH

(the WITCH OF HARJU was one!)
aesthetic: red/black. simple. primarily curse through blood and can transform into any animal if they have its blood.
rite of passage: killing something.
elderly witches: don't bleed. their veins become thick, dark and coagulated and skin is ashen/pale. veins very visible.
(ritualistic)
(cuts all over body from past rituals)

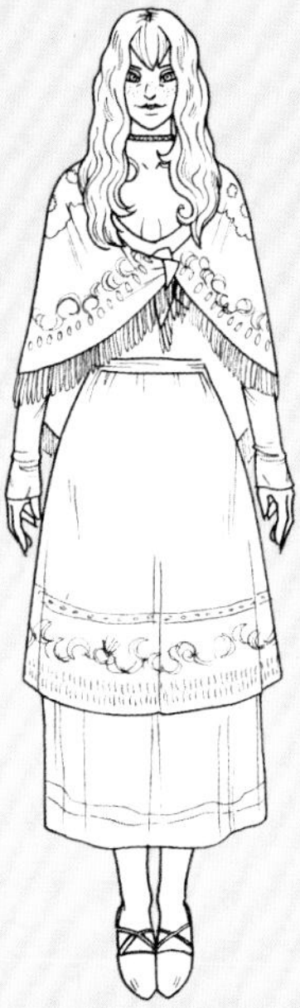

(the original ZOYA who killed THOMAS!)

RAT-CATCHER WITCH

aesthetic: masquerades as trustworthy to help towns but later takes advantage of the deal.
rite of passage: boil rats and eat them.
elderly witches: work in the coven by sending younger witches out to the towns. they are often the reason the town is doing badly. each witch followed by a different plague, be it rats, boils, famine...
(pied piper/rumplestiltskin)
(charmer)
(works in plagues)
(often look good/innocent)

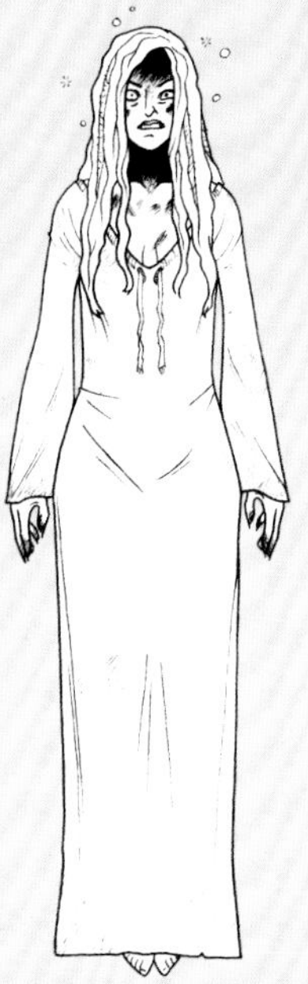

NECROMANCER

aesthetic: simple robes, bodies painted with designs made with ash. psychotic.
rites of passage: super druggy and full of smoke. (natural witchdoctor psychedelics)
elderly witches: can master shadows but the more they are able to master the shadows the less they are able to control their corporal form.
(unkept hair)
(a few natted dreads)

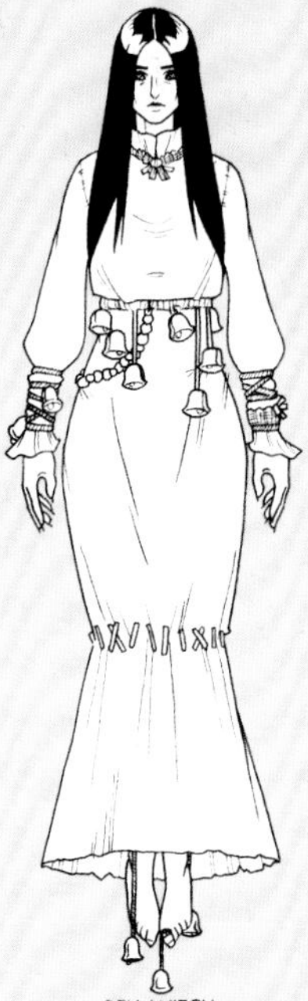

BELL WITCH

aesthetic: covered in bells, have siren-like voices. a group is BAD JUJU - can cause you to go deaf, permanently.
rites of passage: summon something cursed through song? hanged?
elderly witches: gradually lose their vision but their hearing grows tenfold.

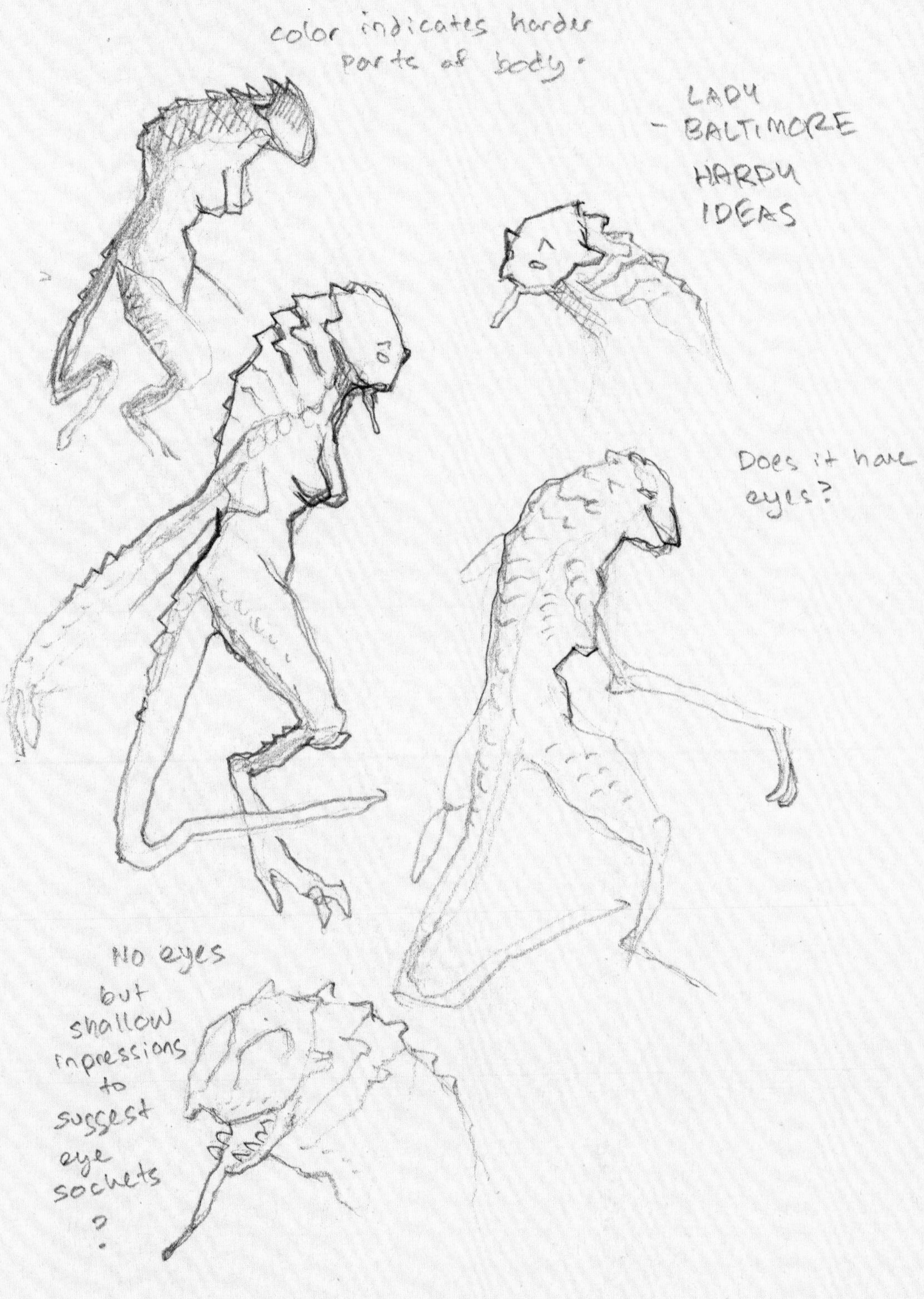
color indicates harder parts of body.
LADY - BALTIMORE HARDY IDEAS
Does it have eyes?
No eyes but shallow impressions to suggest eye sockets ?

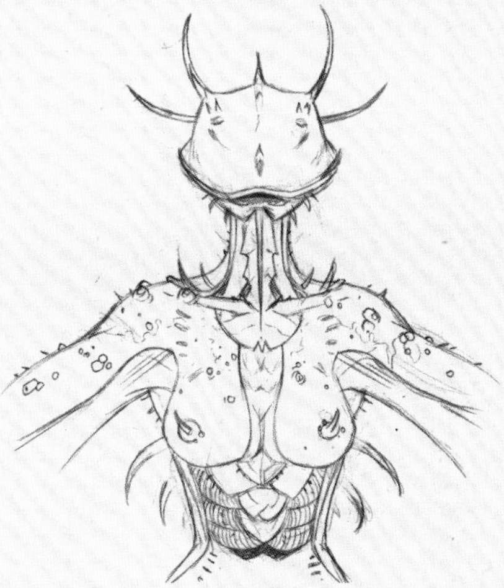

Horseshoe crab head acts like a paper shredder. Once locked onto a hand/foot/limb, when the victim pulls it back out it's a nub.

It's pretty hollow, so I'm thinking it could even fit a head in there.

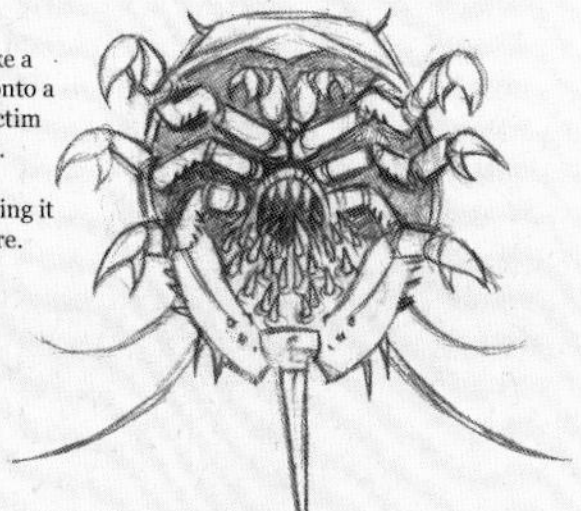

If you want the chin-tail to stand out more, I can shorten the other spines to be punky little spikes.

Looking beyond regular bat wings and looking at octopus between-leg-webbing reference, though it might actually end up looking the exact dang same.

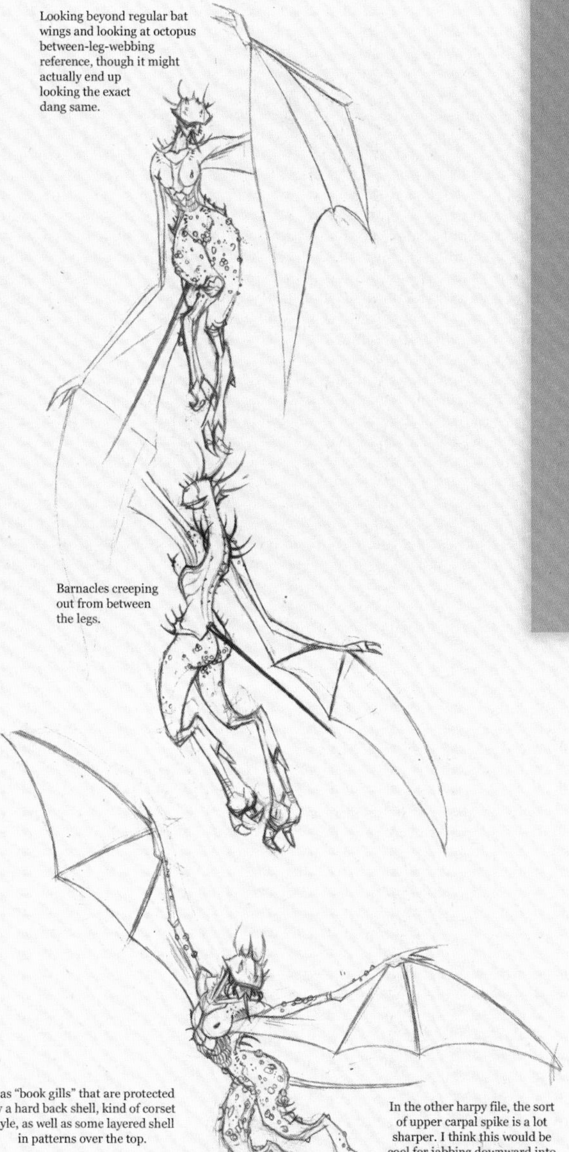

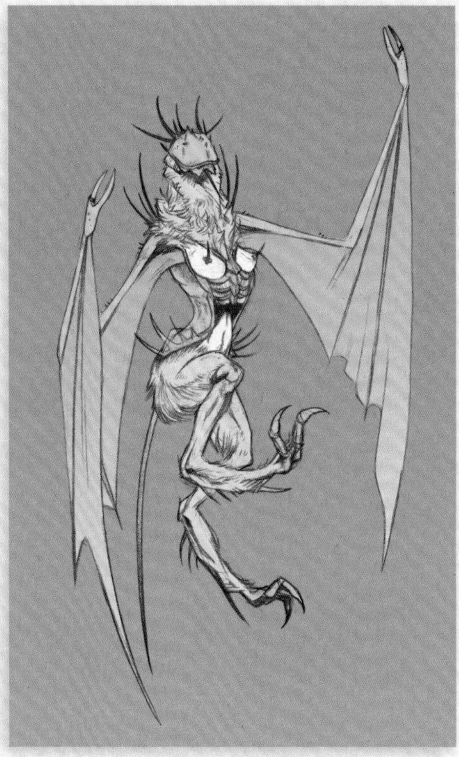

Barnacles creeping out from between the legs.

Has "book gills" that are protected by a hard back shell, kind of corset style, as well as some layered shell in patterns over the top.

This would be a great weak spot to aim for, though I'd imagine trying to get past their talons of death would still make it difficult.

In the other harpy file, the sort of upper carpal spike is a lot sharper. I think this would be cool for jabbing downward into people's shoulders or chest, kind of locking down into the body, and then using the two claws on the foot to lift them up.

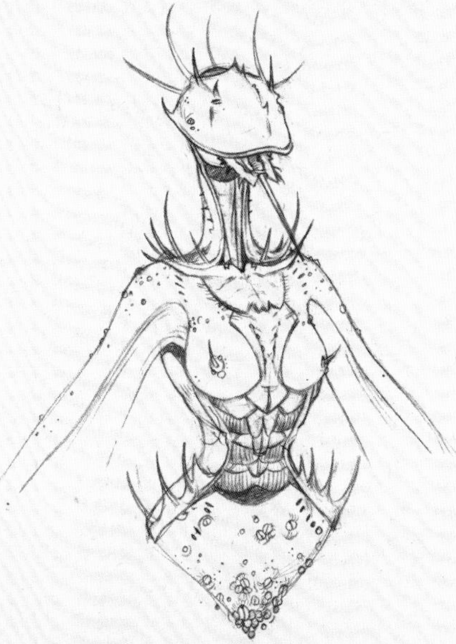

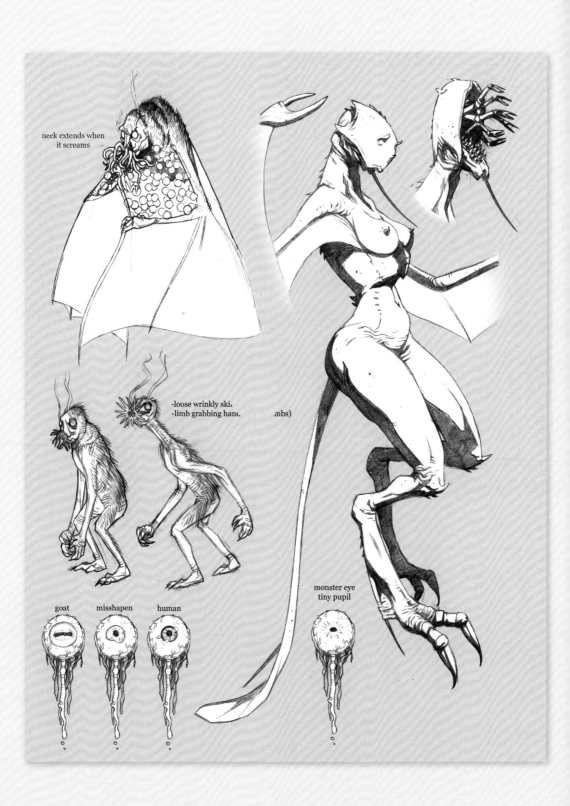

neck extends when
it screams

-loose wrinkly ski
-limb grabbing hand   mbs)

goat   misshapen   human

monster eye
tiny pupil

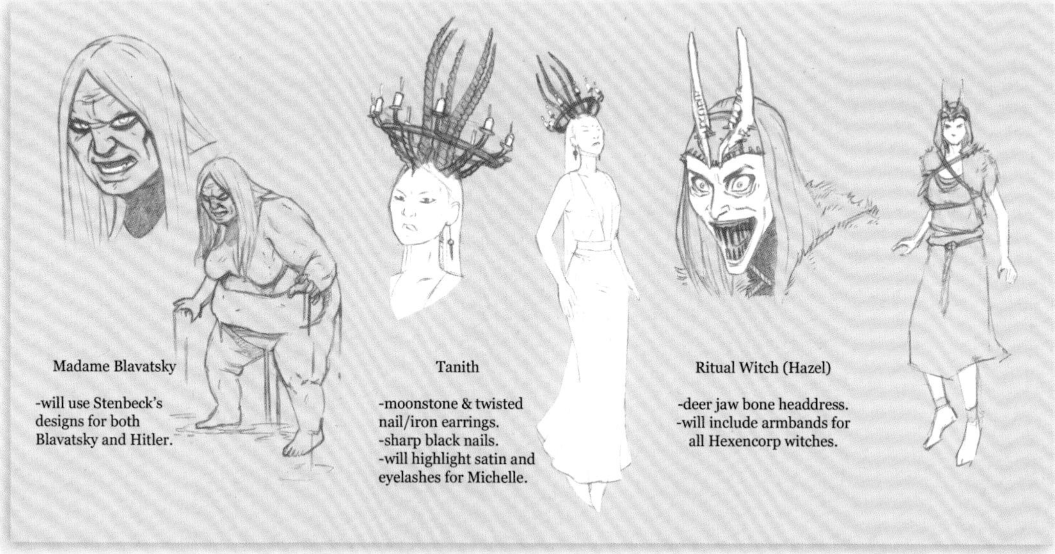
Madame Blavatsky
-will use Stenbeck's designs for both Blavatsky and Hitler.
Tanith
-moonstone & twisted nail/iron earrings.
-sharp black nails.
-will highlight satin and eyelashes for Michelle.
Ritual Witch (Hazel)
-deer jaw bone headdress.
-will include armbands for all Hexencorp witches.

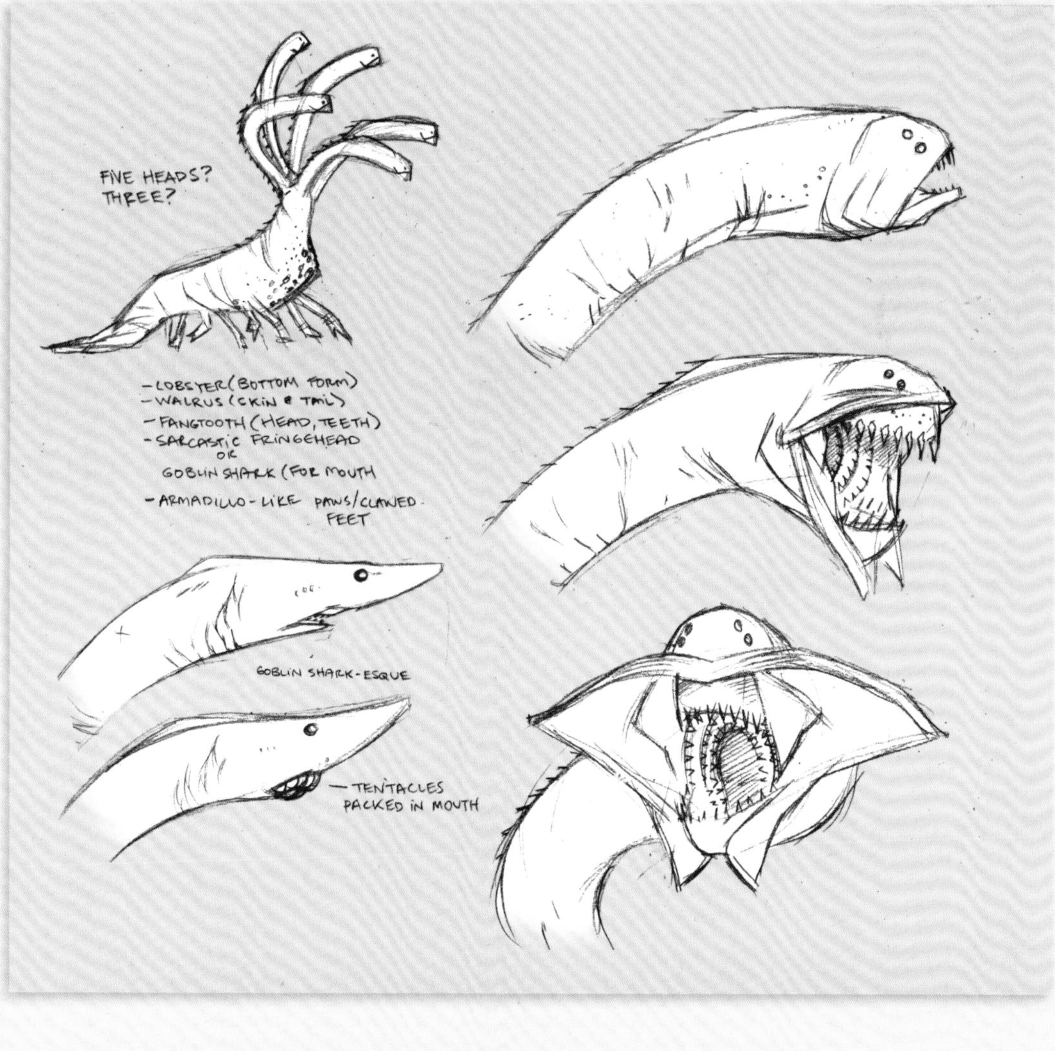
FIVE HEADS? THREE?
-LOBSYER (BOTTOM FORM)
-WALRUS (SKIN & TAIL)
-FANGTOOTH (HEAD, TEETH)
-SARCASTIC FRINGEHEAD OR GOBLIN SHARK (FOR MOUTH
-ARMADILLO-LIKE PAWS/CLAWED FEET
GOBLIN SHARK-ESQUE
-TENTACLES PACKED IN MOUTH

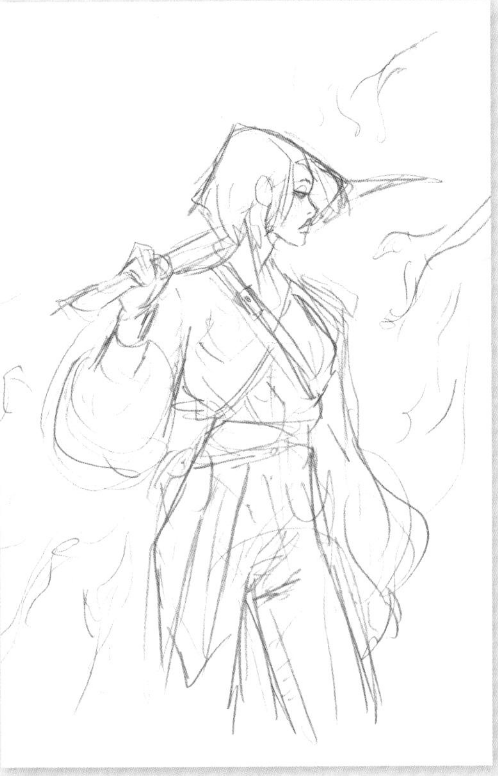

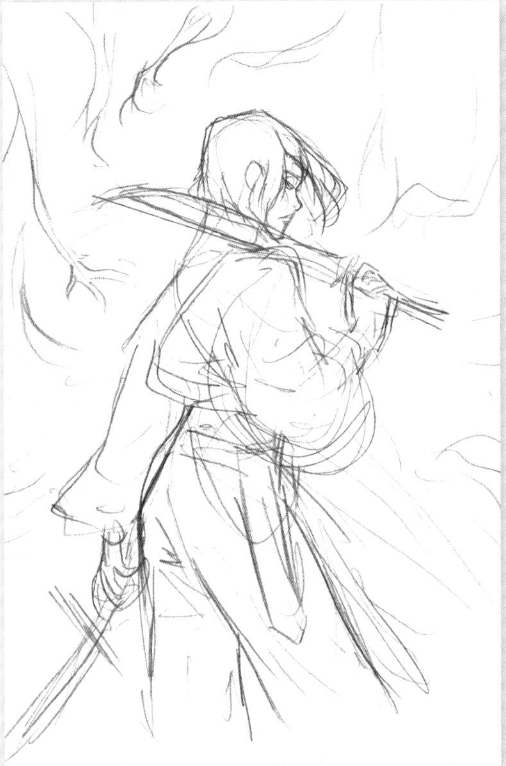

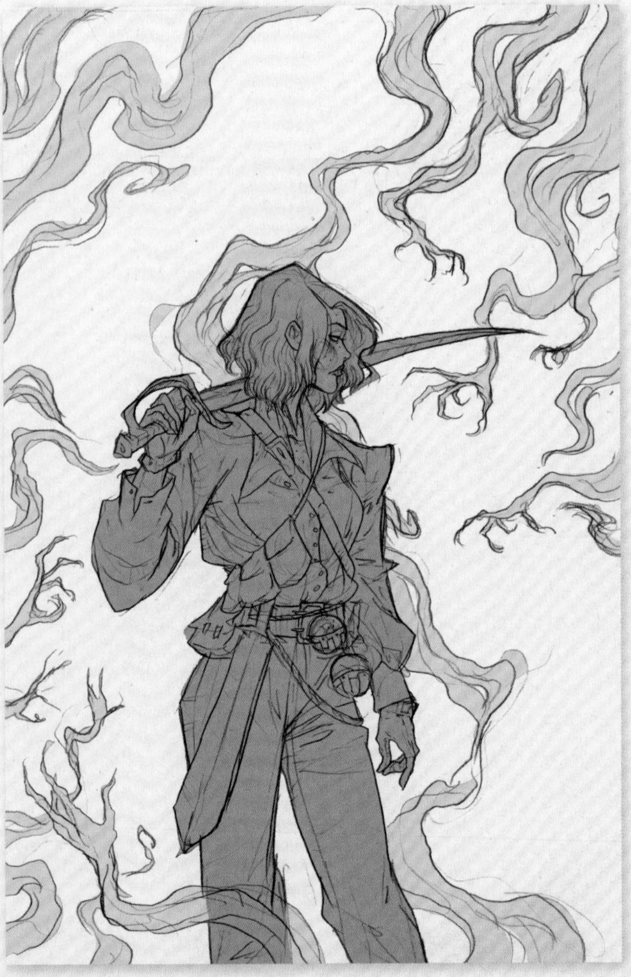

Abigail Larson's sketches (*top*) and pencils (*left*) for the first issue.

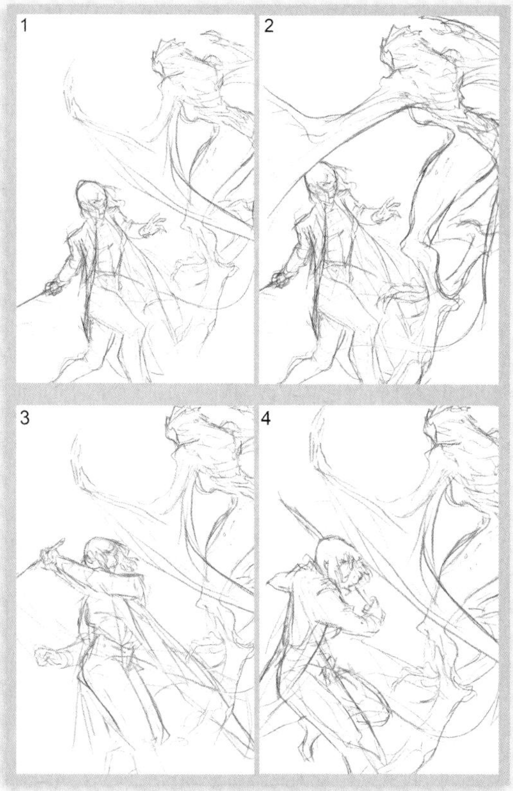
1
2
3
4

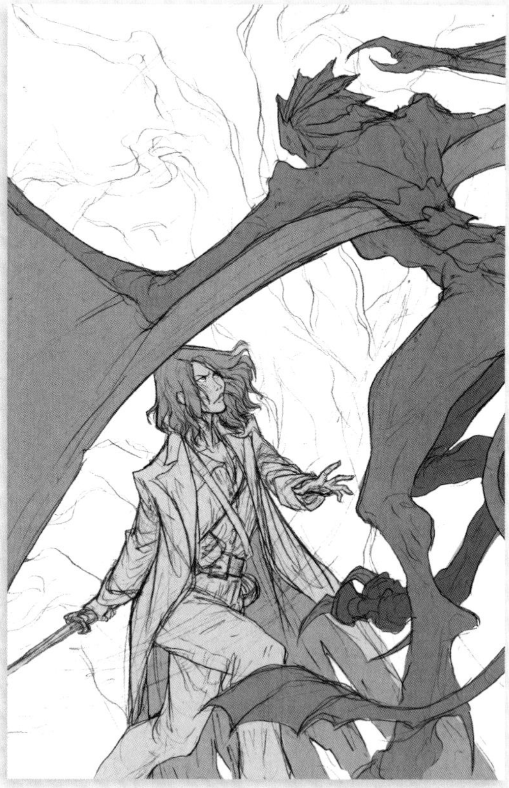

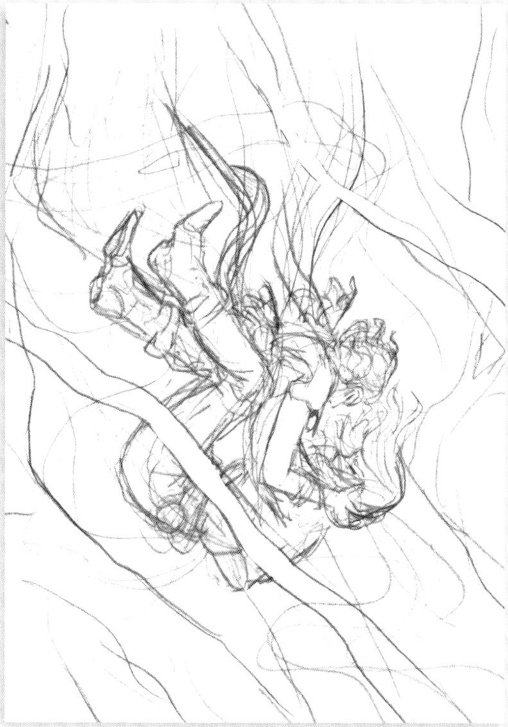

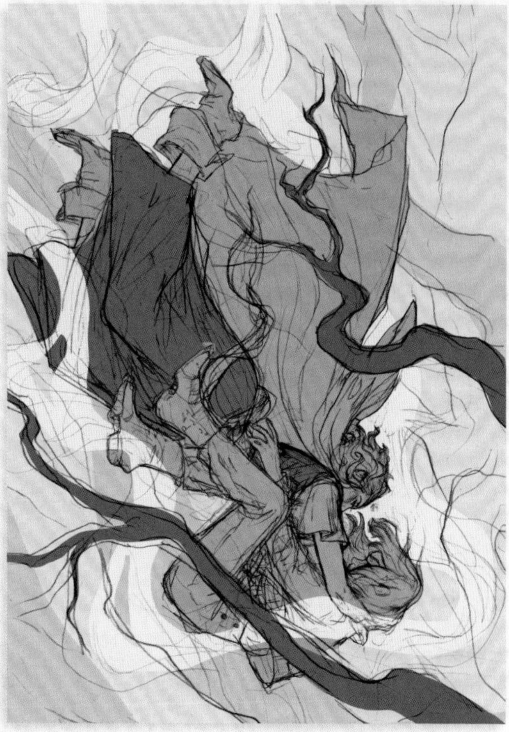

Her sketches and pencils for #2 (*top*) and #3 (*bottom*).

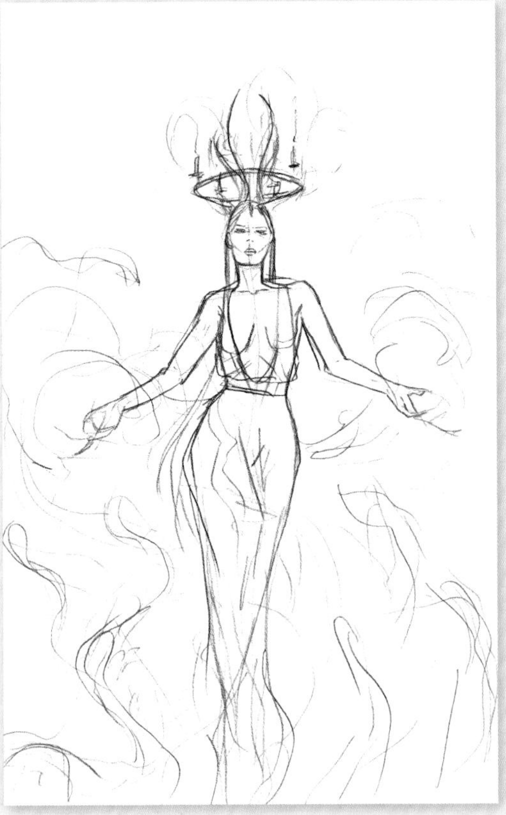

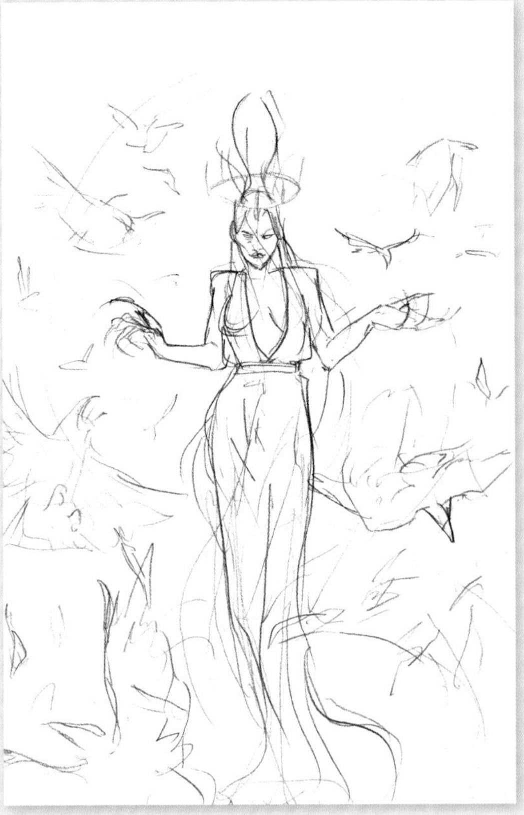

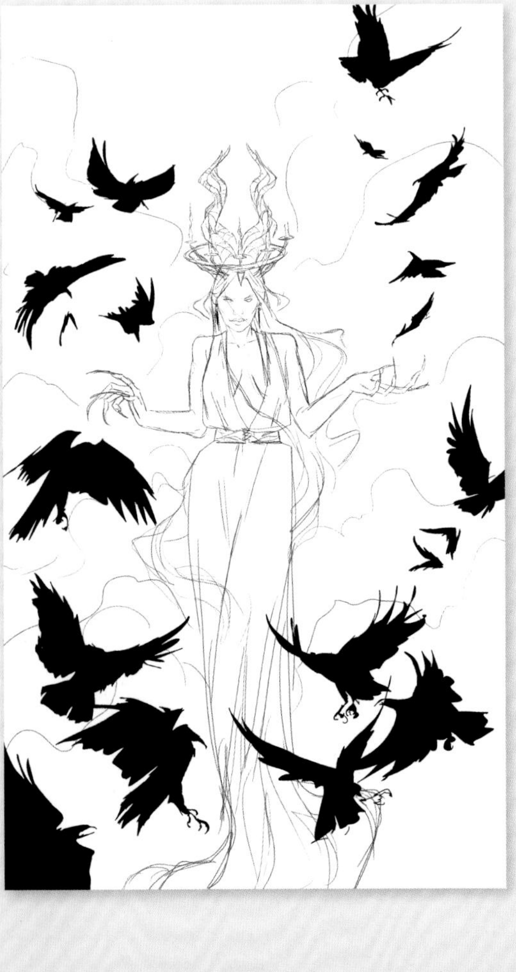

Abigail sent two poses for the Tanith cover (*top*) and her pencils (*below*).

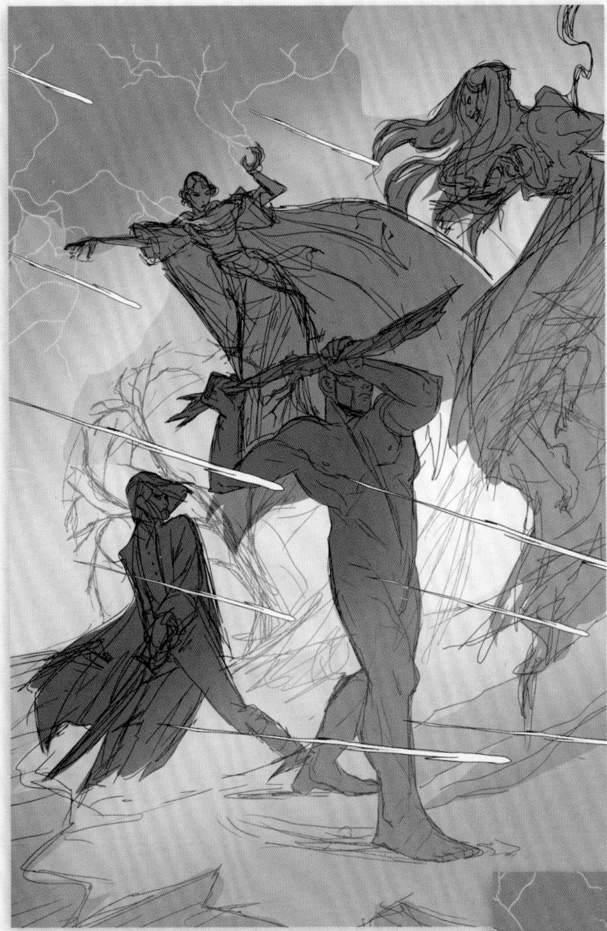

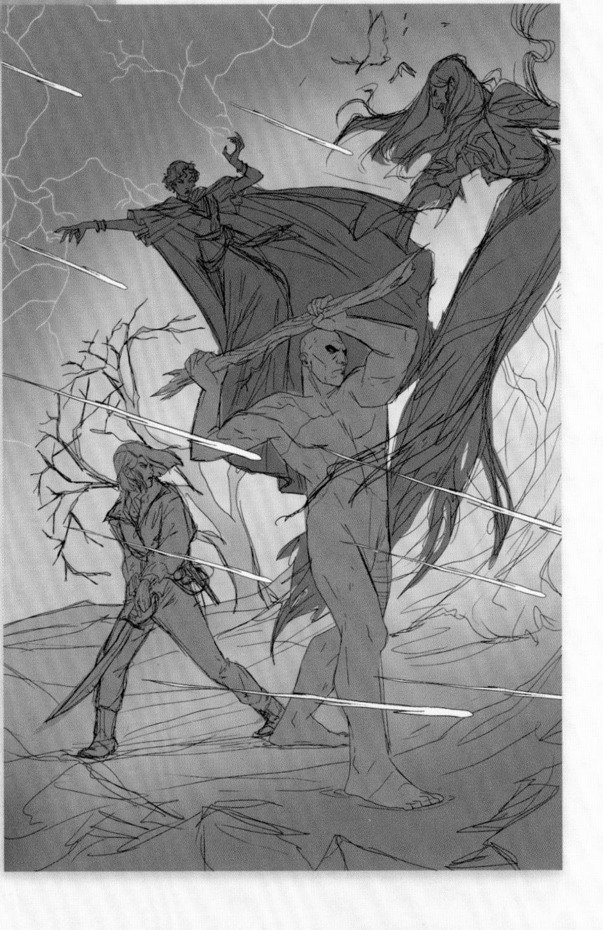

Sketches for the final issue. We decided to show the golem's face and let readers look forward to him being there, a hint toward the greater Outerverse connections.

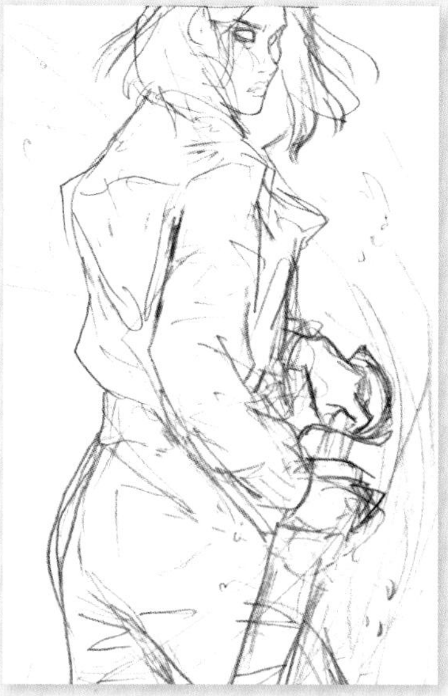

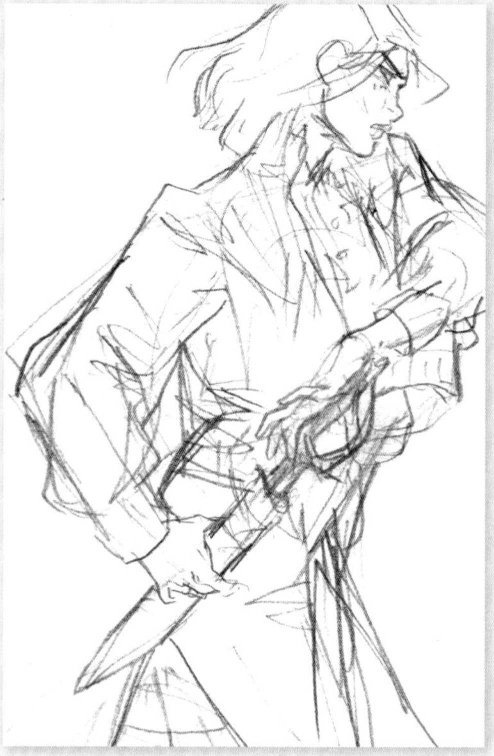

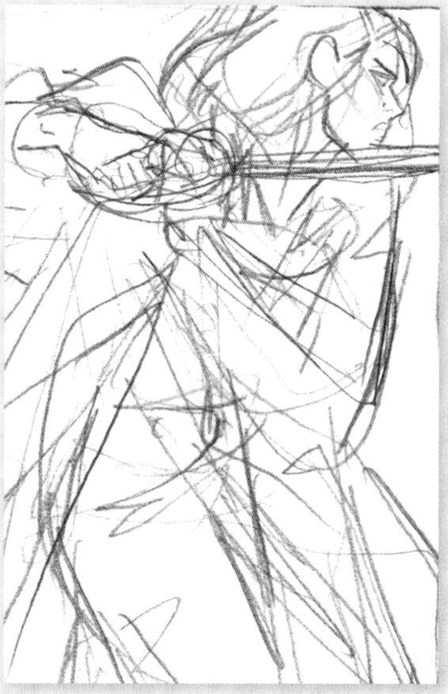

Abigail's sketches for the collection cover. We loved all of these options, but went with the top left sketch on the facing page.

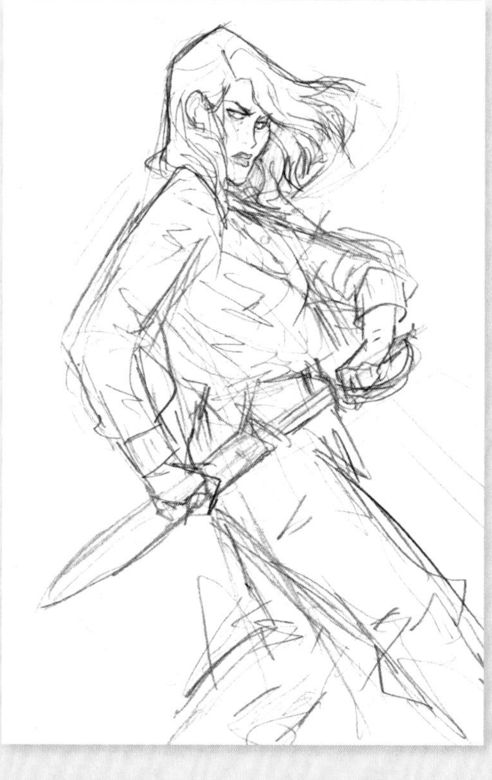

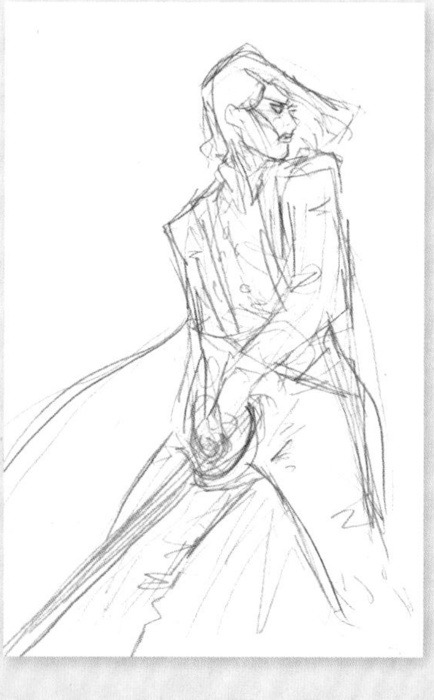

Our only note on this sketch was to make Sofia's stance stronger, and Abigail sent us the two options below with room for the logo either at the top or bottom. Usually we keep the logo at the top, but Sofia looked so perfect that we wanted her face to command the cover.

Following page: Bridgit's variant cover for the first issue, an exclusive for Jetpack Comics and Forbidden Planet UK.

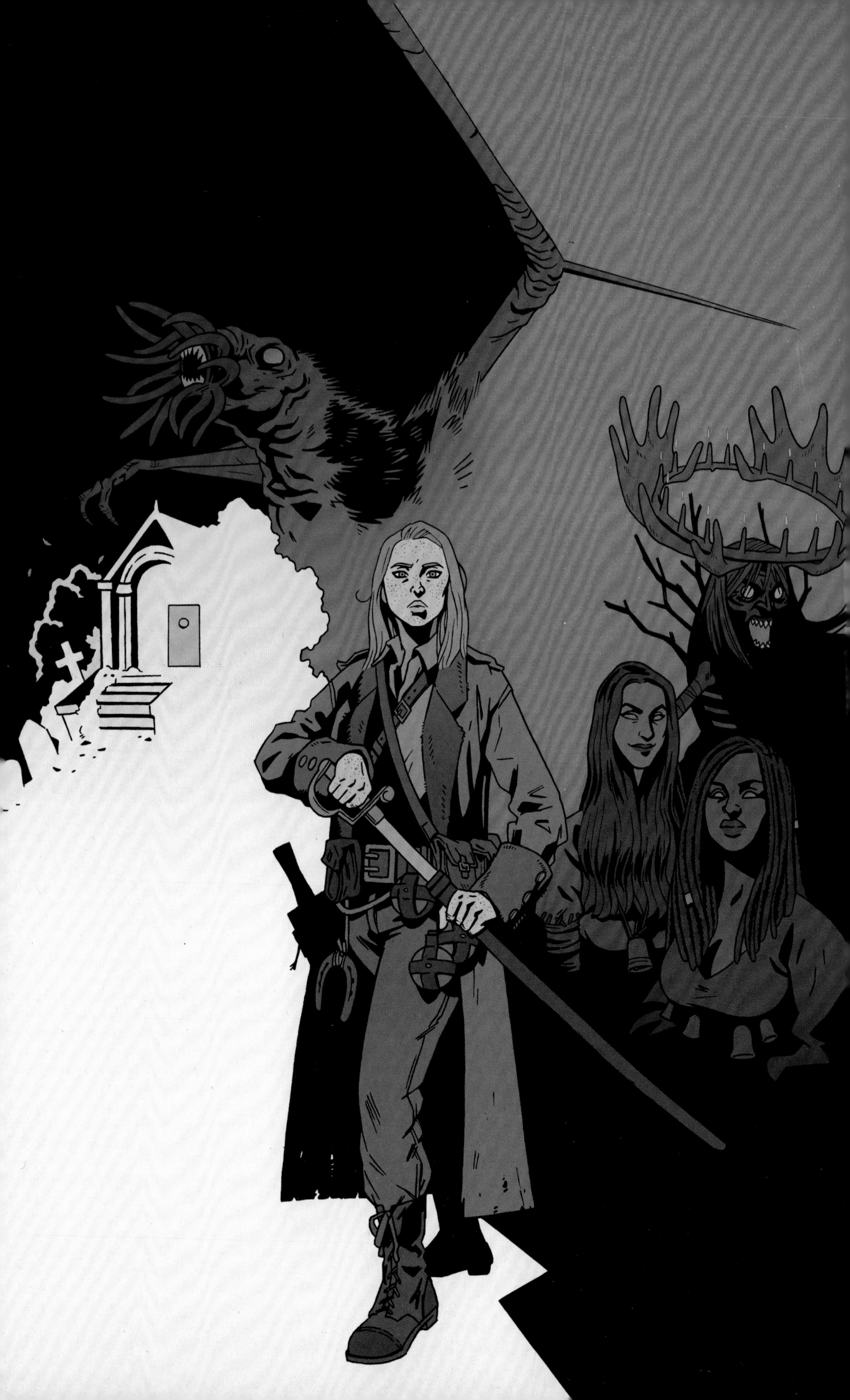